YOUR SOCIAL WORK PRACTICE PLACEMENT

From Start to Finish

IAN MATHEWS, DIANE SIMPSON & KARIN CRAWFORD

Los Angeles | London | New Delhi
Singapore | Washington DC

Los Angeles | London | New Delhi
Singapore | Washington DC

SAGE Publications Ltd
1 Oliver's Yard
55 City Road
London EC1Y 1SP

SAGE Publications Inc.
2455 Teller Road
Thousand Oaks, California 91320

SAGE Publications India Pvt Ltd
B 1/I 1 Mohan Cooperative Industrial Area
Mathura Road
New Delhi 110 044

SAGE Publications Asia-Pacific Pte Ltd
3 Church Street
#10-04 Samsung Hub
Singapore 049483

Editor: Kate Wharton
Assistant editor: Laura Walmsley
Production editor: Katherine Haw
Copyeditor: Jane Fricker
Proofreader: Neil Dowden
Marketing manager: Tamara Navaratnam
Cover design: Lisa Harper
Typeset by: C&M Digitals (P) Ltd, Chennai,
   India
Printed in Great Britain by CPI Group (UK) Ltd,
Croydon, CR0 4YY

© Ian Mathews, Diane Simpson and Karin Crawford 2014

First published 2014

Library of Congress Control Number: 2013946253

British Library Cataloguing in Publication data

A catalogue record for this book is available from the British Library

ISBN 978-1-84920-178-0
ISBN 978-1-84920-179-7 (pbk)

MIX
Paper from
responsible sources
FSC® C013604

CONTENTS

ABOUT THE AUTHORS

Ian Mathews is a Senior Lecturer in Social Work at the University of Lincoln and a founding member of Green College, Oxford. Ian is a Fellow of the Higher Education Academy and a registered social worker. Prior to moving into higher education, Ian gained substantial practice experience in both health and social care, as a practitioner and manager. Ian teaches on a range of undergraduate and postgraduate social work programmes and has a particular interest in adult care, mental health and spirituality.

Diane Simpson is a Senior Lecturer in Social Work at the University of Lincoln. Diane is a registered social worker and a Fellow of the Higher Education Academy. Diane's social work career was in children and families social work in statutory and voluntary settings. Diane holds the Practice Teachers' Award and has been approved as a Stage 2 Practice Educator. Diane teaches across on the undergraduate and postgraduate social work programmes with particular interest in practice learning, readiness to practise and child development.

Dr Karin Crawford is a Principal Teaching Fellow and Director of Education and Students in the College of Social Science at the University of Lincoln. Karin is a registered social worker and Senior Fellow of the Higher Education Academy. Karin has previously practised in both health and social care, as a practitioner and manager. This experience spanned statutory, voluntary and private sectors including general nursing, social work, policy development and the management of both adult and children's care management services.

INTRODUCTION

CONTEXT AND AIMS OF THIS BOOK

> Indeed we have only the most general ideas of what we are trying to produce, what constitutes the essential skill of the social worker, and consequently still more varied ideas of how to set about it. (Younghusband, 1959: 28)

Over 50 years ago, Eileen Younghusband was commissioned by the government to identify a strategic approach to the training of social workers. The outcomes of her committee's deliberations were followed by the Seebohm Report in 1968, which established social work as a generic profession and engendered the creation of generic Social Services Departments from 1970. The social work qualification itself progressed from being a certificate to a diploma and finally to being an all degree award from 2003. In the intervening 54 years since Younghusband's perceptive observation, social work as a profession has come under scrutiny many times through a series of reports and studies. Following the Scottish Executive's 21st Century Social Work Review entitled *Changing Lives* (2006), which offered a relatively broad vision of social work as a force for social and community development and cohesion, the discussion paper *The Changing Roles and Tasks of Social Work* offered a similarly broad definition of social work, asserting that:

> Social work faces both opportunities and challenges. Fundamentally we do not believe that what social work has to offer has significantly changed in recent years. Nor, although they will take different forms, have the essential social and individual challenges it faces changed. However the context clearly has. The time is now right to explore the nature of a new contract between social work and its stakeholders. Social work and social workers deserve and are entitled to receive support, recognition and respect. Nevertheless, this respect must be earned in the sense that social work must be prepared to respond flexibly and creatively to the new service environment. (Blewett et al. 2007: 36)

Nevertheless, the inquiry following the death of Peter Connelly in the same year resulted in the setting up of the Social Work Task Force which produced its final report, *Building a Safe, Confident Future*, in 2009. The Social Work Reform Board was established to implement the Task Force's core recommendations (Social Work

Reform Board, 2010a). Included within the Task Force's recommendations were core requirements related to determining readiness for practice prior to assessed practice placements through clearly defined progression points; establishing new arrangements (standards) to ensure the provision of sufficient high-quality practice placements, which are properly supervised and assessed, for all social work students; and explicitly linking the new qualifying degree to the Assessed and Supported Year in Employment (ASYE). The Social Work Reform Board also saw the transfer of the regulation of social work education from the General Social Care Council (GSCC) to the Health and Care Professions Council (HCPC) and the establishment of The College of Social Work (TCSW) in 2011. The HCPC and TCSW have together issued a set of regulatory and advisory documents which will inform all social work qualifying programmes in England.

Throughout these changes, there have been questions raised about the overall quality of social work placements. For example, Lord Laming's review of child protection (Laming, 2009) following the death of Baby P (Peter Connelly) identified that newly qualified social workers were able to enter employment in children and families settings without having had placement experience of this type of work. Similarly, the Social Work Task Force (2009), whilst not supporting Lord Laming's proposition to introduce specialist training, emphasised that universities needed to provide 'high-quality' placements that equipped students for the rigours of qualified practice. In specific terms, the Social Work Task Force (2009) was concerned about the quality and sufficiency of learning opportunities and was keen to ensure that students experience complex work whilst on placement, including safeguarding and statutory interventions.

Thus the Social Work Reform Board (2010b) issued new standards setting out requirements for the qualification of practice educators. In line with the recommendations of the Social Work Task Force (2009), 170 placement days are now required to allow for greater time to be spent on preparation for practice skills which will be jointly planned and delivered between universities and employers (Social Work Reform Board, 2011; TCSW, 2012a). Students will also need to have one placement that includes statutory functions. The definition of statutory relates to the work undertaken, rather than the characteristics of the placement; such work will include a combination of assessment (including assessment of risk), operating within a legislative context, use of power and authority, interprofessional collaborative working and working under pressure (TCSW, undated (a)). Students will still be required to experience two qualitatively different placements, either in terms of the type of work undertaken, the nature of the agency or modalities of working (Social Work Reform Board, 2011; TCSW, 2012a).

Running parallel to the initiatives in practice learning, the Reform Board also developed the Professional Capabilities Framework (PCF) (TCSW, 2012b, 2012c), which shows a career pathway for social work practitioners from entry to the degree programme and on through the social worker's entire career. There are nine areas of capability in the PCF: professionalism; values and ethics; diversity; rights, justice and economic wellbeing; knowledge; critical reflection and analysis; intervention and skills; contexts and organisations; and professional leadership.

Within this context, the chapters in this book are primarily intended to support student social workers' learning through practice placements. Additionally, the text will be of interest to your practice educators and on-site supervisors, who, although qualified practitioners, support and assess student social workers in practice. The text, therefore, very explicitly addresses knowledge, skills and values for professional practice, being informed and underpinned by core regulatory documents, in particular:

- The Professional Capabilities Framework (PCF) as defined by The College of Social Work (TCSW, 2012c);

- Standards of Conduct, Performance and Ethics as prescribed by the HCPC (HCPC, 2012a);

- The Standards of Proficiency for social workers in England as prescribed by the HCPC to be achieved for entry to the social work register (HCPC, 2012b);

- Standards for Education and Training (SETs) as prescribed by the HCPC (HCPC, 2012c);

- The Subject Benchmark Statement for Social Policy and Social Work (Quality Assurance Agency [QAA], 2008).

The book sets out to be a logical guide, or handbook, that identifies the very real practical challenges, opportunities, potential pitfalls and processes that you, as a student social worker, are likely to encounter on placement learning. Additionally, the text challenges you to critically engage with your practice learning setting, questioning, observing, reflecting, challenging and analysing your experience of practice.

SCOPE OF THE BOOK

The chapters in this book focus primarily on the context of the first placement experience, although much of the material will be relevant to placement experiences across the whole of the qualifying degree. Thus you will find the chapters particularly relevant, supportive and informative if you are new to the experience of assessed practice work. The book takes a broad approach to social work education and practice learning; thus whilst the contextual professional and regulatory documents drawn upon hail from an English perspective, the text has wide relevance across the four countries of the United Kingdom. Furthermore, we acknowledge the complexity of different levels of placements and different ways in which placements are organised and assessed by universities, giving some examples and comparisons as appropriate.

Within this introductory section, whilst setting out the aims and scope of the book, it is equally important, in our view, to be clear about the limitations of the text. For example, this book does not cover social work theories and methods in depth, but within each chapter, you will be directed to further sources as appropriate. Additionally, the book does not and cannot duplicate practice handbooks that are provided by your university as part of your course; rather, it is intended that this book is like having a 'virtual tutor' with you through the placement, so that you are able to quickly locate guidance and reassurance about particular concerns, experiences, expectations and challenges as they arise. Thus we believe you will find the book distinctive, engaging, practical and relevant as you move through periods of learning and assessment in practice.

THE STRUCTURE AND CONTENTS OF THE BOOK

The book is structured to reflect the 'life course of placements', hence its subtitle 'From Start to Finish'; so working through the chapters sequentially will aid logical, progressive learning, and support easy searching for specific guidance. Thus the chapters take you through learning about pre-placement preparation; starting out on placement; the middle of the placement; and ending the placement.

After this introductory section, you will find eight main chapters followed by a brief conclusion after Chapter 8 and a glossary of terms and abbreviations. The chapters are effectively paired as shown below; the first chapter in each pair covering both 'processes and practicalities' before the second chapter explores the knowledge, skills and values of particular relevance and importance at that stage of practice learning.

- Chapters 1 and 2 cover pre-placement preparation;
- Chapters 3 and 4 explore the early stages of placement;
- Chapters 5 and 6 cover the middle stages of placement;
- Chapter 7 and 8 consider the final stages and ending of placement.

Across the book we aim to reflect the diversity and complexity of practice learning, alongside the diverse needs of students. In order to fully meet the aim of being interactive, practical and relevant to you as you learn in practice, you will find that the chapters include a number of distinctive and interesting features threaded throughout the text. For example, you will read case study examples and reflections developed from real students' experiences, actual examples of real student work, reflective and learning activities, practical checklists, 'top tips', summaries of relevant literature and research and each chapter closes with annotated suggestions for further reading/web resources. Throughout the chapters you will read extracts headed 'student voice' where social work students that we have worked with offer their experiences of first and second placements in relation to the topic in the chapter. Through all of these features, particularly the 'further reading', you will be guided to expand particular aspects of your learning that are realistically beyond the scope of this text, for example detailed sources on social work theories and methods. Also included is a clear glossary of terms and abbreviations within the final section of the book.

We hope that you enjoy using this book to support your practice learning in social work and that it helps you to prepare for tangible, real issues, to reflect and to work through ways to address them and learn from them.

PART I
PREPARATION FOR THE PLACEMENT

1

PROCESSES AND PRACTICALITIES

Chapter summary

When you have worked through this chapter, you will be able to:

- Explain the purpose of a social work placement;
- Outline the preparation for placement procedures;
- Describe the purpose and content of readiness for direct practice assessments;
- Understand the role of the pre-placement meeting;
- Reflect upon your own readiness for direct practice and consider ways of preparing for placement.

INTRODUCTION

This chapter considers the practical tasks you will need to complete to ensure a successful start to placement, including the completion of documentation and the placement application form. We ask you to reflect upon and consider your level of capability as a beginning social worker and to identify your learning needs so that you and your practice educator can prepare for your placement. Most universities will have a person or team of people with designated responsibility for practice placements (although they may have different job titles) and in this chapter we introduce you to the work of this person or team and outline key steps in both applying for placement and demonstrating that you are ready for practice. Students usually find placements exciting and also a little nerve

wracking; we hope this chapter will guide you through some of the early processes associated with getting ready for starting placement.

WHAT ARE SOCIAL WORK PLACEMENTS?

Social work placements are varied, diverse and unique. Over the last few years, placements have been developed in a range of non-traditional settings which may not be
automatically associated with the practice of 'traditional' social work; this includes
schools, voluntary organisations, private agencies, placements within organisations
led by service users (Doel et al., 2007) and placements with individual service users as
part of the personalisation agenda (Tickle, 2009). This may mean that the person in
the agency who takes day-to-day responsibility for organising your placement and the
work you undertake, sometimes called a practice supervisor, work-based supervisor
or on-site supervisor (in this book we use the term on-site supervisor for people who
take this role), is not a qualified social worker. This does not mean that your placement will be of inferior quality as all placements are audited under the framework for
Quality Assurance in Practice Learning (QAPL) which was first introduced in 2010
by the General Social Care Council (GSCC, 2010) and has recently been revised by
The College of Social Work and Skills for Care (2012). Many of these 'non-traditional'
placements offer invaluable learning and development opportunities for social work
students that would not be available within 'traditional' placements such as those
provided by local authorities.

From 2013, all social work qualifying programmes will provide a placement
structure that consists of 30 days' readiness for practice, a first practice placement of 70 days and a final practice placement of 100 days (TCSW, 2012a).
In general terms, work placements provide students with the opportunity to
acquire skills pertinent for employment, evaluate their practice and knowledge
and inform future employment choices (Fanthome, 2004). However, for social
work students, placements are an opportunity for you to learn about the professional practice of social work, apply theory to practice situations and demonstrate proficiency and capability in social work skills, values and theory. From
September 2013 all students will be assessed against the Professional Capabilities Framework (PCF) (TCSW, 2012b, 2012c). During placement you will need
to show your practice educator that you have met the requirements of the PCF,
which measure your understanding and application of social work knowledge,
values and skills, and your capabilities as a beginning social worker across nine
domains set at different levels of proficiency and complexity for each placement.
Importantly, you will have to pass each assessed practice learning experience in
order to progress in your studies. It is therefore crucial to have a clear view of
the knowledge, values and skills that you already possess and what your learning
needs for placement are (see Chapter 2).

As a starting point, this first activity asks you to think about your first placement.

Activity 1.1

My first placement

Thinking about your first social work placement, work through the questions below and complete the right-hand column of the table.

Questions	My initial thoughts
Which service user group would you like to work with?	
Where would you want your placement to be?	
What are you most looking forward to about your placement?	
Do you have any worries about placement?	

PREPARING FOR YOUR FIRST PLACEMENT

All placements and all students are individual; as such the period prior to placements can cause students anxiety. Placement providers respond to requests for placements at different speeds, pre-placement meetings take place at different times and practice educators may not be available to provide a placement in precise alignment with the university's calendar; inevitably this means that students will know at different times when their placements are confirmed. For some, confirmation and organisation of the placement will not be received until close to the start date or placement commencement period. Whilst university staff and placements teams will be familiar with such processes and may not seem anxious about the uncertainty, this can be a worrying time for students. It is therefore important to be able to cope with your anxieties and to carefully manage your communications with the university's placements team – time spent by staff helping you manage your emotions may well be better spent organising and confirming placements. This is not meant to discourage you from contacting your placement team, merely to reassure you that they will not have forgotten about you.

COMPLETING RELEVANT DOCUMENTATION

Part of demonstrating your readiness for practice involves completing paperwork and documentation in a timely fashion; this section outlines some of documentation you will be asked to complete, often right at the very start of your social work studies.

ENHANCED CRIMINAL RECORDS BUREAU (CRB) OR DISCLOSURE AND BARRING SCHEME (DBS) CHECK

Within the first few weeks of commencing your course, you will be asked to complete a Criminal Records Bureau (CRB) or Disclosure and Barring Scheme (DBS) check, which will formally record any cautions or criminal convictions you may have. The Disclosure and Barring Scheme undertake CRBs (see: www.homeoffice.gov.uk/agencies-public-bodies/dbs/about-us1/what-we-do/before-the-dbs/). Your university will probably have asked you to disclose any cautions or criminal convictions at interview and it is important to be completely open and honest. Having a conviction or caution (where you have admitted guilt to the police) does not necessarily preclude you from social work training but it does depend on the nature of the offence and when the offence occurred. As a profession, our primary duty is to protect the wellbeing of service users and some offences may mean that you are potentially unsuitable for social work. Failure to disclose a caution or conviction may be regarded as an attempt to deceive your social work programme and could result in the instigation of formal readiness for practice procedures which may result in the termination of training. The importance of vetting staff for work with vulnerable service users, and in particular the role of the CRB check, came to prominence following the murders of Jessica Chapman and Holly Wells by their school caretaker, Ian Huntley, in 2002 (Bichard, 2004).

DECLARATION OF SUITABILITY FOR PRACTICE

As a social worker in training, you are expected to comply with the Health and Care Professions Council's (HCPC) Guidance on Conduct and Ethics for Students (HCPC, 2012a) and you may be asked to sign to say that you have read and will comply with these standards. Whilst this is generic guidance for students in all professions regulated by the HCPC, the document sets out the standards expected of students during their training. The expectations include ethical practice in relation to your conduct with service users, guidance on disclosure of information to your education provider should any circumstance impair your fitness to practise and requirements to maintain your professional development, knowledge and skills and to be aware of when these are insufficient (HCPC, 2012a).

Typically a declaration of suitability for practice will also ask students to disclose any physical or mental health issues, disciplinary offences or involvement with statutory services that may impair or be relevant to fitness to practise. Deciding what is relevant and what not can be difficult, but our advice is to disclose information even if you are unsure of its relevance. The HCPC places the onus on practitioners and students to take responsibility for their own health and character and to recognise when they are physically or mentally unfit to practise or when their conduct would preclude them from doing so. In practical terms, this requires students to inform the university if any issue arises that might affect their suitability for practice (HCPC, 2012a).

It is also possible that universities will ask whether you, or anyone in your immediate household, have been users of social care services (as an adult or a child). Again, past or current involvement with social care services does not automatically preclude you from the profession, but some concerns (e.g. safeguarding issues) may lead your university to make enquiries about your suitability.

OTHER DOCUMENTATION

There are other important processes and documents that you need to consider prior to the commencement of your placement. For example, if you are intending to use a car whilst on placement, you need to ensure that you have obtained business insurance. Some insurers will provide this at no additional cost, but others will charge. If you do not have, or cannot afford business insurance, you must not use your car to transport service users or for any business travel. Be aware that your placement provider may ask to see all of your vehicle documents including your car insurance, your driving licence and a current MOT certificate. You need to ensure that all of your documentation is current, as if placements require a car driver, they will not allow you to start until you are able to prove that you are appropriately insured and safe to drive on their behalf.

AN IMPORTANT REMINDER ABOUT DOCUMENTATION

The documentation that you complete and compile is part of your preparation and readiness for practice processes. Your university programme may ask to see some or all of the documents before you can proceed to placement. Additionally, placements may ask to see this documentation to ensure that you are a suitable candidate for a student placement within their organisation. It is not unknown for some organisations to ask you to complete a further CRB/DBS check specifically in relation to your placement with them; this will depend upon the organisation's policies and procedures.

We are aware of situations where students have lost or misplaced documentation or where paperwork has been damaged, making it illegible. In these circumstances, you will need to obtain new or duplicate documentation, which could potentially delay the start of your placement. It is therefore vital that you store the documentation in a safe place where it cannot be damaged. Also, universities may require you to have a CRB/DBS check that is less than three years old, so students on part-time courses or who have interrupted studies may need to renew their CRB/DBS. Our advice is to buy a folder to place these documents in, which you will be able to show during readiness for practice processes (if required) and also to placement providers.

Your documentation acts as a 'passport' to placement (Doel, 2010: 3) and it is important that you make sure you keep this up to date. In the event of any change in your circumstances, such as health issues or criminal convictions (including speeding tickets), you will need to disclose this information to the university (HCPC, 2012a; Parker, 2010a) no matter how minor you perceive this to be.

Top tips – Preparing your documents

- Store documentation safely

- Buy a folder to store all key documents

- If your circumstances change (e.g. CRB/DBS, health), you must inform your university

---

Activity 1.2

Keeping track of key documents

Work through the table below and complete the two empty columns as you locate and collate the necessary documentation. We have left some room for you to add any other documentation that might be required by your university.

Documentation checklist	Tick when complete	Where have you stored this document?
Complete CRB/DBS documentation		
Read the HCPC Guidance on Conduct and Ethics for Students		
If required, obtain business use on car insurance		
Make sure you driving licence is in date (if applicable)		
If required, make sure your car has a current MOT certificate		
Complete declarations of suitability for practice (if required)		
Complete the placement application form		

COMPLETING YOUR PLACEMENT APPLICATION FORM

As detailed earlier in the chapter, most universities will have a dedicated placement or practice team who will be responsible for guiding you through the placement application process. It is important to be familiar with the structure of placement provision within your university and the processes of applying for placements. Regardless of when placements are scheduled to commence, the application process is likely to take place some months prior to the start date to allow time for placement finding and matching. If you have a particular requirement, such as wanting a placement overseas or perhaps in your home town, which falls outside existing partnerships between your university and local placement providers, it would be wise to alert your placement team to this at the earliest opportunity.

Placement application forms and processes will also vary across universities, so what follows is generic advice on completing the placement application form. Placements can be scarce resources, so it is important to complete your application form with thought and care. It is likely that the application form will provide you with some options about your preferences (e.g. service user group, location, travel). Generally speaking, narrowing your options with specific placement interests may make placement finding problematic; we would therefore advise that you indicate broad preferences (e.g. working with children and families) rather than narrowing your requirements to a specific type of work or placement setting (e.g. Children and Family Court Advisory and Support Service [CAFCASS] or adoption work). Placement application forms are also likely to reflect something about your pre-course experiences and what you envisage your learning needs to be. Your university will probably encourage you to complete a self-audit of your knowledge, values and skills prior to placement so you can identify learning needs to be addressed in placement. Time spent reflecting upon your learning during the degree course and what this means for your future learning needs will be time well spent. It is really helpful if placements know what your strengths and learning needs are as it will help to plan suitable learning opportunities.

If you have any specific requirements, the application form is a good place to make these needs known. Some students are reluctant to disclose details of disabilities or specific needs, but this information can be vital in finding you a placement that can meet your needs. You may also have caring responsibilities that need to be accommodated and placement teams will only be familiar with your needs if you let them know.

Whilst this may be self-evident, it is also important that you ensure that the placement team has your correct contact details (including term-time and home addresses, telephone numbers and email addresses). If you change any of these contact details, remember to let the placement team know so that they can update their records. Additionally, you need to make sure you allow time to review and edit your application, paying particular attention to grammar and spelling as well as content. Sometimes your placement team or academic tutor will be able to assist with placement application forms to ensure you present your information coherently and articulately.

WHAT YOUR UNIVERSITY MAY EXPECT OF YOU

Placement teams/placement coordinators often have to meet the needs of students at different levels of social work training, sometimes at both undergraduate and post-graduate levels. Social work programmes will therefore usually require you to complete documentation well in advance of the placement start period and they will expect you to submit by a specific date in the academic year. Universities will also expect you to consider suitable placements, even if this does not match your view of what an ideal placement would be. All placements are audited as part of quality assurance processes (TCSW and Skills for Care, 2012), so they should be able to meet your learning needs. Social work degree courses are generic and you should not refuse to consider a placement in a setting that you do not intend working in on qualification. Often students find that taking a placement in a setting which they had previously discounted can be a rewarding experience which informs their career choices and adds to their curriculum vitae (CV). There may also be an expectation that you undertake travel to placement and if you receive a social work bursary, there is a portion within it which is earmarked for travel costs. Some placements may reimburse travel costs, but many placements are not able to do so.

Some students may also have valuable information or contacts that can lead to the development of new placements. Universities always need to increase the number and the quality of the placements they provide and we would encourage you to contact your placement coordinator/placement team if you are able to provide new leads or contacts. However, many universities will insist that students should not arrange their own placements. Whilst arranging your own placement may seem an obvious solution to students, this interference in established processes and systems can cause problems for university staff, placement providers and other students. It can also place additional demands on placement providers who may be confused by receiving placement requests from a number of different sources.

PLACEMENT MATCHING

Once you have completed and submitted your placement application form, the university placement team/coordinator will review your information in the light of available placements and other programme demands and make decisions about where to send your application form. Universities will try to match you to your preferred placement setting, based upon the needs and interests you expressed in your application form, although they cannot guarantee an exact match. Some universities will send copies of your application form to potential placement providers, whilst others will hold a formal matching meeting, or there might be a combination of both of these methods. Once placements have received your details, they might be able to make a decision about whether to invite you for an (often informal) interview but in some organisations (such as local authorities), several applications may be given/sent to one person who has the job of finding and matching placements within their organisation. Inevitably, the latter approach will take longer to complete.

READINESS FOR PRACTICE

The social work degree requirements place great emphasis on readiness or fitness for practice, with 30 days being set aside for this process. The readiness for practice arrangements are designed to be robust and are jointly planned, delivered and assessed by universities, service users and employers (TCSW, undated (a)). Whilst there is still flexibility in how readiness for practice processes are configured and assessed, there is an expectation that universities will draw on a range of methods of assessment to determine fitness to practise (Social Work Reform Board, 2011; TCSW, 2012d, undated (c)). The College of Social Work (undated (c)) anticipates that most of the 30 days will be used prior to commencement of the first placement to assist students in developing the necessary skills for practice. However, some days can be retained for more advanced skills development later in the degree programme. The readiness for practice assessment reflects the Professional Capabilities Framework, and an initial level of capability across all nine elements will need to be demonstrated before students can proceed to placement (TCSW, 2012d). The intention then is that only suitable, high quality students will be able to progress through training (Social Work Reform Board, 2010b).

Whilst it is difficult to anticipate the evolution of readiness for practice processes, you will need to be prepared to have your skills observed and examined, your knowledge tested both in terms of academic understanding and the ability to apply this to direct practice, and your values scrutinised to ensure compatibility with and adherence to professional standards. Suggested content of readiness for practice modules includes developing skills in communication and observation, understanding the context in which social work practice takes place, shadowing qualified social workers and the involvement of service users and carers as experts through experience (TCSW, undated (c)). Readiness for practice assessment will occur at several points within your degree programme.

As discussed, a mixture of strategies to assess readiness for practice will be utilised, often involving service users as co-assessors in determining suitability and also co-providers of readiness for practice assessment opportunities (Advocacy in Action et al., 2006; Elliott et al., 2005; Lishman, 2009a). Assessments of readiness for practice are therefore varied and may include:

- An interview with your academic tutor, sometimes with a service user or practitioner;

- A discussion with a service user;

- Role play with opportunities for feedback;

- Shadowing of an experienced qualified social work practitioner, often with a reflective account of your learning from this experience;

- An assessed video of practice or live observation of practice;

- Academic assessment of written work;

- Providing evidence that you have completed necessary documentation (e.g. CRB).

(Advocacy in Action et al., 2006; Doel, 2010;
Elliot et al., 2005; Parker, 2010a)

The PCF at the level of readiness for direct practice requires students to show beginning levels of capability in all nine domains of the PCF, which are presented in Table 1.1. We have included a column for you to keep track of your learning and begin to think about how you have met the readiness for direct practice domain level capabilities. Later in the chapter, Activity 1.3 asks you to map your development in relation to each domain.

Table 1.1 PCF domain level – Readiness for Practice Capabilities (TCSW 2012d)

Domain	Readiness for direct practice domain level capabilities	Where and how this can be evidenced
Professionalism	Describe the role of the social worker Describe the mutual roles and responsibilities in supervision	
	Describe the importance of professional behaviour	
	Describe the importance of personal and professional boundaries	
	Demonstrate ability to learn, using a range of approaches	
	Describe the importance of emotional resilience in social work	
Values and ethics	Understand the profession's ethical principles and their relevance to practice	
	Demonstrate awareness of own personal values and how these can impact on practice	
Diversity	Recognise the importance of diversity in human identity and experience, and the application of anti-discriminatory and anti-oppressive principles in social work practice	
Rights, justice and economic wellbeing	Understand the principles of rights, justice and economic wellbeing, and their significance for social work practice	
Knowledge	Demonstrate an initial understanding of the application of research, theory and knowledge from sociology, social policy, psychology, health and human growth and development to social work	
	Demonstrate an initial understanding of the legal and policy frameworks and guidance that inform and mandate social work practice	
	Demonstrate an initial understanding of the range of theories and models for social work intervention	
Critical reflection and analysis	Understand the role of reflective practice and demonstrate basic skills of reflection	
	Understand the need to construct hypotheses in social work practice	
	Recognise and describe why evidence is important in social work practice	

Domain	Readiness for direct practice domain level capabilities	Where and how this can be evidenced
Intervention and skills	Demonstrate core communication skills and the capacity to develop them	
	Demonstrate the ability to engage with people in order to build compassionate and effective relationships	
	Demonstrate awareness of a range of frameworks to assess and plan intervention	
	Demonstrate basic ability to produce written documents relevant for practice	
	Demonstrate initial awareness of risk and safeguarding	
Contexts and organisations	Demonstrate awareness of the impact of organisational context on social work practice	
Professional leadership	Demonstrate awareness of the importance of professional leadership in social work	

It is clear that you will need to evidence at least a rudimentary level of capability that can be further developed in your first placement. Although universities have different readiness for practice assessments, there is some preparation work that you can do, for example:

- Discuss the readiness for practice process with your academic tutor and ask for guidance on relevant preparation to undertake;

- After reading this text, seek further reading on social work placements to support your learning about social work placements and what they might be like;

- Revise the academic modules you have studied so far and make a note of how these have influenced your knowledge, values or skills; make links to the PCF domain level capabilities for readiness for direct practice as you do this;

- Practise communication and listening skills with your family and friends;

- Write a short statement about your values in relation to the HCPC Guidance on Conduct and Ethics for Students or the values proposed by the British Association of Social Workers (BASW, 2012) (available from: http://cdn.basw.co.uk/upload/basw_112315-7.pdf);

- Read newspapers articles about social work and social care to make sure you are aware of contemporary social work issues and concerns;

- Visit the website of The College of Social Work (www.collegeofsocialwork.org/), which will give you lots of information about current developments in social work practice.

An important component of the readiness for practice process is to test your understanding of the PCF, as this will form the basis of your assessment on placement. You will be asked to demonstrate a detailed understanding of the requirements of the framework whilst on placement and you will need to be familiar with the document prior to undertaking your readiness for practice process.

In order to help you with your preparations, this next activity asks you to complete a self-evaluation of your performance in relation to each of the nine domains of the PCF. Do not worry if you feel unfamiliar with the PCF as we will discuss it in greater detail later in the book. Do not forget to consider the teaching you have received on your course so far, your previous experience and any gaps or needs in your knowledge and skills.

Activity 1.3

Evaluating your knowledge, values and skills in relation to the PCF

PCF	What do I know about this aspect of the PCF?	What sorts of things have I already done that will demonstrate evidence for this capability?	What skills do I already possess in relation to this capability?	What skills, knowledge or values do I need to develop for this capability?
Professionalism				
Values and ethics				
Diversity				
Rights, justice and economic wellbeing				
Knowledge				
Critical reflection and analysis				
Intervention and skills				
Contexts and organisations				
Professional leadership				

When you have completed this activity, read the case study below which introduces Gulshan, a social work student who is soon starting his first placement. In Chapter 2 you will read more about Gulshan and consider what theories would be relevant to his placement.

Gulshan

Gulshan is a social work student; he attends his pre-placement meeting in a busy voluntary agency which works with socially excluded young people in an inner-city environment. The agency runs a variety of group work activities and provides activity weekends away from the city. It also helps young people find work either on a paid or voluntary experience. It has a limited number of 'crisis' beds for homeless young people where they can stay on a temporary basis. Gulshan's practice educator tells him that issues he can expect to encounter on placement include substance misuse, self-harm, poor educational attainment, loss of parental contact, offending behaviour, mental health problems and homelessness. The practice educator already has a number of service users in mind that Gulshan could potentially work with including a young man with learning difficulty who has recently come out of prison and is currently homeless.

Prior to his placement, Gulshan completed Activity 1.3 and evaluated his learning and development in relation to the PCF domains at the readiness for direct practice level. Table 1.2 presents a copy of Gulshan's completed work on Activity 1.3.

Table 1.2 Example case study: Evaluating Gulshan's knowledge, values and skills in relation to the PCF

PCF	What do I know about this aspect of the PCF?	What sorts of things have I already done that will demonstrate evidence for this capability?	What skills do I already possess in relation to this capability?	What skills, knowledge or values do I need to develop for this capability?
Professionalism	That I should behave at all times like a professional.	Good attendance on the social work course. I have been reliable and punctual. I have read the HCPC Guidance on Conduct and Ethics for Students. We have discussed how best to look after ourselves whilst on placement.	I have good time management and organisational skills.	I need to work on how to present myself in meetings with other professionals.
Values and ethics	I have been learning about professional values such as respect, self-determination, confidentiality, empowerment and protecting people from harm.	We have completed a module on Values and Ethics. I have tried to listen to other people's points of view even though they are different to my own. I now know about treating information as confidential.	I believe in treating people with respect and think I'm good at understanding people's experiences and views.	I need to learn how to challenge people effectively. I would like to learn how to manage information in accordance with the Data Protection Act 1998.

(Continued)

Table 1.2   (Continued)

PCF	What do I know about this aspect of the PCF?	What sorts of things have I already done that will demonstrate evidence for this capability?	What skills do I already possess in relation to this capability?	What skills, knowledge or values do I need to develop for this capability?
Diversity	I have been learning about discrimination and anti-oppressive practice. I've also learnt about my own pre-conceptions and prejudices and how these might influence how I see practice situations.	I have taken part in discussions about oppression and have thought about other people's experiences and perspectives. I have been good at listening to what others have to say but felt less confident in voicing my opinions.	I have started to see issues of social injustice and discrimination and that anti-oppressive practice is not about treating everyone in the same way.	I need to develop skills in discussing issues of discrimination and oppression with service users in a clear and understandable way. I need to keep reflecting on my own perceptions and prejudices to make sure they don't interfere with the work on placement.
Rights, justice and economic wellbeing	In university, we have been discussing people's rights and legislation such as the Human Rights Act 1998. I also attended a Welfare Rights session.	During some voluntary work, I liaised with a housing department for a service user.	I have some knowledge of the law and have been learning about discrimination.	I need to know how legislation is applied in real practice.
Knowledge	I have undertaken a range of academic modules that provide theory that can explain situations or how to best intervene.	We have been working on case studies in seminars and also for assignments which need you to think about the role of knowledge in social work practice. Service users came to talk about their experiences of social workers and that really made me think about what sort of practitioner I want to be.	I have developed my communication skills and understand some of the theories and methods. There was an assessed role play as part of the readiness for practice module.	I am struggling to understand how to apply theory to practice.
Critical reflection and analysis	I've noticed that the lecturers talk a lot about criticality for our academic work and when using case studies about practice, we have been asked to think about different ways of helping.	I have been reading about criticality for my assignments and bought some study skills books. Thinking about practice, we have been applying assessment and analysis skills to case studies.	I have learnt never to take things at face value.	I need to develop skills in working with real service users and analysing information.

PCF	What do I know about this aspect of the PCF?	What sorts of things have I already done that will demonstrate evidence for this capability?	What skills do I already possess in relation to this capability?	What skills, knowledge or values do I need to develop for this capability?
		We have been looking at reflective practice and part of the readiness for practice assessment is a written reflective account of my development prior to placement.	I have started to examine and question my own assumptions and views.	
Intervention and skills	In the communications module, I have learnt about counselling models and done activities to try out these skills. We also practised taking a telephone referral.	In my last job before coming to university, I worked in a customer service centre and have a lot of experience of answering the telephone.	I have some telephone skills which have been helpful for listening.	I am concerned about how to write things for service users' files.
Contexts and organisations	The placements team organised a talk from placement providers and the different types of organisations amazed me.	We did an assessment case study using a video and had to consider the range of professionals who might be working with the service user.	I was quite good at thinking about who might be able to help the service user.	I do not have any experience of inter-agency or interdisciplinary work.
Professional leadership	I was unsure whether I would be able to meet this capability at this stage in my career, but I have been taking responsibility for my own learning during the first year of the degree.	I have become a student representative. With some friends, we have set up a study group. I have also set myself a study timetable which has helped me manage other demands on my time. We had some teaching about using supervision which stressed the responsibilities students will have during supervision whilst on placement	My communication and negotiation skills have helped me set up the study group and represent the views of the student cohort in formal meetings.	I would like to work on my confidence in presenting information in formal settings.

COMMENT

Whilst being at a very early stage of his career, Gulshan has still been able to find evidence in relation to each aspect of the PCF. Even small things can count as evidence towards your development in relation to the PCF (e.g. reading about an issue) as you will be able to build upon these small steps and develop increasing complexity as you progress. In common with many other students about to start placement, Gulshan has highlighted learning needs about the application of theory to practice and hopes to build both his skills and confidence in relation to each area. Being able to reflect upon your progress, learning needs and practice situations is vital for social work practice, as we will discuss in Chapter 2 in relation to reflective practice.

WHAT HAPPENS IF YOU FAIL YOUR READINESS FOR PRACTICE ASSESSMENT?

There are a number of reasons why you might fail your readiness for practice assessment. Some are listed below, although this is not an exhaustive list:

- Not demonstrating sufficient understanding of knowledge, skills and values to commence placement;

- Not evidencing a grasp of the requirements of the PCF;

- Failure to complete necessary documentation within the required timescales;

- Issues relating to your Criminal Records Bureau (CRB) or Disclosure and Barring Scheme (DBS) check;

- Inability to relate to service users or to accurately report their experiences;

- Breaches of the HCPC Guidance on Conduct and Ethics for student professionals in training;

- Behaviours that suggest unsuitability for practice with vulnerable service users (e.g. unreliability, lack of honesty and integrity) or raise concern about your health and wellbeing.

If you fail your readiness for practice assessment, what happens next will depend on the reason for failing. For example, if your documentation is incomplete you might be offered another chance to be assessed and it may be possible to conditionally proceed to placement with the requirement that you produce the necessary documents at the earliest opportunity, or by a set date. However, if there are concerns about your understanding of knowledge, values and skills or if your behaviour has caused significant concerns, then you might not have another assessment opportunity. Some issues are so serious that your university may formally invoke university-wide readiness for practice processes, for example serious breaches of professional expectations as outlined in the HCPC Guidance on Conduct and Ethics for Students. This is usually a formal panel of practitioners, service users and academics that will consider the available evidence and will determine whether a student is permitted to continue with their social work studies. If you find yourself in this situation you will be able to present your account to the panel, often with the support of a representative of the Student's Union.

MAKING CONTACT WITH YOUR PLACEMENT/THE PRE-PLACEMENT INTERVIEW

Having received your application form, it is likely that the placement provider will invite you for interview; this is called a pre-placement meeting. You will need to carefully prepare for this meeting; whilst it is not always the case, it is possible that, in some areas, other students are also applying for a placement with the organisation. You may find it helpful to make a list of questions to ask at the meeting (Lomax et al., 2010); for example, information regarding working hours, dress code, what the organisation expects of students, what sort of work you will be allocated, what pre-placement reading and preparation is required, as well as who you will be working with both within the team and externally. You might also have particular needs (e.g. caring responsibilities or specific learning needs) that you wish to discuss with your practice educator so they can make sure these are catered for once the placement begins. There is a lack of research evidence about pre-placement meetings (see research summary below), but we know that there is no prescribed format for this meeting.

RESEARCH SUMMARY

Because of the lack of research about the purpose and function of pre-placement meetings, we undertook a qualitative study (currently submitted for publication) of pre-placement meetings. There was one focus group with experienced practice educators and another focus group with students about to start their first placement.

Our findings were that:

- Pre-placement meetings come in all shapes and sizes with very little consistency about the way they are structured and the things that are required of students;

- Some pre-placement meetings were competitive interviews for the placement;

- Some pre-placement meetings were very formal and others were very relaxed;

- Students experienced some pre-placement meetings as an informal chat whereas others were asked to prepare presentations and attend a panel interview;

(Continued)

(Continued)

- The pre-placement interview makes sure the placement and student are a good match for each other;

- The meeting is the opportunity to be clear about specific needs such as child care responsibilities;

- There were occasions when the student did not attend the pre-placement meeting or offer apologies;

- Practice educators use application forms as a screening tool;

- Practice educators may test out the student's understanding of theory and the level of their pre-placement preparation.

ISSUES FOR PART-TIME STUDENTS

Some social work degrees are offered on a part-time basis and some students who study part-time do so as 'employment-based' or 'work-based' students. It is also then possible, in some regions, that these students may undertake their first placement within their own work setting. However, in some regions this is actively discouraged because, in doing so, students undertaking placements in settings where they have worked or currently work will have particular issues to consider. Whilst there may be no concerns about the content or nature of the work with service users or how to work effectively within an organisation, employment-based students face a number of other challenges. For example, how to make their learning explicit in a setting where they may have worked for some time; students may take certain skills and abilities for granted and therefore may not easily recognise evidence of capability in relation to the PCF. When on placement in their own work setting, employment-based students face particular difficulties in making the transition from practitioner to 'student' (Doel, 2010). This can be exacerbated by the expectations of their manager or wider team and by demands of a (heavy) caseload; for example, colleagues may forget that they are a student and need learning opportunities in the same way as other students; managers may find it hard to provide workload relief and the student can find it difficult to take study leave when the pressures facing colleagues are evident. If you are in this position, we strongly advise you to make sure you discuss your student status with your practice educator so that thoughts and plans for how this can be protected are considered in your learning agreement.

PLACEMENT COUNTDOWN

Our view is that preparation for placement takes place over several months prior to arriving in your placement setting. This final section of the chapter takes you through some of the last-minute preparations you need to make prior to the start of your placement and covers three areas: preparing yourself; organising academic work; and understanding placement roles and responsibilities.

PREPARING YOURSELF

As we outlined earlier, it is crucial to have given some thought to your learning needs prior to placement which will require critical self-reflection and self-evaluation. Your practice educator will appreciate you sharing your ideas of your learning needs as you arrive in placement and your progress towards meeting these can be reviewed during supervision throughout placement. We suggest that you make a written note of your learning needs prior to placement start and use these to inform your learning agreement.

There might also be practicalities to consider, such as ensuring that you understand the dress code of the agency. For example, some settings will not allow you to dress in jeans and may expect you to cover tattoos or remove piercings. Many social care and social work placement settings require smart casual dress, unless you are attending an event which has a specific type of dress code (e.g. court attendance or outdoor activities with young people). Some students unwittingly fall foul of what are largely unwritten dress codes within organisations by over- or under-dressing. You may also need to consider how people such as co-workers, managers, service users and other professionals may view the wearing of short skirts, shorts, strapless tops, open shirts or other items of clothing that could be seen as being unsuitable. Your practice educator will be able to advise you on these issues and you need to remember that you are representing yourself and your profession on placement. The key is to dress modestly in a way that is most suitable for the professional work you are undertaking.

It is also important to make sure you are organised for your journey to placement. Thinking about what time you will need to get up, making sure you set your alarm clock, planning your travel route (via public transport or car) and having a trial run of the journey are all essential aspects of your planning. Your placement may provide you with a diary or give you access to an e-diary. If not, you will need to purchase one as maintaining an up-to-date diary will be essential if you are going to effectively manage your time on placement and fit in the demands of practice and academic work.

If applicable, you might need to make arrangements for family and caring commitments. This tends to be less stressful if you know well in advance the start date of your placement and whether there will be any breaks during the placement (e.g. Christmas or half-term holidays). Negotiating time off for school holiday periods may not always be possible and will be dependent upon the academic timetable. If in doubt, speak to your module coordinator for placements as they will know the key dates for placement-related activities (e.g. marking, practice assurance/assessment panels, examination boards) and will be able to tell you if there is any flexibility on the placement dates. You might need to plan, or at the very least consider, how you are going to manage the work/life demands that you will face. Home commitments will vary from student to student, but *all* students need to think about how they will find time for study whilst being on a full-time placement, how to ensure they have some leisure time and how they will manage relationships with family and friends when they are extremely busy.

A real student, who we refer to as David, offers the following advice about how to manage a work/life balance:

Student voice – David

The majority of people have to find a balance between work/life. Whilst on placement I have had to find a work/life/academic balance which has been incredibly difficult and the only way I found to do this is through being incredibly organised. It's not just a case of organising your working day, but also organising your 'free time', the closer you get to the end of placement the more every hour counts. Book your academic work into time slots just as you would your work appointments, but make sure you also have time slots for you and your family.

Consider David's advice and your reading so far in this chapter as you complete the following activity.

Activity 1.4

Managing work/life pressures

Spend some time thinking about your personal commitments and write a list of the things you will need to manage or organise prior to placement and then consider some potential solutions to how you might manage these.

Managing work/life pressures	
Issue to manage	**Possible solutions**

COMMENT

Of course, it is not possible for us to know the particular challenges that you may face, but commonly students completing this activity are struck by the level of goodwill and support they are likely to need from family and friends during their studies. This informal support is crucial to completion but is often unacknowledged (Mathews et al., 2009).

ORGANISING ACADEMIC WORK

Prior to starting placement, you need to make sure that you have all of the documentation relating to placement. This may seem a particularly obvious recommendation, but from our experience it is one that students often neglect. There might be a number of documents which will guide you through placement. Students usually focus on portfolio building during placement to evidence their skills in relation to the PCF. It is sensible to organise a folder for your portfolio and make sure you are familiar with its requirements. However, there might also be other placement documentation that you need to be familiar with such as those which outline people's roles or explain what to do in the case of absence from placement.

You need to be aware of what you are being assessed against whilst on placement, so make sure you read the placement documentation with care. Keeping up to date with portfolio work throughout the placement is the most effective way of managing the practice and academic assessment elements of placement and at the heart of this are good organisational skills.

Top tips – Preparing for placement

- Read all of the placement documentation
- Prepare folders or files (electronic or paper) to put placement documentation and evidence in
- Start as you mean to go on – get organised and stay that way
- Keep on top of the portfolio requirements throughout the placement – never leave this until the last minute

---

UNDERSTANDING PLACEMENT ROLES AND RESPONSIBILITIES

Reading the placement documentation will provide you with the necessary information about who is who in placement. You will be allocated a practice educator who will be responsible for assessing your practice during placement, writing the final report on your progress and making a decision about whether you have passed or failed the assessment in relation to the PCF. Eventually all practice educators will be registered and qualified social workers with additional training in teaching students (TCSW, 2012e). Until these changes are fully implemented, however, your practice educator may not be a qualified social worker. You might be based with your practice educator all the time but some students will be placed in settings where their practice educator is not present full-time. In these circumstances you will be provided with an 'off-site' or 'long-arm practice educator'. The practice educator will also provide you with supervision which tests out and supports your learning regarding application of theory and values. If your practice educator is in placement all the time, they will supervise the work allocated to you and sometimes this element of supervision is shared with the manager of the team. You should be prepared that supervision will be both supportive and challenging, as part of the practice educator's role is to challenge your thinking, your developing knowledge and values.

If you have a placement where the practice educator is off-site or long-arm, then there will be someone who is based in placement who will take responsibility for day-to-day management, support and supervision; this role may be called practice assessor, practice supervisor, on-site supervisor or work-based supervisor. We use the term 'on-site supervisor' in this book. The on-site supervisor will allocate work to you, as well as providing daily guidance and support. They will write reports for your portfolio, but do not make the decision to pass or fail. On-site supervisors may also supervise work allocated to ensure you adhere to agency standards.

As a student social worker in placement, you will be required to adhere to professional standards of behaviour (e.g. the PCF as well as the HCPC Guidance on Conduct and Ethics for Students) and also agency policies and procedures (e.g. recording policies). Placements will expect you to show a beginning level of professionalism and you will be expected to be accountable for your practice. This will mean making sure you undertake the work allocated to you (with support and guidance) and adhere to placement work practices (e.g. signing in and out of the office; keeping to health and safety requirements). If you cannot go into placement, you will need to let your practice educator, and possibly the university module coordinator, know and provide a valid reason for this. If absence is because of illness and is prolonged (more than seven days), you may be asked to obtain a doctor's certificate to explain this absence.

CONCLUSION

This chapter has introduced you to the key processes in preparing for a placement. Placements are an exciting component of the social work degree, but the requirements and expectations prior to placement may seem rather onerous; however, the placement team/coordinator and academic staff will guide you through these steps in a sequential manner, which will hopefully mean that the tasks involved seem less overwhelming. Preparing for placement is a lengthy process that takes place over many months and it is important that you engage with these requirements in a proactive way. Being organised is key to successfully managing some of these processes and will certainly be beneficial when you start placement and have to manage the concurrent demands of placement and academic work.

FURTHER READING

Doel, M. (2010) *Social Work Placements: A Traveller's Guide*. London: Routledge.
Renowned for his work on practice learning, Doel uses the analogy of a 'travel guide' and takes the reader through the placement journey. This is an accessible and easy to read book which will appeal to those who think conceptually using metaphors.

Lomax, R., Jones, K., Leigh, S. and Gay, C. (2010) *Surviving Your Social Work Placement*. Basingstoke: Palgrave Macmillan.
This is a highly practical book which covers all aspects of student placement. It is well grounded in practice wisdom and experience.

INTERNET RESOURCES

The Social Work Reform Board (SWRB): www.education.gov.uk/swrb

The SWRB was established to build on the work of the Social Work Task Force (SWTF) which made 15 recommendations about the reform of the social work profession that considered initial education, a continuing professional development framework for qualified practitioners, supportive employment infrastructures, workforce planning models and the creation of a College of Social Work.

The College of Social Work (TCSW): www.collegeofsocialwork.org/

From the beginning of 2012, The College of Social Work became the lead professional organisation for social work. The college represents social work as a profession and advocates on behalf of its members and the profession as a whole. The PCF and the relevant domain capability levels can be found on this website at: www.collegeofsocialwork.org/pcf.aspx

The Health and Care Professions Council (HCPC): www.hpc-uk.org/

The HCPC became the regulatory body for social work on 1 August 2012. It maintains the register of qualified social workers and ensures that social workers are fit to practise, that they do so in a manner that is commensurate with professional standards and maintain their continuing professional development. Originally known as the Health Professions Council the regulatory body was renamed to reflect the inclusion of social work.

2

KNOWLEDGE, SKILLS AND VALUES

Chapter summary

When you have worked through this chapter, you will be able to:

- Identify the knowledge you need prior to going on placement and consider the importance of 'knowledge' in social work practice;

- Develop an understanding of social work theory and why it is required in practice;

- Discuss why a recognition of social work values is necessary to pre-placement preparation;

- Appreciate the importance of reflection as a skill for improving practice;

- Understand how effective anti-oppressive practice draws on social work knowledge, values and skills that inform one another and are often interrelated.

INTRODUCTION

In this chapter we introduce you to some of the knowledge, values and skills that you need to consider as you prepare to go on placement. We appreciate that you have much to think about at this time and a number of practical arrangements to organise, but now is the best time to clear your thoughts and thoroughly prepare for the demands that lie ahead. Often students tell us that they wish that they had prepared more before the start of their placement, as the demands of casework and learning a bewildering array of new processes, organisational paperwork and ways of working, to say nothing of portfolio building, can be very time consuming once placement starts. Consequently, the time you spend on preparing beforehand can make a real difference to the quality of your work.

In this chapter you may feel that we spend a disproportionate amount of time thinking about knowledge and, as an example of one aspect of knowledge, how an understanding of theory is of importance. This is deliberate as it is easier to consider the values you need to demonstrate and the skills you require, once your practice on placement has commenced. This is not to suggest that these topics are entirely absent from this chapter, but you may find that certain chapters concentrate more on particular themes or issues that are of significance to a particular stage of placement. After we have encouraged you to think about knowledge and theory we then discuss the role of social work values and skills, highlighting how the skills of reflection are crucial as a way of processing and understanding your ideas and experiences. Finally, we introduce the concept of anti-oppressive practice and use it as an example of how knowledge, values and skills can sometimes fuse together and become difficult to disentangle. Do not worry if you feel that you only have a limited understanding of some of the concepts we discuss in this chapter as we will re-visit them on a number of occasions throughout this book and this chapter is purely an accessible and thought provoking introduction.

WHAT IS KNOWLEDGE?

Throughout this book and throughout your placements you will be working with the concepts of knowledge, values and skills. Therefore, it is important to start by considering the meanings of these key terms in order to clarify thinking and support your further learning.

Activity 2.1

Understanding knowledge

Consider these questions and make some short notes in response. We suggest that, for this activity, you do not refer to the Internet or other sources, but initially try to note down your own ideas:

- What is 'knowledge'?
- What different types of knowledge inform social work practice?

COMMENT

'Knowledge' is one of those complex terms that we casually use and intuitively understand, but rarely take time to critique. For example, in recent decades there has been an increasing emphasis on 'evidence-based practice' not just in social work, but in other allied professions such as nursing and occupational therapy (Mathews and Crawford, 2011). Government, the general public and practitioners want to know that professional activity is based on reliable 'evidence' that promotes best practice and positive outcomes; this, however, raises a question. Is evidence the same as knowledge? We would argue that it is not. The term 'evidence' is increasingly defined within a scientific frame of reference which argues that it can only be produced using research techniques which have a clear, scientific rationale (Alcock and Ferguson, 2012; Thompson and Thompson, 2008). Knowledge, however, is a more open and fluid term which lacks the rigour and certainty that evidence may seem to provide. For example, Trevithick (2008: 1214) suggests that:

> ... knowledge involves gathering, analysing and synthesizing different theories (explanations) in order to arrive at some kind of tentative understanding, hypothesis or judgement.

Evidence, of course, may underpin and inform knowledge, but it is only one of the influences that we need to consider when we think about the composition of knowledge. For example, in 2002 the Social Care Institute for Excellence (SCIE), whose role it is to identify, enhance and disseminate the knowledge base for good practice in social care, commissioned a team of researchers 'to explore the types and quality of social care knowledge' (Pawson et al., 2003: vii). The Knowledge Review subsequently produced for the SCIE is useful as it identifies five potential sources of knowledge that inform social work practice.

RESEARCH SUMMARY – TYPES OF KNOWLEDGE FOR SOCIAL WORK PRACTICE

- *Organisational knowledge* – knowledge which derives from social care and other allied organisations, through the provision, management and governance of social care. This type of knowledge is often generated by senior managers who are responsible for interpreting local and national policies and issuing guidelines for staff to follow. Often this organisational approach describes and prescribes the context for the delivery of social care services.

- *Practitioner knowledge* – this type of knowledge stands in contrast to organisational knowledge as it is produced by the 'hands on' work of practitioners who have worked, often over many years, with service users from similar backgrounds experiencing similar issues. This experience and 'know how' is accumulated and shared with other colleagues and over time the 'collected wisdom' of a team or organisation grows and matures.

- *Policy community knowledge* – this type of knowledge derives from bodies such as central government, local government, audits, reviews, commissions and 'think tanks'. Consequently, this knowledge is formally produced often in response to new legislation or government policy by civil servants, politicians and legal experts who work together to produce guidance which steers service provision.

- *Research knowledge* – knowledge which is produced via academic enquiry often by university staff or by people in large organisations such as the NHS or major charities. It often involves funding from government or a research council and uses scientific methods of enquiry leading to publication.

- *Service user and carer knowledge* – this final type of knowledge parallels practitioner knowledge as it also comes from what can be learnt from direct experience. This time it derives from being on the receiving end of social care provision as a service user or from the experience of providing care to a dependent person. Increasingly social care organisations and universities use service users to enhance their credibility and ability to conduct research, and service user organisations themselves are also increasingly active in carrying out research.

(Adapted from Mathews and Crawford, 2011; Pawson et al., 2003)

We hope that you find this typology helpful in developing your understanding of knowledge. There are of course other ways of categorising and considering the knowledge that underpins practice and there are a number of limitations and contradictions inherent within this model. For example, the subjective and interpretative nature of both practitioner and service user knowledge stands in contrast to the objectivity of academic research with its emphasis on scientific method, yet all three types of knowledge are seen to be equal within the model and of significance to practice. As you commence placement and begin to gain experience we recommend that you return to this typology and use it as a framework for discussing the different sources of knowledge that you use to inform your work and to enhance your criticality.

In the next section of this chapter you will learn about one aspect of knowledge, social work theory, which is crucial for you to understand and be able to use from the start of your placement. Theory and theoretical observations can emanate from a range of different sources including a number of the knowledge sources that we noted above. Whilst the precise origin of many theories can be difficult to trace, often theory is created via scholarly activities such as formal research and academic debate and is best seen as an example of research knowledge (Pawson et al., 2003).

SOCIAL WORK THEORY

A feature of the demand for social work practice to be more evidence-based has been a parallel and related call for it to better relate theory to practice (Humphrey, 2011; Parker and Bradley, 2010). From experience we know that students (and practitioners) find this difficult and sometimes classroom-based teaching fails to easily transfer to practice (O'Sullivan, 2011). Whilst this book is not primarily about theory, and is certainly not intended to be a 'handbook of theory for students', it may be helpful to pose a series of questions to help us explore this important aspect of placement activity.

WHAT IS THEORY?

Oko (2011: 6) suggests that theory is 'a set of related ideas and assumptions that are drawn upon to help explain a particular phenomenon'. Whilst Payne (2005: 5) states that 'a theory is an organised statement of ideas about the world'. Both of these straight-forward definitions tell us that a theory is simply a way of organising ideas about a particular topic or issue. Often theories derive from research into practice or human behaviour and they are always open to challenge and revision as our insights change and develop. Oko (2011) rightly warns that many theories are based on assumptions about how the world works and we could go further and suggest that all theories contain elements of subjectivity and ideology. This is perhaps most explicitly seen in the more 'radical' sociological or social work theories which question the basis of capitalist society and are often explicitly influenced by a socialist or Marxist perspective.

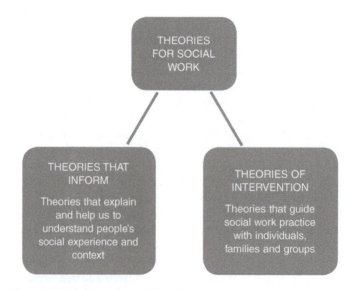

Figure 2.1   Categories of theory for social work

Equally, a number of authors (Humphrey, 2011; Parker, 2010a; Thompson, 2006) suggest that social work practice 'borrows' theory from a range of disciplines including sociology, psychology and social policy. This eclecticism is not necessarily problematic and could be seen to offer a depth and breadth to our theoretical understanding which other professions may lack (Mathews and Crawford, 2011). As a final thought in this introductory discussion, we want to suggest that most theories used in social work can be divided into two related categories. First are those theories which help us to explore and understand the individual and social context of the service user, for example theories of social exclusion, oppression, attachment and power, which may be collectively entitled 'theories which inform'. There is a second group of theories, however, which we will label 'theories of intervention'. These theoretical methods and models guide the interventions we make into the lives of families and service users; examples may include crisis intervention, systems theory and the task-centred approach.

WHY DO WE NEED THEORY?

In our view there are at least two reasons why social work students on placement need to understand and use theory. The first is summarised by Parker (2010a: 20):

> ... theories and models guide social workers' actions and provide explanatory frameworks that make effective interventions possible and, in doing so, they contribute to ethical, evidence based and accountable practice.

This quotation echoes our previous point that theory offers an 'explanatory framework' and assists practitioners to understand the context of their intervention. It then suggests that good use of theory makes 'effective interventions possible'. It could be argued that due to the fluidity and complexity of the situations routinely faced by social workers, a sound grasp of theory is not going to be sufficient by itself to ensure effectiveness (Mathews and Crawford, 2011). Parker (2010a) also implies that practice which is informed by theory is more likely to be accountable and ethical. In other words, the use of theory provides a framework which helps us to explain 'why we did what we did', particularly to those people to whom social work is responsible, such as service users and managers. Additionally, it gives an audit trail to our thinking, provides evidence on which to base our practice and helps us to make defensible decisions.

The second reason why social work students preparing to go on placement need to gain an understanding of theory is entirely pragmatic – it is a key requirement of the Professional Capabilities Framework (PCF). As stated in Chapter 1, the PCF level readiness for direct practice requires students to show beginning levels of capability in all nine domains of the PCF, including the knowledge domain which requires students to:

> Demonstrate an initial understanding of the application of research, theory and knowledge from sociology, social policy, psychology, health and human growth and development to social work.

Demonstrate an initial understanding of the legal and policy frameworks and guidance that inform and mandate social work practice.

Demonstrate an initial understanding of the range of theories and models for social work intervention. (TCSW, 2012d)

As you will see from these requirements, the domain confirms the eclectic nature of social work knowledge and acknowledges that the profession draws on a range of the social sciences including sociology and psychology. It should also be helpful to remember that at this stage of your professional development, only a 'limited understanding' of theories and models is required.

Student voice – Amelia

When we studied theory in the modules at university, before going onto my first practice placement, I found it really hard to understand what it was all about and why we were bothering; to be honest, I didn't always enjoy this part of the modules. But when I knew where my first placement would be and I discussed this with my tutor, I went back over some of the theory we had learnt and it seemed more interesting, important and relevant to what I would be doing.

In this chapter, so far, we have considered what theory is and why we need it; following Amelia's experience, we now turn our attention to the practical use of theory. Even at this pre-placement stage you need to be thinking how you will integrate theory into practice and which theories may be especially useful in your placement setting. In order to help you with your thinking we return to the example of Gulshan to whom you were introduced in Chapter 1.

Activity 2.2

Understanding theories when preparing for practice

In Chapter 1 you read about Gulshan, a social work student who was preparing for a placement in a busy inner-city voluntary agency that works with socially excluded young people. Gulshan already knows from his practice educator that he is likely to be working with young people who experience a range of complex issues – such as learning difficulties, substance misuse, loss of parental contact, offending behaviour, mental health problems and homelessness. Practice in the agency often involves supporting young people to find work experience, supporting young people by the provision of crisis beds and working with them through group work activities and activity weekends.

Now that Gulshan has some preliminary information about his placement and the needs of service users he will be working with, which theories do you think he should consider as part of his preparation for direct practice?

Divide your answer into 'theories which inform' and 'theories of intervention'.

COMMENT

From the information Gulshan has already received it seems that his placement is going to be a busy one and there are a number of 'theories which inform' that he needs to consider. For example, the agency offers a service to young people who are homeless and experiencing a crisis – so theories which explore and explain the nature of crisis might be useful. Gulshan also needs to know about the social context within which the agency operates so knowledge of social exclusion and theories of poverty, such as the cycle of deprivation, will also be required. He also needs to consider the different models of mental illness and look at some of the theories which attempt to explain such damaging behaviours as substance misuse and self-harm. Examples of 'theories of intervention' that he could consider include crisis intervention, systems theory and task-centred work. Understanding of these placement-specific theories needs to be complemented by knowledge of other more generic theories concerning communication, relationship building and the use of self, all of which have a broad applicability across placement settings. There are clearly many other theories or theoretical concepts that Gulshan could consider which you may have identified. Whilst your practice educator should not expect you to have an in-depth knowledge of theory, they will expect you to have thoughtfully considered the work undertaken in your placement and to have completed a considerable amount of preparatory work.

So far in this chapter we have concentrated on the related concepts of knowledge and theory and thought about their importance as you prepare to go on placement. We have also implied that both theory and knowledge contain elements of bias and subjectivity. One of the influences that may affect knowledge and theory is the value base of the person who creates or uses them. We are sure that as part of your course you will have been learning about the importance of values to the practice of social work, and we now want to concentrate on how a consideration of values is essential at this early stage of your placement experience.

SOCIAL WORK VALUES

Throughout the short history of professional social work a number of authors and bodies have attempted to define those values which may inform or underpin professional practice. Father Felix Biestek (1961), an American Roman Catholic priest, is credited with being amongst the first to formulate a set of values to guide practice in the 1960s. His list of values, which have been replicated and re-worked on a number of occasions, include:

- *Individualisation* – recognition that the situation or issue faced by a service user is unique to them;

- *Purposeful expression of feelings* – the opportunity as a service user to express emotions and feelings which in turn can be used to initiate change;

- *Controlled emotional involvement* – the development of a professional relationship based on empathy which maintains an appropriate boundary between the worker and a service user;

- *Acceptance* – to be recognised in your own right as being a person of worth and value;

- *Non-judgemental attitude* – not passing judgement on other people;

- *Self-determination* – promoting the ability of people to make choices and to take decisions;

- *Confidentiality* – not disclosing personal information obtained from within the professional relationship.

The listing of social work values is however problematic as there is a danger that important principles, such as engagement with structural issues, are disregarded or that the list takes on the form of a mantra, lacking in substance or clarity (Shardlow, 1991). It is also worth noting that social issues, our understanding of them and the context of practice has moved on significantly since Biestek's attempt to articulate the value base of the profession and it could be argued that more recent views should take precedence. Nonetheless, his list is helpful as it encourages sound practice and supports working with individuals in a non-judgemental and respectful manner. There are of course other more contemporary values or ethical statements that guide practice of which you need to be aware. For example, the Health and Care Professions Council's Guidance on Conduct and Ethics for Students (HCPC, 2012a; available from: www. hpc-uk.org/assets/documents/10002C16Guidanceonconductandethicsforstudents. pdf) is an important document as it clearly articulates the personal and professional conduct required from students as they embark on their professional career. Crucially, this guidance is based on ethical principles and clearly reflects the value base of social work. You also need to be aware of The Code of Ethics for Social Work published by the British Association of Social Workers (BASW, 2012; available from: http://cdn. basw.co.uk/upload/basw_112315-7.pdf).

We would encourage you to thoughtfully consider these attempts to articulate the value base of social work as all of them add to our understanding of practice. At this time of preparation you should also familiarise yourself with the value requirements that need to be demonstrated and embedded in your practice on placement which derive from the Professional Capabilities Framework for Social Workers in England

(TCSW, 2012c). Specifically, by the end of your first practice placement (TCSW, 2012g) you need to be able to:

- Understand and, with support, apply the profession's ethical principles;

- Recognise and with support manage the impact of own values on professional practice;

- Identify and with guidance manage potentially conflicting values and ethical dilemmas;

- Elicit and respect the needs and views of service users and carers and, with support, promote their participation in decision making wherever possible;

- Promote and protect the privacy of individuals within and outside their families and networks, recognising the requirements of professional accountability and information sharing;

By the conclusion of your final placement you should be able to demonstrate competency in the following values and ethics (TCSW, 2012f):

- Understand and apply the profession's ethical principles and legislation taking account of these in reaching decisions;

- Understand and with support manage the impact of own values upon professional practice;

- Manage potentially conflicting or competing values, and with guidance, recognise, reflect on and work with ethical dilemmas;

- Demonstrate respectful partnership work with service users and carers, eliciting and respecting their needs and views and promoting their participation in decision making wherever possible;

- Recognise and promote individuals' rights to autonomy and self-determination;

- Promote and protect the privacy of individuals within and outside their families and networks, recognising the requirements of professional accountability and information sharing.

As you can see from these final expectations, you have some way to go! In all that you do over the course of your social work education, both in the classroom and on placement, you need to demonstrate that your knowledge, understanding and insight is incrementally increasing. Professional values can sometimes be difficult to evidence and tend to be overlooked by busy students on placement who sometimes overly concentrate on the more practical work of placement to the detriment of incorporating values. This is why ensuring that values are regularly discussed in supervision from the start of your placement is vital. As part of preparing to go on placement, you may find it helpful to carefully consider the values and ethics within the PCF (TCSW, 2012f and 2012g) and begin to think how you might evidence them in practice and in your portfolio.

SOCIAL WORK SKILLS — THE EXAMPLE OF REFLECTION

From working through the previous sections in this chapter, you will have gained an understanding of the concepts of knowledge and values for social work practice. Social work skills can be thought of as the means by which we apply our knowledge and values in practice. Trevithick defines a skill as

> ... an action with a specific *goal* that can be *learnt*, that involves *actions per-formed in sequence*, that can be organized in ways that involve *economy of effort* and *evaluated* in terms of its relevance and effectiveness. Although these characteristics have been described separately, they interweave and overlap. (2012: 155, emphasis in original).

Trevithick (2012) draws on 80 different generalist skills and interventions in her text, with particular attention to communication skills. Throughout the chapters of this book you will also learn about a range of skills, hence here in this chapter we deliberately focus on the skills of reflection and reflective practice. In our view, effec-tive reflection is a key social work skill that enables the practitioner to integrate knowledge, theory and values in their practice (Thompson and Thompson, 2008). Reflection is a key term in social work and, as with all of our core concepts, it is open to interpretation. One definition we particularly like comes from Humphrey (2011: 106):

> Reflection is about acquiring new insights in relation to any given phenom-enon, including ourselves, other people, theories and cultures. It involves an inward journeying as we need to process these new insights within our own minds, and also an outward journeying insofar as we discuss these new insights with other people including peers, supervisors, service users and carers.

This statement emphasises that reflection focuses not only on ourselves, but also enables us to consider learning and the challenges that we have encoun-tered from other sources. Reflection is seen as a two-way process. First there is an internal process where we consider for ourselves what we have seen, done and learnt, which is followed by a second stage where this thinking is shared with other people.

The concept of reflection, and the use of reflecting, have become something of a 'mantra' in social work in recent years and a range of social work authors have writ-ten extensively about the process and purpose of reflection (e.g. Brookfield, 2009; Ixer, 1999; Nathan, 2002). Interest in how professionals make use of reflection originates from the work of American social scientist Donald Schön (1983), who devised a two-fold classification of how professionals acquire the skills and knowledge which are essential to their role. He describes the first approach as being 'technical-rational', where a situation always responds in the same way to the same set of actions. Consequently, a practitioner can learn the skills required to solve the problem through demonstration, mentoring and modelling. Schön had a range of mainly scientific disciplines and professions in mind when he devised this term, such as elements of dentistry, surgery or engineering which he argued may be learnt in this way. Other professions, however, like social work which work directly with people, often at times in their lives when they are experiencing significant change, vulnerability and uncertainty, may find a technical-rational approach to be inadequate. This is where the skills of reflection are important as it allows us to process and critique the complexity and fluidity of the situations that we may encounter. Schön's second approach is more relevant to social work and is entitled 'reflection-in-action'. This occurs as the professional actively considers and critiques their actions, thoughts and feelings whilst performing their duties.

RESEARCH SUMMARY – IXER'S FIVE-STAGE MODEL OF REFLECTION

Ixer (1999) proposes a five-stage model of reflection which can be used in social work practice.

1. A problem or issue is identified that is of concern. It has to be a significant problem which requires considerable thought to solve;

2. The practitioner considers the problem and gains a fuller understanding of what it is and why it has happened;

3. Tentative hypotheses and solutions to the problem are constructed;

4. These hypotheses are subjected to scrutiny, critique and reasoning; this may involve other people such as your practice educator or manager;

5. The solution is put into practice and tested. (Adapted from Parker, 2010a: 30)

Ixer's model provides a description of the process or stages of reflection. As you have read from the description of Schön's (1983) concept of reflection-in-action, this type of reflection can encourage flexibility and enable plans to alter and be responsive to changing situations.

Activity 2.3

Using Ixer's five-stage model of reflection

Think about the placement setting you may be going to and identify a significant problem which needs careful consideration prior to you starting work. This could be a range of things and it may be helpful to think back to some of the issues you have previously identified in this chapter. For example, you may have thought about the organisational culture of your placement, or have concerns about the type of work or the service user group you will be working with, or maybe you are worried about how you will physically manage to combine your personal commitments, study and the demands of placement. Using Ixer's model, reflect on your problem and try to devise a possible solution.

COMMENT

This exercise is a difficult one to complete at this stage of your placement preparation and our aim is purely to encourage you to think how reflection may work in practice. In order to test the model we will use the example of Jasveer.

CASE STUDY

Jasveer

Jasveer is a social work student who is going on placement to a school for children with special needs. She has been told in her pre-placement meeting that a number of the children can be aggressive and volatile and she is concerned as to how she will manage these challenging behaviours. Using Ixer's (1999) model, Jasveer might adopt the following approach:

Step 1: Jasveer has been thinking about her placement since her pre-placement meeting and has been reflecting on what her practice educator said. She is looking forward to going on placement and working with a service user group of which she has no experience. There are a number of challenges that she is expecting to face, but she is most concerned about how to manage the behaviours mentioned by her practice educator and is worried that she will not be able to cope.

Step 2: Jasveer undertakes some background reading on children with special needs and challenging behaviours and asks a friend who is a teacher about her experience. She learns that sometimes violence and aggression can occur due to a lack of stimulation, an unmet need, or frustration arising from an inability to verbally communicate.

Step 3: Jasveer makes a preliminary list of ways in which she might manage challenging behaviour and keep herself safe in the classroom.

> **Step 4**: She then discusses her ideas with her friend and makes an appointment to see her university tutor. At the meeting Jasveer tells her tutor about her concerns and her coping strategies. The tutor acknowledges the validity of the issue, discusses her fears and makes some further suggestions. The tutor agrees to contact the practice educator to make her aware of Jasveer's concerns.
>
> **Step 5**: Prior to starting placement, Jasveer visits the school to observe how her practice educator manages her class and discusses different behaviour management approaches with the staff.

We appreciate that this example is unsatisfactory as clearly Jasveer will not be able to test out her solution until she commences her placement. Nonetheless, we hope that you have found this introduction to reflection helpful as it is a skill which requires time to develop and is critical to the success of your placement. Many universities require students to keep a reflective diary or log whilst on placement in which they record their thoughts and feelings and share them with their practice educator during supervision. Such tools are helpful, not least because they compel students to step aside from their busy schedules, casework pressures and portfolio building, and take time to value and thoughtfully consider their work. Even at this stage, it is helpful to get into the habit of recording your reflections; this initial exercise might be useful to discuss at your first supervision session.

KNOWLEDGE, VALUES AND SKILLS – PREPARING FOR PRACTICE

As we have already discussed, preparing to go on placement can be stressful as there are a range of practicalities and arrangements that need to be in place before you will feel able to leave home for that first day at your 'new office'. Throughout this chapter, we have been exploring how, as part of your preparation, you also need to give consideration to what knowledge, values and skills you already possess and what you need to acquire either before or during your placement. Whilst this may appear to be a daunting prospect, self-reflection and thoughtful preparation are key to a successful placement.

This initial thinking is not easy as potentially readers of this text will be going on placements with a wide range of social care providers who will require very different sets of knowledge and understanding. For example, some placements will be within the private, voluntary or independent sector and may have a very particular ethos or way of working. Some placements will be provided by large local authorities and will have a clear statutory emphasis. Others may be within small organisations, where you will be expected to undertake a number of different roles and functions. Who you potentially work with will also be different. Some of you will know prior to going on placement that you will be predominantly working with a specific service user group, whilst other placements will be more generic in nature. It is worth noting, however, that even if your placement is with a particular group of service users, you will encounter many service users, carers and people from outside of your specialist area. For example, if you are working with children, parents (adults) will form a core component of the work you do. The geographical nature of the placement also needs to be considered. Some placements will be in large busy urban areas with an ethnically and culturally diverse population. Others will be in isolated rural areas with significant pockets of deprivation where arranging services and even visiting people (especially in winter) can be a real problem. In other words, placements come 'in all shapes and sizes' and what you need to know or acquire can differ markedly from placement to placement.

Activity 2.4

Preparing for placement: knowledge, values and skills

Spend some time thinking about where you are going on placement. Then make some notes in response to the following questions:

- What knowledge do I already have or need to acquire before I go on placement?
- What values do I already demonstrate or need to acquire before I go on placement?
- What skills do I already have or need to acquire before I go on placement?

(Adapted from Lomax et al., 2010)

COMMENT

These are difficult questions and we expect that you have provided a diverse range of responses. At this stage you may only have a limited awareness of your placement and may not know what knowledge, values and skills you are expected to take with you. Nonetheless, this exercise is helpful as it prompts you to think about your preparation and gives you time to ask questions of yourself and those who will be supporting you on placement. You are also aware now of how standards and capabilities from The College of Social Work and the Health and Care Professions Council provide helpful guidance to the level of knowledge, values and skills you are expected to have at different stages of your professional development.

Table 2.1 presents an example of a response to Activity 2.4 from a student who is going on placement with a Crisis Resolution Home Treatment Team (CRHT) provided by a Mental Health Trust.

As you can see, this student has done some initial thinking about her placement, but needs to think further about the work she needs to do before entering the team. For example, working within the National Health Service (NHS) may be a new and very different experience for her as it has its own organisational culture, emphases

Table 2.1 A personal reflection of the knowledge, values and skills that need to be taken on placement (adapted from Lomax et al., 2010)

	What I already know	What I need to acquire
Knowledge	I know about the social model of mental health. I know what 'mental illness' is.	What is home treatment? Think about theories relating to 'crisis'. Look again at specific mental illnesses – schizophrenia, psychosis, etc.
Values	I am non-judgemental. I am open with people. I try to be honest and trustworthy in all that I do.	Valuing people for who they are and learning to look beyond the label of their illness. Not being judgemental about people who misuse substances.
Skills	I have good communication skills. I have past experience of running groups. I have past experience of assessment work.	Report writing. Process recording. Working with medical and nursing staff. Working with service users who are very poorly.

and priorities which are different to other organisations. This placement will also be primarily engaging with people of working age. If the student has only got previous experience of working with children, she may need to think how she can best transfer and use her past experience and knowledge. You may have noted that there are some contradictions within the response. She claims to be non-judgemental, but acknowledges that she may need to reconsider her value base regarding people who misuse substances. This recognition, we would argue, is a strength as it demonstrates a degree of personal insight and gives both the student and her practice educator something to work on. Finally, the student claims to know what mental illness is. We would hope and expect that any certainty around such a complex and contested topic would be challenged by the experiences and new knowledge she receives on placement. Like her, you may find it helpful to revisit Activity 2.4 once you are established in placement and see how your thinking has changed.

Additionally, you may find it useful to further divide the knowledge, values and skills you have identified into those components which are general and applicable to all or most social work settings, and those elements which are specific to your placement. Using the example of the student who is about to go on placement with the CRHT, amongst the specialist knowledge that she will need to acquire is an understanding of the Mental Health Acts 1983 and 2007 and the Mental Capacity Act 2005. Another more generic skill she will need to develop, however, is how to communicate effectively with mentally ill people and their carers, as good communication skills are required by all students on placement.

Another consideration that you will need to take into account is which other professions will be represented on your placement and how this might affect what you need to know. In a CRHT a student will be working with a range of colleagues including community psychiatric nurses, occupational therapists, consultant psychiatrists and psychologists. On some occasions and in some fora, the student may be the only representative from a social care background. In the contemporary world of health and social care the majority of you will be working within a multidisciplinary, interprofessional framework where you will 'rubbing shoulders' with a range of fellow professionals on a regular basis. Consequently, you are going to need to know how to professionally relate to other workers from other disciplines across a range of potentially complex situations (Crawford, 2012). For example, you may need to know how to conduct joint visits, how to appropriately record in a multidisciplinary way, how to skilfully deal with disagreement and conflict, and crucially how to articulate what your role is and understand what other professionals do.

Top tips – Consolidating your knowledge pre-placement

- Remember that you already possess knowledge and skills which are valuable and can inform your practice on placement

- Remember to revisit the academic work you have already produced on your course as this is an invaluable source of knowledge

- Use and return to the exercises within the early chapters of this book as a means of consolidating your knowledge

---

So far, in this chapter, we have largely considered knowledge, values and skills as though they are distinct and separable concepts. The reality is, however, that there are genuine difficulties in separating knowledge from the skills required to put that knowledge into practice, whilst simultaneously recognising the explicit role that values have in shaping practice. In this final section of the chapter we introduce a key component of practice which highlights this difficulty.

ANTI-OPPRESSIVE PRACTICE – THE FUSION OF KNOWLEDGE, VALUES AND SKILLS

Embedded within the various guidance and values requirements we considered earlier in this chapter, you will have noted the significance of such concepts as social justice, providing choices and options, and working in partnership with service users and carers. These personal and professional values inform and underpin what has become known as 'anti-oppressive practice'. Like a number of terms we have already mentioned, the phrase anti-oppressive practice is widely used but difficult to define and open to a range of interpretations (Thompson, 2006). It is beyond the scope of this book to critique the nuances of this term, but we will return to consider its importance at a number of different stages of your placement. For the moment, a brief discussion will help us place our thoughts into context.

Anti-oppressive practice recognises that social work operates within established political and organisational systems which give practitioners significant power and authority over the people they work with (Smith, 2008). Consequently, social workers can oppress people, either deliberately or unintentionally, through the misuse of their power. Social workers also need to be aware that some people, or groups of people, are discriminated against by society and that practitioners have a moral and professional duty to work in ways which recognise these inequalities and fight against them (Ferguson and Woodward, 2009; Mulally, 1993). Anti-oppressive practice then requires an active consideration of our own practice and the practice of others, a view as to how the organisation we work for operates, and a wider understanding of structural and institutional oppression. We would argue that a sound value base is necessary if anti-oppressive practice is to be demonstrated, but knowledge and skills will also be required. We will return to our discussion of anti-oppressive practice on many occasions throughout this book, but for the moment we purely want to use it as a vehicle to discuss the interaction between knowledge, values and skills. In order to clarify our thinking, let us return to Jasveer, who you may remember has been given a placement in a school for pupils with special needs.

Activity 2.5

Knowledge, values and skills for placement

Early in her placement Jasveer overhears a teaching assistant making racist and disablist comments about a child from a travelling family who has significant learning difficulties. She decides to challenge the person about their views.

- Which values will Jasveer need to demonstrate?
- What knowledge will she need?
- What skills will she have to use?

COMMENT

Jasveer will need to demonstrate a commitment to a range of values from the PCF which she needs to meet at the end of her first placement experience (TCSW, 2012g). For example, the need for her practice to be informed by the requirement to 'elicit and respect the needs and views of service users and carers' and that she applies the profession's ethical principles. Her challenge has been driven by her desire for social justice, the search for equality, and an awareness of the corrosive nature of disablism and racism. Equally, in order to challenge her colleague in a mature and constructive way she will need to demonstrate values of respect, honesty and working in partnership. In terms of knowledge, Jasveer will need to know about racism, disablism, how travelling families can often face discrimination and how these damaging influences affect the lives of people. Later she will need to know how to use supervision as an opportunity to reflect on the situation, the effectiveness of her challenge and how any repercussions can be managed. Alongside knowledge and values, Jasveer will also need to demonstrate a range of skills such as assertiveness, appropriate body language and clear communication if she is to talk to her colleague in a suitable manner.

We hope that you can see from this brief example that knowledge, values and skills often intertwine and inform one another and that it is sometimes difficult to separate them in practice. This is not a negative and provides further evidence for our assertion that social work is a complex activity which requires a breadth of insights and behaviours. Part of your task on placement is to develop your practice so that it is explicitly characterised by all of these components. From an early stage in your placement you may find it helpful to revisit Activity 2.4 and use it as a tool to identify the knowledge, values and skills that you either intend to use or have used in your work.

Top tips – At the start of your placement

- Do not be daunted (or over-confident) at this early stage in your placement

- Remember that social work is a complex and demanding task that draws on a wide range of knowledge, values and skills; you can never know everything there is to know about social work

- Be prepared for those times on placement when you feel unskilled, confused and demoralised

- Remember that you are on placement to learn

CONCLUSION

In this chapter we have introduced you to some of the knowledge, values and skills that you need to consider as you prepare to go on placement. We seem to have spent much of the chapter thinking about knowledge, in particular how an understanding of the place of theory is important. In subsequent chapters we will address this imbalance and will concentrate more on the role of values and skills once you have commenced your placement practice. Having considered the concept of knowledge for practice, the chapter turned to briefly consider the role of values and skills, particularly looking at the skills of reflection in practice as a way of integrating knowledge, theory and values in practice through processing and understanding your ideas and experiences. Having explored the three core concepts of knowledge, values and skills, you were then encouraged to reflect on, as part of your preparation for practice, the knowledge, values and skills you already have and what you need to acquire either before or during your placement. Finally, in order to demonstrate how social work knowledge, values and skills inform one another and are often interrelated, we introduced you to the concept of anti-oppressive practice and used it as an example of how knowledge, values and skills can sometimes fuse together and become difficult to disentangle. All of these topics are of considerable significance to making social work practice effective and successful, not only at this preparatory stage, but throughout your placement. You will need to take time over the next few months to review and update your developing understanding; we will return to these demanding themes later in this book in order to encourage and stimulate your learning. Despite the challenges of the subject area, we hope that you have enjoyed this introduction and will make good use of the resources we have identified below which will further inform your thinking and practice.

FURTHER READING

Beckett, C. (2006) *Essential Theory for Social Work Practice*. London: Sage.
This is an excellent and eminently readable text on social work theory which provides various activities which 'bring alive' theoretical issues.

Mathews, I. and Crawford, K. (2011) *Evidence Based Practice in Social Work*. Exeter: Learning Matters.
This book analyses the different sources of knowledge that underpin and inform professional practice. It presents a critical view which questions recent emphases on evidence to the detriment of knowledge and explores in greater detail many of the themes we have alluded to in Chapter 2.

Thompson, S. and Thompson, N. (2008) *The Critically Reflective Practitioner*. Basingstoke: Palgrave Macmillan.
Whilst not written solely for social workers, the content of this book offers very relevant further learning on reflective practice. With particular regard to your practice learning experience, there are helpful chapters on writing reflective accounts, recording and assessing reflection and integrating theory and practice.

INTERNET RESOURCES

The 'Community Care' website: www.communitycare.co.uk/Home

This site is an excellent resource which features comment and analysis of contemporary issues in social care as well as providing a useful archive of accessible materials. It also has a very useful jobs section.

PART II
THE BEGINNING OF THE PLACEMENT

3

PROCESSES AND PRACTICALITIES

Chapter summary

When you have worked through this chapter, you will have:

- Considered how to manage pre-placement emotions;
- Identified last minute pre-placement preparations;
- Obtained an understanding of induction processes;
- Received information about key placement processes within the first few weeks of placement such as learning agreements;
- Explored important placement issues such as personal boundaries and data protection;
- Identified the different ways in which you might learn in placement.

INTRODUCTION

This chapter considers how you can make a positive start to placement. We begin by thinking about the days immediately prior to commencement of placement, particularly helping you think about managing emotions that may arise before you enter the placement, as well as the last-minute arrangements and preparations that you may need to consider. The chapter then moves on to discuss the early weeks of placement, giving guidance that will help you settle into the placement setting. We discuss the induction period, providing valuable information about placement processes, data protection, professional boundaries, reflective practice, being observed and using supervision.

IMMEDIATELY PRIOR TO ARRIVAL ON PLACEMENT

ACKNOWLEDGING AND MANAGING EMOTIONS

In the days immediately prior to arriving in placement you may be feeling a range of emotions, some positive and some negative; this is entirely normal. Indeed, research with social work students in the United States (Gelman, 2004; Gelman and Lloyd, 2008) identified a range of concerns experienced by students prior to placement, including being sufficiently well informed and experienced to cope with practice, whether they would be able to work effectively with service users or establish a good working relationship with their practice educators, and worries about achieving work/life balance.

In the first activity of this chapter you are asked to make a list of your hopes and fears before you commence placement. This activity serves two purposes: first, it helps you think about how you will manage your concerns and expectations, and second, at the end of the placement this activity will be a useful reflection tool enabling you to consider the progress you have made. No doubt your university will require you to keep some sort of reflective account *during* your placement, but these usually do not ask you to consider your feelings prior to the start of placement. However, this activity is likely to be useful to you when reflecting, and writing about your overall learning.

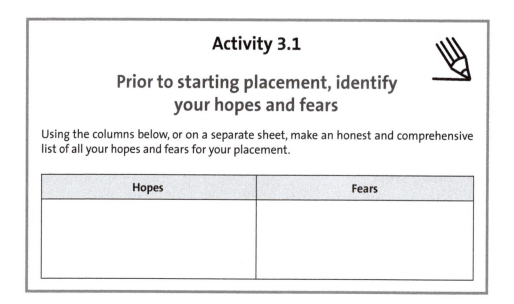

Activity 3.1

Prior to starting placement, identify your hopes and fears

Using the columns below, or on a separate sheet, make an honest and comprehensive list of all your hopes and fears for your placement.

Hopes	Fears

COMMENT

We asked a number of students who were due to go on their first placement to complete a similar activity. Table 3.1 presents some of the hopes and fears about placement these students identified.

Table 3.1   Examples of students' hopes and fears about their first placement

Hopes	Fears
• Expand knowledge/to learn	• Failing
• Build a good relationship with people on placement/get on with others/establish good relations/ relationship building	• Ageism/age – not being taken seriously
	• Not getting on with colleagues
	• (Too much of a) workload
• Build confidence and self-esteem	• Stress
• Have fun/to enjoy the experience	• Fitting in other commitments/juggling study, work and family/ maintaining family life (guilt issues)/child care/no energy to do university work/having no social life/managing family life and work
• Understand the work/for it to make sense	• Lone working/being left unsupervised

The students we worked with identified a range of hopes and fears which echo those identified by Gelman (2004) and Gelman and Lloyd (2008). For example, they were keen to learn and develop their knowledge and skill base and to increase their confidence as professional social work students. Students can return from placement 'transformed' by their experiences and feeling positive about their abilities. However, the students in the above example also mentioned a number of worries about starting the placement that related to their own presentation and skill level and also the demands the placement would place upon them. These anxieties also reflect the challenging nature of social work in terms of undertaking assessments, making decisions, dealing with difficult interpersonal interactions and being emotionally resilient. In many ways, the same concerns may continue into qualified practice although you are likely to feel more confident as your skills and knowledge increase.

In preparing for your placement, it is worthwhile thinking about how you will manage the hopes and worries you have noted and to identify some coping methods you will use to manage these issues; finding ways to cope is an aspect of emotional resilience which we will return to in Chapter 5. Activity 3.2 invites you to think about how you may do this. In pre-empting your hopes and fears and thinking about solutions or strategies to deal with them, we hope you will feel better equipped and more confident about starting placement.

Activity 3.2

Managing your hopes and fears

Take the list of hopes and fears that you identified in Activity 3.1 and transpose them into the first column of the grid below. Then think through some possible ways in which you might address them, in the right-hand column.

(Continued)

(Continued)

Your hope or fear	What will you do to manage or cope with this?

We asked the same group of students (as in Table 3.1) to identify how they could manage their hopes and fears and their responses are detailed in Table 3.2. Although we cannot tie the strategies to a particular hope or fear, we have categorised student responses into themes which address issues identified in the hopes and fears activity. We trust this gives you a flavour of the range of possible solutions and hopefully that it will trigger some ideas for your own coping strategies.

Table 3.2 Students' strategies for managing hopes and fears prior to their first placement

Making the most of the learning opportunities in the placement:

- Ask plenty of questions (there is no such thing as a stupid question)
- Not being afraid to ask for help and guidance
- Speak up when doubting self
- Ask for learning opportunities
- Do in-house training
- Ask to shadow an experienced staff member
- Listen
- Express your feelings
- Know whistle blowing policy and complaints procedure/know lone working policy
- Remind people you are not qualified yet
- Get stuck in!
- Appear confident

Developing time management and organisational skills:

- Create a study timetable
- Organise
- Good organisational skills
- Time management
- Keep a diary and record of work
- Buy diaries to plan/be prepared
- Keep up to date with work
- Keep time aside for work

Be informed:

- Read, read, read – e.g. the portfolio
- Read a chapter before bed
- Do background reading
- Read relevant texts
- Look over level one work to refresh your memory
- Get to know the PCF

Looking after yourself:

- Taking time out – minimum 30 minutes a day
- Give yourself breaks so you do not overload (yourself)
- Get regular sleep
- Make time to relax and reflect
- Reward yourself when you meet targets and deadlines
- Be aware
- Write down anything that is on your mind

Having a supportive network:

- Ask family and friends for support
- (Have) a close support network/talk with friends (being mindful of confidentiality)
- Use each other for support
- Create study groups to help with workload
- Chat on the discussion board on Blackboard (virtual learning system)/use Blackboard for discussions
- Remember your friends are there to help
- Have (placement) tutors on speed dial!

Keeping the needs of the service user in mind:

- Take time to empathise
- Put yourself in their situation

Practice makes perfect:

Role play (i.e. before a face-to-face meeting)

Practical strategies:

- Do shopping online
- Learn to budget

COMMENT

There are some practical strategies within the student responses, such as ensuring that you are prepared and organised for placement. As discussed in Chapter 1, readiness for placement clearly involves developing organisational skills (e.g. having a diary) and planning times for study and recreation. A study timetable is invaluable as it is easy to let the novelty of placement, and your enthusiasm for working with people, get in the way of managing any academic assessment. It is also important to be well informed before and during placement. The students focused on making sure they read enough to support their knowledge, but importantly also identified that they needed to refresh their understanding of modules studied prior to commencing placement. Students may forget to apply previous learning whilst on placement and miss a good opportunity to make connections across their learning.

It is vital to make the most of learning opportunities available to you. Asking questions is a crucial aspect of this, but so is observing other practitioners and asking for opportunities that will develop a specific skill or expand your knowledge in some way. As discussed in Chapter 1, prior to entering placement you should have identified your learning needs for the placement and learning opportunities should be developed to address your needs. One crucial aspect of maximising learning opportunities, which these students did not consider, is the use of supervision, which we discuss later in this chapter. Supervision will also assist you in developing coping strategies to manage the stresses and strains of practice. The students quite rightly emphasised the importance of looking after yourself and becoming an emotionally resilient practitioner, which is one of the requirements of the 'professionalism' capability within the PCF.

Undoubtedly, having a support network is key to a successful placement. As we have discussed elsewhere (Mathews et al., 2009), support networks, formal and informal, are crucial in completing the social work degree and it is likely that you will forge supportive relationships within placement as well as with other students and university staff. It is, however, necessary to be mindful of issues of confidentiality and data protection when using these sources of support, but used wisely they can be pivotal to your learning (Mathews et al., 2009). The practice educator is likely to be your main source of support and guidance during placement and this relationship is known to be critical to placement outcomes (Lefevre, 2005; Urbanowski and Dwyer, 1988).

LAST-MINUTE PREPARATIONS

Just before you start placement, it is important to confirm arrangements with your practice educator. You will need to know what time to arrive in placement and who to contact if there are any problems or difficulties. If you have not already done so, you need to confirm the placement hours. Some placements will have an inflexible working pattern, for example if you are required to work different shifts. Many social care placements will have set working hours, but there may be flexibility within these times. Long working hours or outside of office working may be typical of many settings, so you may find yourself working longer hours than expected.

You might want to give your practice educator your phone number(s) and likewise they may give you theirs. This can be helpful if arrangements change as no social work setting is totally predictable.

Activity 3.3

Final preparations

Consider the following list of final preparation activities. You may wish to add more activities that are particular to your placement or personal contexts. Use the grid below to add your own thoughts, timescales and comments in order to make the list useful to you.

	Comments
Agree a placement start time with your practice educator	
Make sure your practice educator has your contact details; they may also give you theirs	
Make sure you know the placement working hours	

THE FIRST FEW WEEKS OF PLACEMENT

The rest of this chapter discusses the first few weeks of placement, examining induction processes and aspects of social work practice that will enable you to begin working within organisations and teams as well as with service users.

THE INDUCTION PROCESS

During the first two or three weeks of placement, the focus will be on induction. Whilst you might be 'raring to go' and want to start work with service users immediately, the induction process is a core component of helping you to settle into placement and to understand the placement organisation (Maclean and Harrison, 2009; Maclean and Lloyd, 2008; Walker et al., 2008; Williams and Rutter, 2010). Your practice educator is likely to have an induction plan for the first few weeks of placement which will help you and the placement maximise available learning opportunities. The level of structure to the induction varies from placement to placement (Ford and Jones, 1987; Lomax et al., 2010; Walker et al., 2008) and you may either find that your practice educator, in conjunction with the on-site supervisor where relevant, has arranged a full induction process for you, or expects you to organise this yourself or possibly something in between these two approaches.

In Figure 3.1 we present six aspects of the induction process. This is followed by an activity for you to complete, possibly in conjunction with your practice educator, to help plan your induction (although the placement agency may have a formal pre-determined induction process that they follow). We then go on to explain and discuss each of these elements of the induction process.

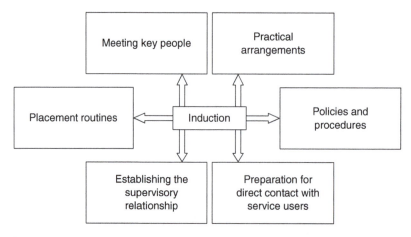

Figure 3.1   The induction process

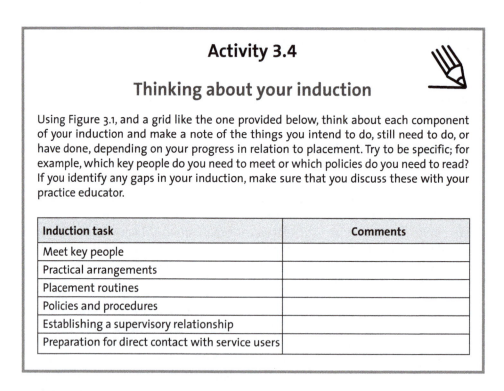

Activity 3.4

Thinking about your induction

Using Figure 3.1, and a grid like the one provided below, think about each component of your induction and make a note of the things you intend to do, still need to do, or have done, depending on your progress in relation to placement. Try to be specific; for example, which key people do you need to meet or which policies do you need to read? If you identify any gaps in your induction, make sure that you discuss these with your practice educator.

Induction task	Comments
Meet key people	
Practical arrangements	
Placement routines	
Policies and procedures	
Establishing a supervisory relationship	
Preparation for direct contact with service users	

COMMENT

As you can see from Figure 3.1 and Activity 3.4, induction processes generally include six key components. There are other ways of conceptualising and presenting the induction process but they share many similarities with this structure (Maclean and Harrison, 2009; Maclean and Lloyd, 2008; Walker et al., 2008; Williams and Rutter, 2010):

MEETING KEY PEOPLE

The first few weeks of placement will require you to get to know people within your placement setting – team members, organisational managers and administrative staff, i.e. all the people that you will be working with on a daily basis. It will be helpful to know about your immediate colleagues as they will provide ongoing support and learning opportunities to you and will be a valuable source of learning during your placement. You will also need to be clear about people's roles and responsibilities during placement. In addition you will need to visit other agencies significant to your placement setting work in order to introduce yourself, meet other professionals and find out what other services they provide.

PRACTICAL ARRANGEMENTS

There are some practical issues that you will need to address during the first few days and weeks of placement. For example, you will need to know how to access the building (keys or key cards may be issued to you for this purpose or you might be given codes for door locks). You may also be issued with an agency identity card. You will need to be given a tour of the building and introduced to any systems which may exist within the placement setting (e.g. booking rooms or signing in/out procedures). In many organisations, there will also be issues relating to accessing IT systems and you might need to attend in-house training before you can access these systems. You will also need to know systems for managing post (incoming and outgoing), access to stationery, as well as the more mundane issues about tea/coffee funds and car parking. You will also need to know what equipment you can use (desk, computer, phone, photocopier) and the agency expectations about the use of such equipment. It is also likely that you will have to present your CRB/DBS and car documentation (insurance/MOT/driving licence) to your practice educator and/or on-site supervisor, upon arrival in the placement. You should be clear from the outset about the personal use of IT equipment (e.g. accessing personal email and social networking sites) and phones. Our advice is to clearly separate your professional and personal lives and not to bring your personal world into a professional arena. Clearly, there may be exceptions to this (e.g. family crises) but these should be the exception rather than the rule. Remember: at the end of the placement, you will need to return any equipment provided to you, so please keep it safe.

BECOMING AWARE OF PLACEMENT ROUTINES

Each placement will have an established pattern of routines which you will need to know. These include team meetings, shift handovers, regular fire alarm tests and normal working patterns. You may be in a team which works beyond the stated working hours (this is particularly common within statutory settings) and you will need to establish what your team, practice educator and/or on-site supervisor expect of you. Working additional hours is not uncommon in social work, but there will be procedures and processes for taking time back – usually called 'TOIL' or time off in lieu. All teams are unique and there will be unwritten 'rules' and ways of behaving within every placement setting which people may not remember to tell you about (Lomax et al., 2010). In Chapter 4 we return to this theme and discuss the importance of 'organisational culture' further.

POLICIES AND PROCEDURES

Each organisation will have its own set of policies and procedures as well as some shared ones in each geographical location (e.g. safeguarding procedures for children and adults). It is important that you familiarise yourself with these procedures during the first part of your placement and know where to find them as and when you need to revisit them during your placement. Most policies and procedures are local interpretations of law or statutory guidance, so being aware of them is a crucial aspect of showing your understanding of the legislative framework. The PCF requires that you show a progressive and developing knowledge of the legal and policy framework in your setting from the start of the placement to the end (TCSW, 2012f; TCSW, 2012g) so finding out about policies and procedures will help you provide evidence for this PCF requirement. You will probably be asked to read a range of policies and procedures, including but not limited to:

- Information governance and data protection
- Health and safety procedures including first aid, risk assessment, fire processes
- Professional boundaries
- Lone working
- Safeguarding
- Whistleblowing
- Record keeping
- Use of equipment (e.g. IT/telephones)
- What to do if you cannot attend placement/time off because of illness or personal issues.

ESTABLISHING YOUR SUPERVISORY RELATIONSHIP WITH YOUR PRACTICE EDUCATOR

Your practice educator will be pivotal throughout your placement. One of the first things you need to do is to establish a supervisory relationship which outlines your expectations of each other. This is usually formalised within a learning agreement or contract for the placement which the university normally contributes to or countersigns. Your practice educator, and where relevant the on-site supervisor, will offer you formal supervision throughout the placement and you will either find that dates for supervision are set at the beginning of the placement or negotiated on a weekly basis. If you have a preference about this you need to let your practice educator and/ or on-site supervisor know.

PREPARATION FOR DIRECT CONTACT WITH SERVICE USERS

The induction process will also help you prepare for contact with service users. This may be direct or indirect preparation, but both are important for your development. Indirect preparation may include shadowing other workers during your first few weeks of placement so you can see the different approaches and styles practitioners have. You might also be asked to read case files prepared by different practitioners to compare and contrast writing styles and think about the method you will adopt.

Student voice – Anya

In the following example, Anya discusses some of the challenges she encountered in organising shadowing opportunities. If you encounter problems in securing indirect learning opportunities, it is important to raise this with your practice educator or on-site supervisor.

When I started placement a new, full-time member of staff started at the same time and another staff member was changing role. While we were able to share our experiences and learn together to a degree, I found this left me competing for shadowing opportunities, particularly with more experienced workers. These are vital in the first few weeks of placement. The constraints on shadowing experiences limited the exposure to working methods and approaches of staff members and inhibited my ability to identify 'best practice'.

I can understand the vested interest that the organisation had in training the paid staff member and this contributed to my reluctance to speak up. I feel that had I done so my learning experience would have greatly been enhanced.

Direct preparation includes reading case files relating to the service users you will be working with or making an appointment to see a service user. Your practice educator will select specific pieces of work for you to be involved with, which will supply evidence of your ability to meet the requirements of the PCF and also to address your learning needs. You might feel nervous about meeting a service user for the first time and your practice educator and/or on-site supervisor may role play situations with you or ask you 'what if' scenarios to help your preparations. Initially, you may find that you are working as part of a team or co-working with another person rather than being expected to manage a piece of work by yourself. Clearly, this will also depend upon whether this is a first or final placement, as generally more autonomy will be expected of a final placement student. However, by the end of a first placement, it is likely that you will be working independently to some degree.

INDUCTION FOR PART-TIME STUDENTS UNDERTAKING PRACTICE IN THEIR EMPLOYMENT SETTING

As discussed in Chapter 1, some readers may be undertaking the social work degree as part-time students, possibly supported and funded by their employers. If students are studying part-time and are to undertake a placement within their own team or setting, they may not require the same induction to the placement setting. However, it is important for students who are, what we might term, 'employment-based', to establish themselves as a student within their own workplace (Doel, 2010). If you are in this position, then central to this will be workload relief which is negotiated with your manager and your practice educator (if this is not your line manager). You will also need to negotiate with your colleagues about your student role and ask for learning opportunities (e.g. shadowing) in the same way as other students. Whilst you may be an established and experienced practitioner within your workplace, this is the first time that you have been a student there and you need to make good use of the learning that is available to you.

LEARNING AGREEMENTS

An important task during the induction period will be the negotiation and preparation of a learning agreement, which is a contract between the student, practice educator, on-site supervisor (if applicable) and the university tutor. The learning agreement establishes boundaries and expectations for the placement, outlining your entitlement as a student (e.g. to receive supervision, to be provided with learning opportunities), the responsibilities of the practice educator (to assess the student, to provide learning opportunities) and your expectations of each other (Maclean and Harrison, 2009; Walker et al., 2008). A learning agreement usually considers issues such as working hours, study leave and what sort of work will be allocated to you to help you meet the requirements of the PCF as well as your individual learning needs. It may also discuss what to do if concerns or issues arise during your time on placement (e.g. usually that there will be an attempt to resolve the problems, but if this is not possible, to contact the university). Practice about learning agreements varies from university to university; some universities visit you at the beginning of the placement to discuss the learning agreement, but others do not. However, time spent discussing and preparing the agreement is time well spent as it provides clarity about placement planning and expectations. Universities use the learning agreement to satisfy themselves that appropriate and sufficient learning and assessment opportunities in relation to the PCF are available and the agreement will usually form the basis for the mid-point review.

ABSENCE FROM PLACEMENTS

This may sound obvious, but you must inform your practice educator and on-site supervisor, if you have one, if you cannot attend placement. As you will be aware, you have to complete a set number of days in placement (70 for the first placement and 100 for the second placement) and it is crucial that you keep a note of the number of days spent engaged in placement-related activity. You will therefore need to keep a note of any absences and make up time for any days not in placement. You might also be required to let the university placement tutor know when you are absent so they are aware of how many days need to be added to your placement.

DATA PROTECTION

When you arrive in placement, it is likely that you will be required to manage a significant amount of confidential information. It is crucial that you make yourself aware of the agency's policies and procedures for handling such information. These procedures will determine how you record information, what system is used for recording and storing data securely and timescales for destruction of information. Key legislation and policy regulating data protection are the Data Protection Act 1998 (National Archives, 1998) and the Caldicott principles (Caldicott Committee, 1997). The Health and Care Professions Council requires students to work in accordance with data protection legislation and placement organisational policy (HCPC, 2012a). Being able to work within legislative frameworks is a requirement of the PCF domains for first and final practice placements (TCSW, 2012f; TCSW, 2012g) as well as meeting the standards that qualified social work practitioners have to meet, the HCPC's Standards of Proficiency (HCPC, 2012b).

Table 3.3 The Data Protection Act 1998 and its implications for social work practice

The principles of the Data Protection Act (Schedule 1, Part 1, Data Protection Act, 1998)	Implications for social work practice
1. 'Personal data shall be processed fairly and lawfully'	Make sure you adhere to the organisation's policies regarding gathering, recording, storage and destruction of information.
2. 'Personal data shall be obtained only for one or more specified and lawful purposes, and shall not be further processed in a manner incompatible with that purpose or those purposes'	You need to be clear why you are asking for specific information from service users and that you use that information for the reason given.
3. 'Personal data shall be adequate, relevant and not excessive in relation to the purpose or purposes for which they are processed'	Do not be gratuitous in the amount and nature information you request – you need to understand why you need the information and not ask for information that is not required.
4. 'Personal data shall be accurate and, where necessary, kept up to date'	You need to check the accuracy of information and keep record keeping up to date. Develop a system or routine for completing recording in a timely fashion.

(Continued)

Table 3.3 (Continued)

The principles of the Data Protection Act (Schedule 1, Part 1, Data Protection Act, 1998)	Implications for social work practice
5. 'Personal data processed for any purpose or purposes shall not be kept for longer than is necessary for that purpose or those purposes'	You need to know how long your agency retains information for. Handwritten notes should be destroyed using a secure method.
6. 'Personal data shall be processed in accordance with the rights of data subjects under this Act'	People have access to their records, so be mindful of the content of records and reports that you write. It is good practice to share your recording with service users if possible.
7. 'Appropriate technical and organisational measures shall be taken against unauthorised or unlawful processing of personal data and against accidental loss or destruction of, or damage to, personal data'	You need to safeguard information when working on computers, during conversations and when taking data out of the office. Follow agency policies in relation to managing information.
8. 'Personal data shall not be transferred to a country or territory outside the European Economic Area unless that country or territory ensures an adequate level of protection for the rights and freedoms of data subjects in relation to the processing of personal data'	Seek advice from organisation's nominated person if you need information to be transferred outside of your organisation and specifically outside of the European Economic Area.

Table 3.3 lists the implications of the Data Protection Act for social work practice. It is worth spending time in supervision discussing these issues as the appropriate handling and management of information is complex and sanctions for breaches of data protection can be severe (Information Commissioner's Office, 2012). The Information Commissioner's Office has produced an informative DVD about data protection and handling data called *Data Day Hygiene*, which demonstrates issues of data protection and governance in a health care setting but the advice is transferable to social work settings (available from: http://ico.org.uk/news/video). Here are our 'top tips' for ensuring your compliance with data protection.

Top tips – Data protection

- Do not talk to your family and friends about your work other than general statements – do not discuss individual service users

- Make sure you are familiar with agency policies and procedures on data protection

- NEVER check agency records for your family (including yourself!), friends or neighbours

- Disclose any conflict of interest, e.g. if you know a service user or if you were yourself or a family member a service user with a particular organisation

- Do not add service users as friends on your Facebook account/ social networking media and make sure you carefully manage information about yourself using the privacy settings. Do not mention your placement on any social networking site. This

---

includes information about colleagues, service users, geographical location or the type of work you are doing.

- Do not keep personal information on your personal storage devices or computing equipment – use IT equipment provided by the agency
- Do not leave confidential information unattended
- If you have to take information out of the office, follow the agency procedures for this
- If you have to take information home, ensure that it is securely stored and transported in a closable bag or briefcase
- When printing and filing paper records, be careful not to mix up service users' information and put the wrong paperwork onto files
- Make sure you anonymise academic work which discusses your practice with service users

---

It is also important that you think about how you will manage the interface between information relating to your placement and your academic studies. Most universities require students to write about their work with service users as an integral part of the practice curriculum. Whilst most universities will ask you to anonymise your work, you still need to exercise caution. For example, we would discourage you from using people's initials for anonymisation (it would be better to use a pseudonym and make it clear that you have done so). You also need to consider that some service users' situations are so identifiable that even with anonymisation, merely describing their situation might make them known to readers of your work. It is likely that your university will provide guidance on how they want the portfolio to be anonymised, so please make sure you understand and comply with this. At the moment, many universities require submission of a paper portfolio, which will be returned to you once it has been marked. You need to think about how you will store your portfolio once it has been returned and make a decision about when you will destroy it and how this can be done in a secure manner.

If you have a specific educational need, such as dyslexia, you may have been provided with software to support your learning needs. You will not be able to complete confidential placement work on your personal IT equipment, so it is important to make sure that your placement is aware of any equipment or software you need *prior to* starting placement. Increasingly, students with additional learning needs wish to digitally record supervision sessions; this is likely to be acceptable, but you need to have a secure way to manage audio files, especially if service-user names are discussed. We encourage you to discuss these arrangements with your practice educator so that issues of confidentiality and data protection can be managed effectively.

PROFESSIONAL BOUNDARIES

Professional boundaries provide a framework within which social workers practise proficiently and equitably with service users and in a way that safeguards the interests of service users, organisations and practitioners (Cooper, 2012). The General Social Care Council (GSCC) produced guidance on professional boundaries (GSCC, 2011) which is still available on The College of Social Work (TCSW) website; this documents the complexities of establishing professional boundaries and provides crucial advice on how to work appropriately with service users. The requirements of the 'Professionalism' domain of the PCF (TCSW, 2012c) also expect students to be aware of professional boundaries. At the point of starting placement, you will only be required to describe professional boundaries, but by the end of the first placement you will need to 'show awareness of professional boundaries' and also have demonstrated professional behaviours such as honesty and reliability with service users as well as understanding a range of responses to safeguarding concerns (TCSW, 2012d, 2012g). Similarly, the HCPC stipulates that students should adhere to professional standards and behaviours, including respectful interactions with service users (HCPC, 2012a). Students may find it difficult to appropriately form professional boundaries with service users and face challenges such as:

- Establishing professional relationships when the service user is a similar age to themselves;

- The appropriateness of sharing personal information about themselves;

- The use of social networking media;

- The appropriate use of authority and managing power dynamics as a student social worker.

It is important to establish working relationships with service users that safeguard their interests, protect them from harm and are transparent and professional. This requires you, as a practitioner, to work within legislative, policy and organisational frameworks and to be accountable for your own practice. The aforementioned guidance regarding professional boundaries produced by the GSCC (GSCC, 2011) explores the complexity of establishing appropriate professional boundaries as well as providing a list of questions that can help you gauge whether professional boundaries are appropriate or not.

HOW WILL YOU LEARN ON PLACEMENT?

You will find that there are a number of different ways to learn within your placement setting (Maclean and Caffrey, 2009; Maclean and Lloyd, 2008). As well as working directly with service users, a number of other learning opportunities will be available to you (see Figure 3.2 which outlines a range of possible learning opportunities on placement). It is important that you actively engage with these learning opportunities in order to get the most out of your placement. As you can see from the diagram, there might be different elements or levels within the learning opportunities. Additionally, many of the processes may be interrelated; for example, supervision is a learning opportunity in its own right, but it might also support other opportunities such as learning from mistakes or challenges and critical reflection.

There may be other learning opportunities that are available to you which do not appear in the figure. It would be useful to make a note of them as placement-related

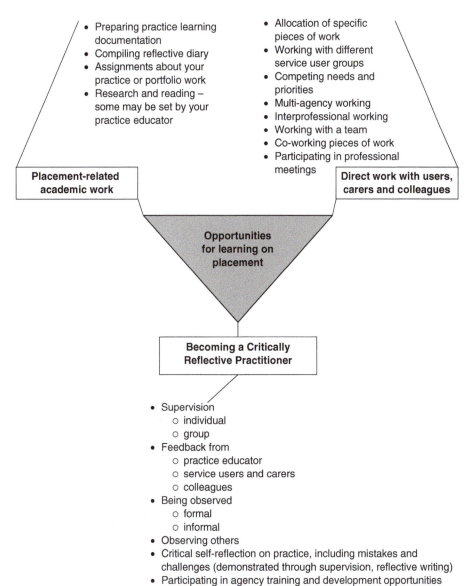

Figure 3.2 Opportunities for learning on placement

academic work usually requires you to evidence your learning and to be clear about how you have developed during placement.

OBSERVING OTHERS AND BEING OBSERVED

Placements give you the chance to observe others and to learn from them, some-times via shadowing experienced practitioners but also from working jointly with them (co-working). Feedback, from service users, colleagues and your practice educator, will also be crucial to your development and it is important that you are able to listen, accept and learn from feedback, both positive and negative. Inevitably, being assessed by your practice educator means being observed directly working with service users. These 'direct observations' usually form a discrete section within your portfolio and it is important to prepare and plan for any observation of your practice. You will learn more about this in Chapter 5.

Learning alongside others is also at the heart of social work placements and is informed by an understanding that learning to be a professional takes place via participation in the social context provided by a 'community of practice' through which practice competence and professional identity emerge (Wenger, 1998). Engaging with the wider team, the organisation and the profession as a whole are therefore crucial to your learning, as well as helping you to develop an understanding of what it means to be a social worker.

CRITICAL REFLECTION

As discussed in Chapters 2 and 4, learning also takes place from reflecting on practice and many professional training programmes promote the importance of critical self-reflection (Shardlow and Doel, 2009). Social work portfolios, which chart your learning and development throughout placement, usually require you to demonstrate reflection on your practice. This then is a key skill that you need to acquire and the PCF domain 'Critical reflection and analysis' requires that by the end of the first placement, students, with support from others, can 'use reflection and analysis in practice' (TCSW, 2012g). Additionally, the PCF domain of 'Professionalism' for the end of the first placement (TCSW, 2012g) requires students to be able to recognise their limitations and to identify future learning needs; this requirement is also reflected in the HCPC guidance about student conduct (HCPC, 2012a). Reflection about practice is seen as a way to critically evaluate practice and to analyse or make sense of practice situations in the light of theory and knowledge as well as helping you consider the gaps in your knowledge and skills and how these might be addressed. Try to get into the habit of critically reflecting on all aspects of your practice. Whilst it might be tempting to only focus on events where things went well, a great deal of learning can take place when you faced challenges or did not think you had performed well (i.e. learning from mistakes).

In order to develop effective reflective skills, you will need to find time and space for reflection (Oelofsen, 2012), which can be problematic as placement settings often experience times of significant demand when quiet contemplation may be mistaken for inactivity! Oelofsen (2012) identifies a number of prerequisites for successful reflection:

- Setting time aside to reflect;

- Deciding how to reflect – either in isolation or collaboratively;

- Being receptive to thinking and learning that comes from reflecting on practice.

Therefore, learning may not always be comfortable and the skills of critical self-reflection may take some time to develop as the following extract from a student,

Megan, at the end of her first placement highlights. Megan was on placement in a children and families setting and describes some of the dilemmas she faced.

Student voice – Megan

At the start of placement I was aware of some situations I would not feel comfortable in, especially setting out professional boundaries with service users of a similar age. I received a referral on service users who were domestically violent towards each other. The female service user was the same age as me; therefore my initial concern was how would I maintain the professional boundaries? When I discussed this case with my practice educator and work-based supervisor they both assigned me additional reading on domestic violence.

At this point I remembered my experience of witnessing domestic violence as a child and I could not get rid of the memories or lock the feelings away as I thought I had done. Working with these service users brought all the same feelings back that I had as a child. I became very withdrawn and forgetful at placement because all I kept thinking about was my own experience and how I would cope again. I did not say anything because I was too excited for my first referral and I didn't want to have it taken away. Eventually when my practice educator asked if I had done the additional reading I broke down and explained everything. My on-site supervisor was also called in for me to tell her about how I was feeling. As a practitioner this meant a lot to me as I could not have got through that case or placement without all the support I received from my practice educator and on-site supervisor and I cannot express enough how much better I felt and how much better my work was with the service users from then on. It allowed me to set my professional boundaries as I was too focused on my work and it also gave me the courage to do one-to-one work with service users who had experienced domestic violence and how domestic violence affects children.

COMMENT

Megan has been able to reflect upon her placement experiences and understand how previous traumatic experiences can be re-awakened during placement. Whilst Megan initially contained her feelings, this was not an effective coping strategy. The effective use of supervision eventually helped Megan address some of the issues and in turn she was able to work more effectively with service users as well as ensuring her own emotional wellbeing.

You will probably find that your academic work aims to support your ability to reflect on practice. For example, as well as the final pieces of work that you submit, you might be asked to write reflections on your practice to support your understanding of practice issues and your own role. It is important to complete such work as soon as you can after the event in order to capture the experience whilst it is still 'fresh'. In Chapter 2, we discussed Ixer's (1999) model of reflection, and here we offer you a further model adapted from the work of Gibbs (1988) as a way to record your reflections on practice. Your university may provide you with a template to help you with reflective writing, but here is an example which includes some of the key aspects of reflective writing.

REFLECTIVE WRITING – SOME KEY QUESTIONS (ADAPTED FROM GIBBS, 1988)

Using Gibbs' work on structured de-briefing, this table guides you through key processes and questions in reflecting upon an event. Once you have answered the questions in the middle column and reflected upon your experiences, use the right-hand column to consider how this might provide evidence in relation to the PCF.

Structured De-brief	Prompts to help you reflect	Links to the PCF
Description	Provide a narrative account of what took place.	
	Try to get the account in chronological order.	
Feelings, thoughts and actions	Consider your thoughts, feelings and actions: • How did I feel? • What made me feel this way? • What did I think about this situation? • How did I react and behave?	
Evaluation and Analysis	What feedback did I receive (if any) from my practice educator about my practice in this situation?	
	Reviewing the event, I have learnt ….	
	What informed my understanding of this situation (e.g. knowledge, theory, legislation, values, HCPC Guidance on Conduct and Ethics for Students)?	
	Why did you choose that piece of knowledge to help you understand the situation?	
	What alternative theories or approaches could have been used? Why were these discounted?	

Structured De-brief	Prompts to help you reflect	Links to the PCF
	Were there any ethical dilemmas?	
	In the future I would ... (consider alternative courses of action as well as what you would try to emulate again)	
Conclusions (general and specific)	I need to know more about ... I need to develop ...	
Personal action plans	My action plan is (provide short- and longer-term goals):	

Activity 3.5

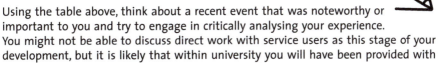

Using the table above, think about a recent event that was noteworthy or important to you and try to engage in critically analysing your experience.

You might not be able to discuss direct work with service users as this stage of your development, but it is likely that within university you will have been provided with some significant events or learning that you can reflect on.

Here is Gulshan's example of using this format to reflect upon a significant event that occurred during the preparation for practice module and he has made links to the PCF domains for readiness for practice (Table 3.4).

Table 3.4 Gulshan's reflections on an incident in the readiness for practice module

Reflective writing – some key questions (adapted from Gibbs, 1998)

Structured De-brief	Prompts to help you reflect	Links to the PCF
Description	Provide a narrative account of what took place. Try to get the account in chronological order. The event was a role play of making a home visit which was undertaken in skills laboratory which is presented as a service user's home. Actors were used to role play the service users and the live video link was observed by tutors. I also had to prepare a written record of the home visit.	**Professionalism –** I dressed appropriately for the role play – smart casual, with trousers and a shirt (I would normally wear jeans for attending university). I also had to be able to explain the purpose of the visit which required me to have an understanding of the role of a social worker.

(Continued)

Table 3.4   (Continued)

Reflective writing – some key questions (adapted from Gibbs, 1998)		
Structured De-brief	*Prompts to help you reflect*	*Links to the PCF*

Feelings, thoughts and actions	Consider your thoughts, feelings and actions:
	
	• How did I feel?
	  I was terrified! I was also shocked at the state of the 'house'
	• What made me feel this way?
	  I have no experience of undertaking home visits. My own value base
	• What did I think about this situation?
	  If I'm honest, I was unsure about the value of a role play because it isn't real. However, with hindsight, I can see this was a helpful activity and I have some areas for development – such as how to introduce myself
	• How did I react and behave?
	  Initially my nerves got the better of me but my performance improved as I went along and was able to get involved in the role play
		Values and Ethics: I became aware that my personal feelings were unhelpful and led me to make assumptions about the service users.
		
		Critical reflection and analysis: I was able to see how my own feelings and attitudes impinged on my initial reaction. My initial reluctance to engage with an artificial situation also detracted from my learning.

Evaluation and analysis	What feedback did I receive (if any) from my practice educator about my practice in this situation? The tutors gave me some balanced feedback – some good, some not so good. Reviewing the event, I have learnt …. The importance of clarity when introducing yourself to a service user. I forgot to say my name or leave any contact details! We also had to make a written record of the visit and there were some significant gaps in the information I produced. What informed my understanding of this situation (e.g. knowledge, theory, legislation, values, HCPC Guidance on Conduct and Ethics for Students)? I was trying to use theory relating to communication – for example, spending some time getting to know the service user and listening to what they had to say. I was also respectful, which is in line with the HCPC requirements – for example, I did not interrupt and I tried hard to make sure I had really understood what the service users had to say. I was conscious of the Data Protection Act 1998 when preparing the write up – I would have been happy to share this with the service users.	**Contexts and organisations and professionalism:** A better grasp of the social work role in that context would have enabled me to be clear about the purpose of the visit and to introduce myself more effectively. **Intervention and skills:** I was able to use knowledge about communication skills and building rapport during the role play – e.g. active listening. I was also able to use written communication skills. There were gaps in my understanding of risk, as evidenced by the omissions in the written record that I produced.

Reflective writing – some key questions (adapted from Gibbs, 1998)

Structured De-brief	Prompts to help you reflect	Links to the PCF
	Why did you choose that piece of knowledge to help you understand the situation?	**Knowledge:** My use of knowledge was mainly about communication skills – establishing a connection with the service user, listening and making sure I'd understood. I was also able to show some understanding of data protection.
	An understanding of communication seemed appropriate given this was an introductory visit that was being role played.	
	What alternative theories or approaches could have been used? Why were these discounted?	
	I didn't think of any others and realise now that this gave me a narrow perspective.	
	Were there any ethical dilemmas?	
	Nothing major.	
	In the future I would … (consider alternative courses of action as well as what you would try to emulate again)	
	I would definitely continue to listen to service users but I also need to keep a focus on the purpose of the visit as my agenda got lost.	
Conclusions (general and specific)	I need to know more about … How to introduce yourself clearly	
	I need to develop … Skills in:	**Critical reflection and analysis:** In examining what I did well/not so well and considering how to improve, this evidences my ability to reflect on my practice.
	1. Explaining who I am and what my role is 2. Keeping a focus on my task or agenda 3. Making sure I capture all relevant information in the written record that I produce	
Personal action plans	My action plan is (provide short and longer term goals):	
	There is another role-play session and I will take this more seriously next time. In the next session, I hope to be able to introduce myself more effectively which will mean including my name.	**Critical reflection and analysis –** is evident in identifying some goals to achieve in the next role play
	This was a planned visit, so I need to develop expertise in how to undertake visits where the service user does not have any notice about this.	
	To try to use other theories about communication – possibly Transactional Analysis.	

COMMENT

Gulshan is able to show a good level of reflection on his own practice and to clearly identify areas for development as well as the things he did well. He could perhaps have been more specific – which theory did he use, what did he mean by there was 'nothing major' regarding ethical issues, which significant informa-tion did omit in the written record? The reflection indicates that Gulshan is questioning his practice (for example, his values regarding the condition of the house). Gulshan has also shown his understanding of how this event can be cross-referenced to the PCF.

LEARNING THROUGH SUPERVISION

Supervision is an integral part of social work practice. Typically, this is an individual process where you meet on a one-to-one basis with your practice educator, although you may be asked to take part in group supervision with other students or within your placement team. Research highlights the beneficial effects of supervision for social work students in increasing student satisfaction with their practice learning opportunities and in helping them manage the complex demands of practice (Kanno and Koeske, 2010). Supervision serves a number of purposes:

- *Support* – it helps sustain the practitioner, helping them to manage the stresses of social work practice;

- *Management* – it manages work allocation and ensures agency objectives and priorities are met;

- *Education* – it has educational or teaching functions, including giving you feed-back on progress. Supervisors may signpost workers to additional training;

- *Mediation* – the supervisor acts as a conduit between practitioners and the organisation, providing a communication link and buffer between them, as well as helping situate the practitioner within the organisation. (Morrison, 1999; Richards et al., 1990)

These supervision functions are equally valid for students as they are for qualified prac-titioners, as they will help you develop competence within the work of the placement through the provision of educational opportunities and guidance. Practice educators and/ or on-site supervisors will also help students 'find their feet' within the organisation and will provide support throughout to help manage the demands of practice. The functions of supervision are intertwined and may occur simultaneously as the example from Megan, given earlier, demonstrates. The educational function came first (making sugges-tions about reading on domestic violence) but this was followed by a supportive response when Megan became distressed. Additionally, in attending to Megan's support needs and the emotional impact that the placement experience was having on her, the practice edu-cator also fulfilled the management function of supervision, by ensuring the needs of the service user could be met and a service provided.

For some students, their placement may be the first time they have received supervision and these are our 'top tips' for making sure you get the most of out of supervision:

Top tips – Making the most of supervision

- Prioritise your supervision sessions; try to avoid cancelling or re-arranging

- Make sure your supervision cannot be disturbed (by telephone calls, other staff)

- Take responsibility for your learning: undertake any preparatory work required of you (e.g. reading); negotiate your supervision agenda with your practice educator; attend on time

- Make sure you have completed tasks set at previous supervisions

- If your supervision does not contain all the ingredients of effective supervision, ask your practice educator to change the format

- Share your reflective journals with your practice educator and use these to support your critical reflection on your practice

- Volunteer evaluation of your practice or ideas about it – do not wait to be asked

- Try not to get defensive when being given (critical) feedback

- Make sure you accept positive feedback

CONCLUSION

This chapter has considered issues relating to starting placement and your first few weeks of practice. As you can see, this is potentially a stressful time but hopefully the information in this chapter has provided you with sufficient reassurance about the process to allay whatever worries you might have. There is a lot of information to take in during this time, but your practice educator will not expect you to know everything all at once.

FURTHER READING

Cooper, F. (2012) *Professional Boundaries in Social Work and Social Care: A Practical Guide to Understanding, Maintaining and Managing Your Professional Boundaries*. London: Jessica Kingsley.

This comprehensive book explains the importance of boundaries and provides ideas on how key boundaries may be established. Potential indicators of when boundaries are in danger of being transgressed are outlined as well as the consequences of breaching boundaries, for both the service user and practitioner. The book contains a number of useful activities which assist self-evaluation and reflection.

Oelofsen, N. (2012) *Developing Reflective Practice: A Guide for Students and Practitioners of Health and Social Care.* Banbury: Lantern Publishing.

This book is a valuable resource for anyone wanting to develop their skills in reflective practice. The book can be read as a whole or by accessing individual chapters, which will be helpful for busy practitioners and students. Each chapter has illustrative examples and activities which are particularly helpful and the whole book builds on one approach to reflective practice. The second part of the book demonstrates how psychological theory can help practitioners understand frontline practice and this is useful in demonstrating how to apply theory to practice. There is an excellent chapter on self-care and recognising signs of stress.

INTERNET RESOURCES

GSCC (2011) *Professional Boundaries: Guidance for Social Workers.* London, GSCC. Available from: www.collegeofsocialwork.org/uploadedFiles/TheCollege/Resources/GSCC_Professional_Boundaries_guidance_2011.pdf

The GSCC guidance on professional boundaries, which can be found on The College of Social Work website (in the section for General Social Care Council Standards), highlights the complexity of establishing and maintaining appropriate professional relationships with service users. There are a number of reflective activities to build your understanding and thinking about professional boundaries.

The GSCC also provides an online interactive quiz about professional boundaries which only takes a few minutes to complete. Although the GSCC has now closed, this activity is still available from: www.gscc.org.uk/professional-boundaries-assessment-tool/

Health and Care Professions Council: www.hpc-uk.org

The HCPC as the regulatory body for social work provides guidance about the standards to be achieved by both qualified and student practitioners.

The Guidance on Conduct and Ethics for Students is available from: www.hpc-uk.org/assets/documents/10002C16Guidanceonconductandethicsforstudents.pdf

The Standards of Proficiency for qualified social workers is available from: www.hpc-uk.org/publications/standards/index.asp?id=569

Information Commissioner's Office: www.ico.gov.uk

This website provides a wealth of information about data protection, information governance and freedom of information. The news section provides short summaries of cases where data protection has been breached and will stimulate thinking about how you will keep confidential material secure.

The ICO also produces DVDs about data protection and information governance which will be relevant to placements. In particular, the DVDs *Data Day Hygiene* and *The Lights Are On* provide illustrations about legislation and how to keep information secure. These are available from: http://ico.org.uk/news/video

4

KNOWLEDGE, SKILLS AND VALUES

Chapter summary

When you have worked through this chapter, you will be able to:

- Identify the knowledge, skill and values you need to consider during the first weeks of placement;

- Develop an awareness of team working and organisational culture;

- Identify communication skills integral to professional practice;

- Understand issues relating to working with risk;

- Recognise the importance of 'reflexivity' as a means of improving practice;

- Correlate social work values and anti-oppressive practice.

INTRODUCTION

At this early stage in your placement you may be struggling to come to terms with the pressures and practicalities of being on placement. To some students, especially those of you who have limited life or work experience, being on placement can seem a daunting and exhausting business. Those of you who are unfamiliar with the inflexibility of work, limited comfort breaks and long working hours may find the first few days of placement especially challenging. At this important time in your development we will be introducing you to a range of relevant issues which are intended to help you make the most of the initial stages of your placement. As with all of the chapters in this book, a range of case studies and interactive exercises are used to encourage and enhance your learning.

First, as you are now settling into your placement environment, we briefly consider what it is like to work in a team and introduce you to the idea that teams and organisations have specific cultures which need to be recognised and worked with. Following this formative discussion we return to a specific purpose of this book, which is to introduce you to a range of skills essential to effective practice. In this chapter we especially consider the acquisition and development of communication skills. Whilst these skills are obviously of significance throughout your placement they are so fundamental to practice that it is right to spend time considering them at this stage. We then address the contested concept of 'risk'. Whilst it may seem a little early to be thinking about such an emotive topic, and we would hope that your workload allocation reflects how early it is on your placement, social workers often work with risk even when they are not expecting to do so. This initial discussion introduces you to a range of critical issues within risk and paves the way for a fuller examination later in this book.

Next, in order to help you to begin to write reflectively, we consider the concept of 'reflexivity', which builds on the work you did in Chapters 2 and 3 on reflection and the nature of knowledge. The critical thinking that reflexivity encourages is essential to your professional development and will help you to analyse and evaluate both your own thoughts and the work of other people. This discussion of knowledge helpfully leads onto our final topic of social work values and anti-oppressive practice where we consider a discrete values requirement embedded in the PCF.

WORKING WITHIN AN ORGANISATION

As discussed in Chapter 3, as part of your introduction to your placement you should have undertaken a period of induction. Within your induction you need to develop a clear idea of who does what in your agency and how managerial processes work. For example, who do I contact if I am absent from work? Or who is responsible for budgets that I may need to access? Seeking answers to these questions may initially seem daunting, but you need to familiarise yourself with your organisation and its way of working in the first few weeks of placement. There will, of course, be considerable differences between the organisations which provide placements to your university. Some agencies will be very small independent projects where a handful of people will undertake every task that needs to be done from cleaning the toilets to negotiating contracts with purchasers. Others will be large statutory agencies which employ hundreds of staff where teams and tasks will be clearly delineated. However your role is configured, your task on placement is to be as responsive as possible to the needs of the organisation and to contribute fully to the work of the organisation. Sometimes this may mean accepting responsibilities that you do not feel comfortable with, or which you may feel are outside your remit; nonetheless, placements really value students who are willing to 'turn their hand to anything'.

It is also important for you to gain an understanding of the 'organisational culture' of your placement workplace. Whilst this is not easy to define, in simple terms it refers to 'the way things are done' within the agency. Edwards (1999) suggest that workers within an organisation share certain values, ideologies and assumptions all of which guide behaviour and performance in the office. Organisational culture is made more obvious through the acceptance of often unspoken 'rules' of behaviour which need to be learnt and followed by the newcomer. For example, the custom of going out for lunch on someone's birthday, the sending (or not) of Christmas cards, what clothes to wear in the office, how to address senior managers, the re-telling of stories and anecdotes which pertain to the workplace or team members, and so on. Organisational culture will be influenced by such factors as managerial style, the structure of the workplace, the size of the organisation and how long the team has been in existence. You may be able to note clear aspects of organisational culture within your placement. For example, some students have noted that NHS teams can be hierarchical in nature with an emphasis placed on qualification and professional status. In contrast, statutory social care teams may seem to be more democratic and tend not to overly regard professional qualification or managerial status. Whilst these observations may be stereotypical you might like to write a reflective diary on how you have found the culture of your workplace in the initial stages of your placement and then reflect back on your writing towards the end of your placement.

Sometimes teams can be difficult places in which to work, especially if the team is undergoing challenge or change, adapting to new circumstances or having to work hard under significant pressure. Teams are nearly always under managerial pressure to perform to their maximum whilst managing scarce resources and assimilating change. In the health and social care sector sickness rates are high and staff turnover is common (Jackson, 2012). Law and policy change at a bewildering speed and managers tend to 'come and go'. Under these circumstances it is not surprising that the atmosphere in the team room may sometimes seem tense or frantic. You also need to consider that your arrival will change dynamics and relationships within the team. For example, it may be that you are the only male in an all female team, or the first student the team has ever had placed with them. You may be nervous about meeting your new team but team members, including your practice educator, may also be nervous about meeting you.

Equally, teams can be very supportive places to work and an invaluable source of emotional and practical support. During your placement you will find that you will need your colleagues to provide you with advice, guidance and support. At other times, you may be the one who is providing support to a colleague who is under strain. Such team working and mutual support is highly valued within social work teams and is an important skill to learn and develop on placement. In Chapter 5 we will be considering the concept of 'emotional intelligence' and how you will need to demonstrate this insight and sensitivity in casework. Without pre-empting that discussion we simply ask you to note that emotional intelligence is also applicable to relationships you form elsewhere in your work, including the way you relate to your team.

COMMUNICATION SKILLS

Wherever you are on placement you will need to either have or gain the ability to communicate with a wide range of people in a range of differing settings. For example, the way you speak with colleagues at a tea break will be very different to how you communicate in a formal meeting where external members or service users are present. The way you communicate with a pre-school child will differ to how you would engage an older person with cognitive impairment. There are a number of good practical and professional reasons why you must learn how to communicate clearly, effectively and consistently. Not least is the fact that you will be formally assessed on your ability to communicate. This is made explicit in the Professional Capabilities Framework which states that:

> Social workers engage with individuals, families, groups and communities, working alongside people to assess and intervene. They enable effective relationships and are effective communicators, using appropriate skills. (TCSW, 2012c)

It is important to note that to be an 'effective communicator' a range of skills and understandings is required. At this early stage of your placement you will need to find out what forms of communication are common in your placement setting, as communication is not confined to the spoken word. For example, if you are working with people with learning difficulty you may need to familiarise yourself with communication methods such as Makaton; or if you are working with deaf people you may need to develop an awareness of British Sign Language. Beyond these specialist communication methods you will also need to consider the multi-lingual nature of contemporary society and know what arrangements are in place to access and pay for translation services. In order to help you with your preparatory thinking about communication we want you to consider the following case study and complete the associated activity.

Katie

Katie has started her placement in Children's Services and as part of her induction is shadowing her practice educator, who has arranged to see a mother and her young child in their own home. The practice educator and Katie arrive at the house at a pre-arranged time, but are kept waiting several minutes before being reluctantly let in. Katie notices that the mother sits on the settee with her arms folded, refuses to look at the practice educator, and answers briefly and with considerable hesitation. As the interview progresses the mother takes every opportunity to interrupt the flow of the conversation by answering her mobile phone, taking the child to the toilet and letting the dog out of the back door. In response to the questions put to her she either shrugs, rolls her eyes or makes a dismissive gesture.

Activity 4.1

Communication skills

Read the case study of Katie's experience and then make some notes of the different types of communication used by the mother during the visit.
    What skills will the practice educator need to use if she is to communicate effectively with the service user?

COMMENT

Like many situations in professional practice this interview does not seem straightforward and will require the practice educator to demonstrate a range of skills and knowledge if she is to effectively communicate with this service user. In terms of the types of communication used by the mother we can immediately sense that the practice educator is not welcome as she is kept waiting for some time before being admitted to the home. These behaviours are referred to as being 'symbolic communications' as they give a clear message without the necessity of open communication (Lishman, 2009b). It may be that the mother was still in bed or attending to her child, but it is not uncommon for service users to be elusive or to refuse to answer their door. The service user then uses a number of non-verbal signals to indicate either her disapproval of what is being said or her unwillingness to engage in the conversation. For example, her body language is closed and defensive, she does not look at the speaker, her answers are limited and she deliberately interrupts the interview. Finally, even when responsive she uses non-verbal gestures such as shrugging or rolling her eyes, which are negative in connotation, rather than positively engaging in the conversation. One clear interpretation of these tactics, whether consciously or unconsciously deployed, is that they are designed to discourage the speaker and to restrict the interview. You will note from this scenario that non-verbal signs, gestures and clues are as important as the spoken word in making or breaking communication. Often it is not so much what is said but what behaviour accompanies or contextualises the conversation that is of significance. You will need to develop your skills of observation and understanding of non-verbal communication and behaviour whilst on placement as this is one of the cornerstones of effective engagement.

The practice educator is going to have to use a diverse set of skills, values and knowledge if she is to successfully negotiate the limitations of the interview. A core value when communicating with difficult to engage service users is 'unconditional positive regard', which is a term developed by Carl Rogers, an American psychologist who is often described as being the founder of person-centred approaches in counselling and social care. Rogers (1961) argued that in order to develop a therapeutic relationship and effect change, a worker had to accept and support a person regardless of what they say or do. Central to this approach is respecting the person and seeking to communicate in an authentic way. That is, as one person to another in a way that respects their views and feelings, whilst being true to your own values and position. Related to this value position is the need for social workers and other professionals to be empathic in their approach. Empathy is both a skill and a value and means trying to put yourself in the place of the other person in an attempt to feel and understand their feelings and views. Whilst this may initially seem complex you need to remember that one of the key skills of social work is the ability to relate to other people, many of whom will be at a point of crisis, distress or transition (Mathews, 2009). Unless you have this ability it is unlikely that you will be an effective social worker.

RESEARCH SUMMARY – UNCONDITIONAL POSITIVE REGARD

Carl Rogers (1902–87) devoted his academic career to analysing the psychological conditions for allowing open communication and empowering people to achieve their full potential. Although influenced by psychoanalytical understandings and principles, such as those developed by Sigmund Freud, he distanced himself from these traditional views and developed a system of person-centred counselling based on the idea that people have innate psychological resources which can be utilised to achieve change and personal growth. The role of the counsellor or social worker was to provide an opportunity where the person could recognise and use their own inner strengths to achieve change. As a key component of this approach, Rogers suggested that often people from damaged or dysfunctional backgrounds who were entering counselling needed to receive unconditional positive regard if the counselling was to be successful. If people had poor self-esteem or generally regarded themselves as inferior or as a failure in life, being valued as a person of worth by the counsellor could be a therapeutic first step to change. Often in social work practice we will encounter people whose behaviour, lifestyle or attitude we find problematical or even offensive. Nonetheless, it is important to set aside our personal views and to work with people in partnership and in a non-judgemental way. This does not mean that we have to approve of their behaviour, but it does mean that we have to do our best to provide a professional and appropriate service (Thompson and Thompson, 2008).

The personal and professional attributes described here will need to be reflected in the communication skills used by the practice educator in the case study of Katie; for example, her non-verbal behaviour needs to be open and welcoming. It may be helpful to smile at the service user and to appropriately acknowledge the child, whilst ensuring that she sits in a position that enables direct eye contact and encourages conversation. The language she uses needs to be clear; conversational flow will be helped by the use of 'open' questions which encourage a response from the listener. For example, questions such as 'how are you?', 'how can I help you?', or 'how is your child getting on at school?' all require a response beyond a simple 'yes' or 'no'. Finally, the practice educator may also consider the use of physical contact. This is not easy to judge as different cultures respond in different ways to physical contact and often there are gender implications to consider. Nonetheless, a simple handshake can communicate respect and acceptance whilst handing a toy to a child may help to 'break the ice'.

We will return to Katie later in this chapter but we want to invite you now to briefly consider two areas where communication can be especially challenging at this early stage of your placement. First, making your first formal telephone call to a service user or fellow professional. Students often tell us that making a telephone call in a crowded office surrounded by experienced professionals is an anxiety-provoking experience. Often students feel inhibited by the feeling that 'everyone is listening to me', or uncertainty about what response they will receive from the person on the other end of the telephone. These insecurities may relate to a lack of confidence and usually lessen as the placement progresses. Nonetheless, it may be helpful to develop a strategy to help you overcome these issues.

Top tips – Making and taking business telephone calls on placement

- Do not be frightened to rehearse a telephone call either with your practice educator or in your own head. Think about what you might say and anticipate the responses of the other person.

- If helpful, make brief notes that will assist you to remember names, key questions or issues – you will find that experienced practitioners do this.

- If you need to refer to written or electronic records ensure that these are available.

- Remember to clearly introduce yourself and your agency. This may seem obvious, but when flustered or anxious even the simplest of information can be difficult to recall. You need to agree with your practice educator what your formal title will be whilst on placement and use this title throughout your communication. For example, 'student social worker' or 'support worker'.

- It is possible that you may not be able to speak to the person you want straight away. For example, you may have to speak first to a receptionist or to another family member. Be prepared for this and be able to explain who you want to talk to. It may be that you will not be able to divulge the reason for your call to this initial person and you need to think how you will respond if asked why you are ringing.

- Consider how you will address the person you are telephoning. This will differ according to context but you need to decide beforehand if you will use their first name, their professional title, or a prefix such as Mr/Mrs/Ms.

- Finally, try to be calm, professional and confident in your manner. Remember that you are representing the agency and your profession, and that first impressions often last.

Second, students often become anxious if they are asked to be a 'first contact point' for their agency. How organisations interact with their service users or potential service users clearly differs, but many agencies will expect students to take part in a weekly 'drop in' session, an open day, or a more formalised system of initial contact in statutory services. By definition, these commitments can be challenging as a diverse range of service users, some already known to the service but many who are not, will make contact expecting a professional and informed response.

Again you may find it helpful to develop a strategy to help you through this experience, for example:

Top tips – Initial contact

- Talk to experienced colleagues who will have worked on the duty rota many times. Try to get a feel of what to expect and what issues are most likely to arise.

- If using an unfamiliar room ensure that you know the layout and where to access any information you require.

- Familiarise yourself with any forms that need to be completed. It is likely that the initial referral form will stipulate what key information is required and will guide your conversation. If not, do not be afraid to devise an 'aide memoire' to help your thinking.

- Ensure that you know who to contact if you receive a query you cannot answer. Equally, be prepared to acknowledge that you don't know the answer to an issue and that you need to seek further advice.

- Remember that you could be the only person the service user will talk to about their problem.

- Make comprehensive notes which will help your practice educator or manager make decisions about risk and priority.

Whilst these situations may feel anxiety provoking, do not forget that the whole purpose of being on placement is to learn. No one will expect a flawless performance from you as you are new to the role and inexperienced. Remember to appropriately seek help and use every opportunity you are given to learn and reflect. In this way your confidence and skill level will increase week by week, and very soon making a telephone call in a crowded office will seem purely part of routine office life.

WORKING WITH RISK

Having experience of initial contact work can be helpful as this will give you an indicator of the type of work that your agency accepts and will help you prepare for your first allocated piece of work. Even so, being allocated your first 'case' can often produce a feeling of anxiety as you begin to decide why, how and when you will commence your intervention. It is likely that your team will have a system to prioritise which referrals or situations are allocated to whom and how quickly. Often a manager will have first sight of a referral and will allocate according to the urgency of the case and who is available and suitably skilled within the team to receive the work. A key variable to be considered is what risks are evident within the case and how might these risks be assessed and managed.

'Risk' is a contentious and fluid term which is used in common language and professional practice to describe a range of events or situations which have the potential to produce an adverse outcome if they were to occur (Blackburn, 2000). Additionally, there is a sense of uncertainty about risk as neither the occurrence nor the outcome can be accurately predicted before the incident happens (Carson and Bain, 2008). Risk, however, should not be uncritically viewed as always being a 'bad thing'. For example, risk is sometimes portrayed as synonymous with 'danger' and something to be avoided or tightly controlled. We would argue, however, that taking a risk can be a positive, life-enhancing experience and is often an integral part of ordinary day-to-day activity. For example, driving a car, attending a concert, asking someone out for a date, going on holiday or talking to a stranger are all everyday activities which are fraught with risk. In terms of our own human development we cannot stand still as all of us need to undergo physical, emotional and social change if we are to achieve our full potential. Many of these transitions are potentially characterised by risk and pain but are necessary for our wellbeing (Walker and Crawford, 2010).

THE DIGNITY OF RISK

American civil rights activist and author Robert Perske was amongst the first to use the term 'the dignity of risk'. Perske (1972) argues, with particular reference to people with learning difficulty, that society and professional intervention tends to over-protect and unnecessarily restrict vulnerable people. This over-protection leads to a lack of opportunity which stifles development and self-esteem and reduces the dignity of the person. Over-protection increasingly disables people by alienating them from their own community and restricting their lives through the use of rules and regulations. Over-protection, it is argued, can be a bigger threat to vulnerable people than any risk of harm that arises from living life. The phrase has been revised and re-worked on a number of occasions and is now often extended to 'the dignity of risk and the right to failure'. Parsons (2007: 1) notes, speaking from a mental health background, that,

> ... there is a double standard for people who are diagnosed with a mental illness and those who are not. People who are not diagnosed have the 'right' to make risky and potentially self-defeating choices without intervention from authorities, clinicians or service providers wishing to protect them from the consequences of their choices. The concept of the dignity of risk acknowledges the fact that accompanying every endeavour is the element of risk and that every opportunity for growth carries with it the potential for failure. All people

learn through a process of trial and error. We learn through taking risks and trying new things and we often learn as much from our mistakes as we do from our successes. When people living with a mental illness are denied the dignity of risk, they are being denied the opportunity to learn and recover.

Activity 4.2

Thinking about risk

In order to help you to consider the complexities of risk further read the following vignettes and make some notes about who or what you think is at risk in each scenario.

Leanne

Leanne is a 16-year-old girl with learning difficulties. She lives with her mother who has mental health problems and her attendance at school is poor as she often stays at home 'to look after Mum'. Leanne has low self-esteem, limited social skills and few friends and has started a relationship with a 40-year-old man whom she met via a social networking site.

Davey

Davey has recently served a lengthy prison sentence for sexual offences against children. He is from the travelling community and has returned home to a site where he may have access to children. He has a diagnosis of personality disorder and is to be supervised by forensic mental health services.

Edith

Edith is an 86-year-old woman with Alzheimer's who lives with her husband in sheltered accommodation. She is increasingly confused, disoriented and aggressive, especially towards her husband and daughter who are struggling to manage her behaviour.

COMMENT

The potential risks within these case examples, and with your own work, can be divided into several broad categories: risk to self, risk to others, risk to the community, risk to an organisation, risk to the worker and risk to other colleagues.

RISK TO SELF

Leanne is placing herself at risk and is potentially leaving herself open to a range of adverse consequences. For example, there is a risk of sexual, financial and emotional exploitation. Edith's disorientation may also place her at risk, especially if she leaves her flat.

RISK TO OTHERS

The most obvious example is Davey, who potentially poses a risk to children and young people with whom he has contact. Edith, however, also poses a risk to her husband and daughter, not only through her aggressive behaviour, but by over-burdening them with her care needs. If they are not able to look after her she may unwittingly place herself at risk of having to consider residential care.

RISK TO THE COMMUNITY

Again Davey poses a risk to the wider community beyond his immediate environment. For example, he could be the man Leanne has met on the Internet or he could be planning to evade supervision by moving around the country. Edith may pose a lesser risk to others but may be aggressive to people she meets or those who provide care to her. The nature and level of this risk would be increased if she mixed predominantly with people of a similar age and frailty.

RISK TO AN ORGANISATION

All three people could pose a risk to the reputation, status or even funding of the organisation or agency which is responsible for their welfare. For example, if the agency does not manage the risk well and serious harm results, contracts may be lost or withdrawn, or staff may be formally and publicly disciplined leading to a loss of reputation. The public, service users and referrers to the service may also lose confidence in the agency, leading to a significant reduction in business.

RISK TO THE WORKER

Contact with vulnerable people and their carers, particularly at times of crisis and uncertainty, or when legal interventions are required, can place workers in a risky position. As mentioned in Chapter 3 you need to be familiar with your placement provider's lone working policies and be aware of risks to your personal safety at all times. Davey is an example of someone who potentially poses a risk to the worker assigned to his case. It is possible that he will resent being supervised and will not cooperate with services. He may have a history of violence and have difficulties managing his anger.

RISK TO OTHER COLLEAGUES

As a competent professional and supportive colleague you also need to be aware that some service users or situations may prove risky to other colleagues. For example, if you are arranging personal care support for Edith you need to be clear what risks are posed to carers assisting her with personal care tasks. Equally, it may be that Leanne does not like female workers and has been known to be verbally aggressive towards them. If this is the case, you need to recognise that potential and be certain to record and pass the information on to your manager or practice educator.

Even at this early stage in your placement, then, you need to be aware of the potential risks and dangers posed by people and situations. Equally, you need to be balanced in your thinking and recognise that sometimes involvement with health or social care organisations or systems poses a risk to service users. For example, the term 'iatrogenic abuse' is used in mental health to describe the abuse experienced by some people as a result of being admitted to the psychiatric system (Tummey and Tummey, 2008). In addition to examples of overt abuse perpetrated by staff or other patients, we know that many people also experience a range of harmful consequences such as the loss of freedom, unemployment, labelling, stigma and side effects to medication as a result of psychiatric treatment. In Children's Services we know that the educational and social outcomes for looked after children and young people are consistently poor (Dimond and Misch, 2002; Scott, 2004). Even worse, as a succession of court cases, public inquiries and compensation claims have demonstrated, over many decades, some children in public care have been systematically physically, emotionally and sexually abused (Ferguson, 2007). Whilst these examples may appear to be extreme you need to recognise that for some people becoming a service user is not always a positive experience and is not without risk. As a practitioner you also need to acknowledge that often there are no risk-free options when working with vulnerable people. Sometimes people choose to place themselves, or others, at risk due to their behaviour, lack of insight or social circumstances. In these casework situations you need to carefully consider, discuss and record the risks and ensure that your practice can be readily defended.

Top tips – Working with risk

- Remember that 'risk' is not always a 'bad' thing

- It is part of human life and development to take risks. Without risk taking we would not develop or move forward in our lives

- Be aware that there are different types of risk

- Adopt a proportionate and balanced view of risk, but do not be afraid to seek advice and guidance from your practice educator and more experienced colleagues

- Reflect the complexity of risk in your portfolio

BEYOND REFLECTION – DEVELOPING REFLEXIVITY

Having made a start in placement and been allocated your first pieces of work you now need to think about how your written work within your portfolio can appropriately reflect the complexity of the issues you face. In Chapters 2 and 3 we argued that reflection is a key skill required by the effective practitioner and introduced you to the ideas of Schön (1983), Ixer (1999) and Gibbs (1998). Over the next few weeks you may be required to produce a reflective log or journal to be read by your practice educator and used within supervision, and possibly to be included in your portfolio (see Chapter 3 for a template). Whilst this type of reflection is of considerable significance we want to encourage you to develop criticality in your overall thinking and encourage you to be reflective in all that you do; not purely when called on to produce a piece of writing.

In recent years there has been an emphasis in social work on 'reflexivity', a term which is relatively new to the profession and is open to a number of interpretations (D'Cruz et al., 2007). One definition that we would like you to consider suggests that reflexivity is:

> ... a critical approach to professional practice that questions how knowledge is generated and, further, how relations of power influence the processes of knowledge generation. (D'Cruz et al., 2007: 74)

You can immediately see that this definition resonates with the debates we had in Chapter 2 regarding the contested and complex nature of knowledge, and the importance of anti-oppressive practice. Reflexivity is the process that the practitioner engages in when they reflect on and question the basis of the knowledge they use to inform their practice. Such a critical approach could, for example, conclude that much of the research and theory used to support social work practice has been produced by white, middle-class, middle-aged men based in European and North American universities (Taylor and White, 2000). If such an assertion is accepted, it raises the question of how reliable, appropriate and relevant is this knowledge given the diverse nature of contemporary social work practice and the fact that the majority of practitioners are women.

Reflexivity, however, goes further still and encourages practitioners to question 'what we know and how we know' it (D'Cruz et al., 2007: 74). The adoption of this critical stance then moves beyond an anonymous and safe critique of what you have read at university and challenges you to consider how you as an individual practitioner have gained, used and interpreted knowledge; for example, the intuitive 'practice wisdom' you have developed and the skills, values and knowledge that you use in everyday practice. Crucial to this analysis is an explicit recognition of power and it is important to raise questions such as: who has the power to create the knowledge used in practice and what interests have been served in the production and use of this knowledge (Sheppard, 1998; Sheppard et al., 2000)? Depending on the context and situation this may be a range of people or organisations including, of course, the individual practitioner. A key understanding is that practitioners often hold power in their work with service users and can decide how to use knowledge for their own purposes. In order to help us think further about reflexivity let us return to our previous example of Katie, who is on placement with Children's Services.

Activity 4.3

Katie's reflections

Katie has returned to the office following her shadowing experience described in the case study. Her practice educator has asked her to reflect on the visit and would like to discuss her thoughts at their first supervision session.

Imagine that you are Katie; consider how knowledge has been used, interpreted and produced during the visit. Make some notes to take into the supervision session in preparation for this discussion.

COMMENT

This is a challenging exercise designed to help you to critically consider the events and context of what could be described as a routine home visit. As a first thought, Katie might be aware that the practice educator had a specific agenda that she wanted to follow at the home visit. There might have been issues that she needed to raise or concerns that she needed to investigate. It is possible that the practice educator possessed knowledge about the mother or her children which was not known by the mother; for example information provided by local school or children's centre or extended family. This information may be biased, subjective or incorrect and almost certainly open to interpretation. In other words, the approach and the actions of the practice educator are going to be shaped by the knowledge she has and how she has chosen to interpret that knowledge. Katie also recognises from conversations that she has had with her practice educator that the family are well known to service providers in the area and have been casually described as 'scroungers' and 'work-shy' by people in the office. Consequently, there are a number of negative perceptions that may impact on the way that the practice educator approaches the family. Katie also reflects on the lack of cooperation received by the practice educator and how difficult it was to hold a conversation with the mother. This, of course, is purely her perception of the encounter and the mother may feel that she was welcoming and communicative. Nonetheless, it may be recorded that the mother was 'sullen and rude' on the case record, which will then become part of the knowledge that informs the perception of the worker who next visits the family. Katie may also consider that knowledge was produced during the visit as the practice educator learnt more about the mother's extended family, her ambition to find employment and her past life. The practice educator later indicated that the information provided by the mother about her family would be invaluable for any court report, but dismissed her desire to find work as being unrealistic. Katie reflected that this new knowledge was being used solely for organisational purposes and outside that specific context was dismissed as being unimportant.

We hope that you can see from this brief example that the practice educator holds considerable power over how knowledge is used, interpreted and passed on. She chooses which knowledge is significant prior to the visit; she has her own perception of the behaviour of the mother which is then relayed to others in the case record, and she subsequently decides which information is important and for what reason. This is not to imply that the practice educator's version of events is 'wrong', but a reflexive approach acknowledges that other interpretations may be equally valid.

SOCIAL WORK VALUES AND ANTI-OPPRESSIVE PRACTICE

Activity 4.3 is helpful as it reminds us of the importance of social work values and how they impact on all aspects of practice. In this chapter we have touched on a number of issues including risk, reflexivity and working within an organisation, all of which require an examination of your value base. In order to summarise and clarify your thoughts on these issues we want to help you think how you might provide evidence for one of the values within the PCF. Let us consider how you might 'Recognise and promote individuals' rights to autonomy and self-determination', which is included in the PCF under the heading of 'Values and Ethics' (TCSW, 2012c).

Thinking specifically about your placement, how do you think you may be able to demonstrate this value in practice? Sometimes promoting 'autonomy and self-determination' is clear to see. For example, you may be supporting a young disabled person to move from their parents' home into independent living accommodation, or be arranging a care package to enable an older person to return home from hospital. Both of these examples contain a degree of risk which could potentially lead to a poor outcome and significant harm for the person involved in the transition. Whilst this possibility obviously needs to be considered you also need to remember the points we raised earlier in this chapter concerning the 'dignity of risk' and how professionals have often denied disabled people the right to take risks with their own lives. Associated with this idea you also need to note that such moves towards independence are described as being a right within the PCF. This of course mirrors a number of rights contained elsewhere; for example within the Human Rights Act 1998 Article 8: 'The right to respect for private and family life', which promotes the right of people to make their own decisions about how and where they lead their lives. On other occasions, however, it may be necessary to think more creatively about how you might evidence this value. For example, you may be able to provide evidence by:

- Supporting a service user to write a letter to an organisation to complain about a poor service they have received;

- Encouraging a young person to join a sports team or a uniformed organisation in an effort to boost their independence and self-confidence;

- Taking a young adult with special needs to a job fair and supporting them to apply for employment;

- Advocating within a family for an older person to refuse to go into respite care;

- Providing information about alternative forms of treatment to a person with cancer.

These are purely ideas and you will note that all of them involve you as a practitioner providing proactive support to facilitate or enable service users to exert influence, to have their voice heard, or to make an informed decision. It is also worth noting that sometimes all of us, including service users, use our right to autonomy and self-determination to make unwise or unusual decisions. For example, the person with cancer may, following your advice regarding alternative treatments, decide to stop all forms of clinical treatment and purely rely on herbal medicine. Whether this is considered to be a 'good' or a 'bad' decision clearly depends on your point of view and the individual circumstances of the patient. Nonetheless, you need to be aware that according to the third principle enshrined in Section 1 of the Mental Capacity Act 2005, 'a person is not to be treated as unable to make a decision merely because he makes an unwise decision'. Whilst practitioners should always seek to promote positive outcomes, encourage personal responsibility and minimise risk, service users have a right to make unwise, even risky, decisions. What they do not have is the right to place other people, especially children or vulnerable adults, at risk as a result or consequence of their behaviour. We need to be aware that there are limits to self-determination and that social workers are required to balance the sometimes competing concepts of 'rights' versus 'risk'. This is the type of complexity that you will meet as your placement progresses and we will return to address these issues later in this book.

CONCLUSION

In this chapter we have considered a range of skills, knowledge and values relevant to the beginning stages of your placement. We commenced by considering the nature of teams and organisational culture. This led to an analysis of communication skills where, using the case scenario of a visit within Children's Services, we encouraged you to think about verbal and non-verbal methods of communication. We then invited you to consider issues relating to risk and how risk taking can be a positive and life-enhancing experience and can protect the dignity of marginalised people. Finally, we returned to reconsider the themes of reflection and anti-oppressive practice, both of which form an ongoing discussion throughout this book. Inevitably we have superficially considered some topics which merit a more detailed analysis. Nonetheless, we hope that you have found this chapter useful. We have identified some resources in the 'further reading' section below which we recommend that you access to further develop your learning, thinking and practice.

FURTHER READING

Hothersall, S.J. and Maas-Lowit, M. (eds) (2010) *Need, Risk and Protection in Social Work Practice*. Exeter: Learning Matters.
Part 1 of this helpful book examines issues of risk, protection and need. It also provides a useful discussion of capacity and incapacity – especially relevant for students who wish to explore the Mental Capacity Act 2005 in greater detail. Part 2 considers risk in a range of service settings such as mental health, older people and children.

Kemshall, H. and Wilkinson, B. (eds) (2011) *Good Practice in Assessing Risk: Current Knowledge, Issues and Approaches*. London: Jessica Kingsley.
This edited book provides chapters on a range of risk assessment practices and critiques current practices and policies relating to risk assessment.

Lefevre, M. (2010) *Communicating with Children and Young People: Making a Difference*. Bristol: The Policy Press.
A comprehensive text which examines why practitioners communicate with children and young people and discusses how this might be achieved.

INTERNET RESOURCES

Diggins, M. (2004) *Teaching and Learning Communication Skills in Social Work Education*. London: SCIE.

Although this source is primarily aimed at educators teaching communication skills, section 4 contains some helpful messages about communication from service users and carers. Available from: www.scie.org.uk/publications/guides/guide05/files/guide05.pdf

For those of you who are interested in a more detailed discussion of the work and philosophy of Robert Perske, his website can be accessed: at www.robertperske.com

PART III

THE MIDDLE OF THE PLACEMENT

5
PROCESSES AND PRACTICALITIES

Chapter summary

When you have worked through this chapter, you will be able to:

- Name the nine Professional Capabilities Framework (PCF) domain levels and consider how to provide evidence of capability in relation to some of these;
- Identify sources of evidence for the assessment of practice;
- Describe how to effectively receive feedback;
- Understand some key skills in beginning practice as a social worker;
- Develop ideas about how to ensure your wellbeing during placement;
- Articulate the processes and practicalities involved during the middle part of your placement and know what to do if things do not go as planned.

INTRODUCTION

This chapter takes you through the middle to the end part of your placement, which is where you will generate most of your evidence in relation to the PCF. The domains of the PCF and potential sources of evidence are discussed and explained alongside guidance on evidence collection. The chapter also considers some of the practical processes relating to the middle of the placement, including mid-point reviews and concerns processes, as well as tasks associated with the social work role such as working with service users, time management, lone working and self-care skills.

THE ASSESSMENT OF PRACTICE

Whilst on placement, the assessment of your abilities in relation to the first or final placement domain levels of the PCF is the responsibility of your practice educator assisted, where relevant, by an on-site supervisor. Your university will typically provide a portfolio or assessment document which you and your practice educator will need to complete throughout the duration of the placement period. This document will usually have some predetermined components that cover practical arrangements (e.g. the learning agreement meeting/contract and a description of the placement setting) and assessment requirements such as observed practice and seeking service user and carer feedback. This first part of the chapter takes you through typical assessment requirements and possible sources of evidence.

WHAT AM I BEING ASSESSED AGAINST?

Whilst on placement, you will be assessed against the PCF domain levels for both the first (70 days) and final (100 days) placement. The pertinent domain levels will probably be identified within the documentation provided to you by your university, but can also be found on The College of Social Work (TCSW) website (see web links at the end of this chapter). There are nine domains within the PCF that provide a structure for qualifying training and post-qualifying learning and development. As this framework is likely to provide the structure for your professional development for many years to come, it is important to be familiar with the domains and the levels appropriate to your stage of development. The PCF is often likened to a fan or rainbow (see TCSW website) but in Figure 5.1 we have represented the nine domains as a jigsaw to reflect their interlocking nature. The importance of holistic assessment practices, instead of competencies based on set tasks, has also been emphasised by The College of Social Work (TCSW, 2012h) and therefore your practice educator and/or on-site supervisor are likely to want an overview of your practice, which can be provided by seeing the whole picture. The jigsaw metaphor also suggests that thinking about a piece of social work practice as a whole may help you to identify smaller constituent parts, or conversely, looking at practice in minute detail, examining its components, may lead to a wider, macro, understanding of a situation.

If you compare the PCF domain levels for the first and final placement, you will be able to see that the expectations about your knowledge and abilities broaden and become incrementally more sophisticated as professional training progresses. Similarly, requirements of autonomous practice and critical enquiry increase. Table 5.1 gives an example of the rising expectations within the domain levels of the PCF by comparing the requirements in relation to 'Contexts and organisations'.

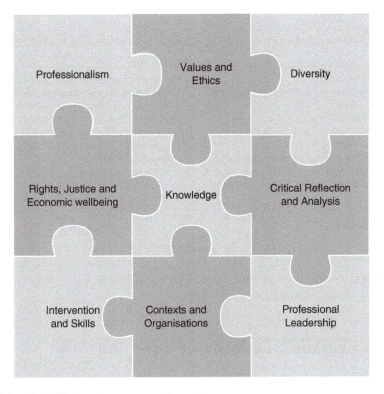

Figure 5.1   The PCF domains represented as a jigsaw

Table 5.1   Comparing the PCF domain levels between first and final placements for 'Contexts and organisations'

Domain descriptor: Contexts and organisations: Engage with, inform and adapt to changing contexts that shape practice. Operate effectively within own organisational frameworks and contribute to the development of services and organisations. Operate effectively within multi-agency and interprofessional partnerships and settings.

FIRST PLACEMENT CAPABILITIES (TCSW, 2012g)	FINAL PLACEMENT CAPABILITIES (TCSW, 2012f)
• With guidance, recognise that social work operates within, and responds to, changing economic, social, political and organisational contexts • With guidance understand legal obligations, structures and behaviours within organisations and how these impact on policy, procedure and practice • With guidance work within the organisational context of your placement setting and understand the lines of accountability	• Recognise that social work operates within, and responds to, changing economic, social, political and organisational contexts • Understand the roles and responsibilities of social workers in a range of organisations, lines of accountability and the boundaries of professional autonomy and discretion • Understand legal obligations, structures and behaviours within organisations and how these impact on policy, procedure and practice

(Continued)

Table 5.1   (Continued)

FIRST PLACEMENT CAPABILITIES (TCSW, 2012g)	FINAL PLACEMENT CAPABILITIES (TCSW, 2012f)
• Understand and respect the role of others within the organisation and work effectively with them • Take responsibility for your role and impact within teams and with guidance contribute positively to team working • Understand the inter-agency, multidisciplinary and interprofessional dimensions to practice and, with guidance, demonstrate partnership working	• Be able to work within an organisation's remit and contribute to its evaluation and development • Understand and respect the role of others within the organisation and work effectively with them • Take responsibility for your role and impact within teams and be able to contribute positively to effective team working • Understand the inter-agency, multidisciplinary and interprofessional dimensions to practice and demonstrate effective partnership working

As you can see from Table 5.1, as you progress there is an expectation that you will be less reliant on guidance from others in understanding the macro, sociopolitical context of social work and in working as a practitioner within policy and legislative contexts, organisations and teams.

FINDING EVIDENCE TO MEET THE PCF DOMAINS

Finding evidence to meet the PCF can initially be daunting until you fully understand what constitutes evidence and how you can successfully prove you have met the capability requirements. The language of the PCF describes the overall standard required and is therefore necessarily abstract and complicated; this may not be especially useful in helping you think through concrete evidence that you could provide for your competence. The knack is to translate the domain levels capability statements into tangible evidence and once you have developed this skill, collating evidence becomes much more straightforward. The extract that follows is from a student's reflective journal about their first two weeks in placement. This extract provides a useful example of how reflections on practice can be related to the PCF domains levels for the end of first placement (TCSW, 2012g).

Student voice – Jessica

The following is an extract from Jessica's reflective journal from her first placement working with young people in a non-traditional placement setting. Jessica recounts her experiences of undertaking an assessment with a young person. Additionally, the first few weeks of Jessica's placement coincided with her young daughter starting school and finding this transition difficult.

During the assessment the young person disclosed some distressing details. I felt tears well up in my eyes and was immediately aware that I needed to control my own emotions in order to continue with the assessment. Reflecting back I think this was a build-up of emotions due to my own anxiety of starting placement and the amount of emotional issues I was dealing with in a short space of time with regards to my daughter starting school and also the young person's issues. I was also aware that I was not giving myself time to reflect on an assessment as they were being carried out one after another.

I realised that I would have to speak to the team leaders and explain that I was finding this somewhat difficult to deal with in some respects as I had not prepared myself for the young people opening up quite so easily. At the end of the day I had group supervision with the team leaders. I felt that it was useful to some extent as I could off-load but they were not social care professionals and it was immediately obvious that they were not qualified to deal with social care issues. They suggested that I just signpost people on as the agency was not equipped due to time constraints and lack of staff to deal with difficult circumstances. They also expressed some concern about ... their lack of expertise and resources to deal with such things. This concerned me as I was then unsure as to my own role on the team.

Activity 5.1

Identifying evidence towards the PCF

Before we comment on Jessica's reflective writing, use this activity to see whether you can identify evidence from this extract that contribute to meeting the PCF (first placement domain levels).

Domain	Evidence from Jessica's journal

COMMENT

Jessica's extract provides evidence towards five of the nine PCF domains; specifically professionalism, values and ethics, diversity, critical reflection and analysis and contexts and organisations. In acknowledging the young person's unique, but traumatic, life experiences Jessica provides some evidence for 'Diversity' and in particular understanding the impact of life events on identity, although this could have been developed further. The acknowledgement of the challenges faced by the young person evoked feelings of distress and sadness for Jessica. She was, however, able to recognise the inappropriateness of allowing this emotional reaction to permeate her interactions with the young person, thus providing evidence for 'Professionalism', particularly in relation to recognition of the impact on her wellbeing, acknowledgement of her limitations and the need for supervision with her on-site supervisor. Moreover, Jessica demonstrated additional self-awareness in her understanding that the assessment with the young person had combined with feelings about her daughter's experiences of starting school, thus providing further evidence for 'Professionalism' through her understanding of her capacity for emotional resilience. In seeking support and advice from the team and on-site supervisor, Jessica demonstrated evidence for 'Contexts and organisations' and in particular her capacity to operate within organisational norms and policies, taking responsibility for her own contributions, demonstrating an understanding of lines of accountability and whilst not in agreement with the views of others, respecting their roles and viewpoints. The questioning of the student social work role within the team and the practices within the organisation indicate 'Critical reflection and analysis' as well as evidencing 'Professionalism' in terms of understanding the social work role within this particular practice placement setting. This uncertainty about practice also suggests that Jessica would be able to provide evidence for 'Values and ethics' given the conflict in approaches between what she was being advised to do and how she thought a social worker might respond. Jessica's capacity for 'Critical reflection and analysis' provides a foundation for all of her evidence. She articulates (but does not make explicit reference to) reflection in and on practice (Schön, 1983) and critically appraises the work she did, the impact this had on her and the organisational response to the needs of the service users which Jessica contrasted with a social work response. Stylistically, Jessica assists the reader with shrewd signposting such as 'reflecting back' which helps the reader identify evidence. Jessica could have improved her writing by supporting her statements with theory.

SOURCES OF EVIDENCE

Evidence for the PCF can be collected from a number of sources, some of which may be included in your portfolio for submission to your university. Activity 5.2 asks you to think about potential sources of evidence within your placement.

Activity 5.2

Identifying possible sources of evidence

Thinking about your placement, possibly in conjunction with your practice educator or on-site supervisor, write down as many potential sources of evidence as you can think of in the diagram below. This will help you clarify the breadth of available evidence and will help you begin to think about what evidence you will be able to use to support claims of your abilities in relation to the PCF. You will also be able to decide which is the best evidence so you can make decisions about what to include in your portfolio or what to write about. At some point, decisions will have to be made with your practice educator about whether the evidence is appropriate, adequate and robust (Walker et al., 2008; Williams and Rutter, 2010).

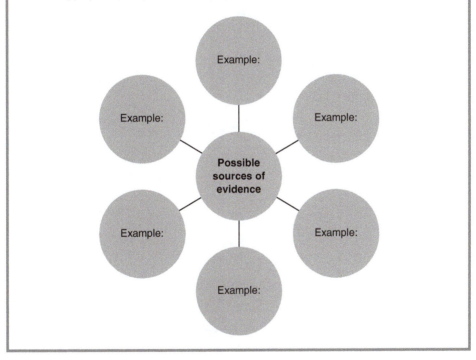

COMMENT

You will probably have identified mandatory elements of your university's placement portfolio as sources of evidence. Whilst the components of portfolios may vary, most universities are likely to have requirements about the inclusion of direct observations of practice, reflective writing and service user and carer feedback. Practice educators and

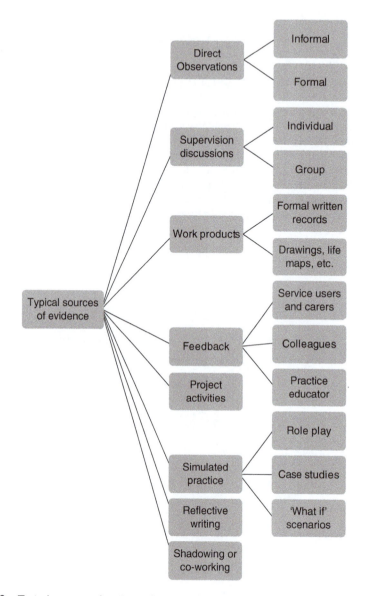

Figure 5.2   Typical sources of evidence for a social work placement

on-site supervisors will also be expected to evidence that they have provided regular, high-quality supervision and include a final report about your development. Figure 5.2 outlines typical sources of evidence used within student social work placements (Lishman, 2009a; Lomax et al., 2010; Maclean and Caffrey, 2009; Parker, 2010a; Walker et al., 2008; Williams and Rutter, 2010). If you refer back to Jessica (student voice), the evidence for capability for the PCF was derived from a reflective journal, although some of the evidence would have been verifiable through the group supervision discussion. Therefore, as you may expect, evidence that can be independently confirmed could be seen as having more weight than reflective claims made by students (Williams and Rutter, 2010). Additionally, sources of evidence can be interlinked; for example, your practice educator may undertake an observation of your practice with service users and compare their own observations with feedback from the service user(s) as well as cross-referencing this with your case recording of the event. Such triangulation of different sources of evidence (Doel et al., 1996; Maclean and Caffrey, 2009; Williams and Rutter, 2010) strengthens the evidence and makes the assessment more valid.

In the sections that follow, we describe these possible sources of evidence to stimulate your thinking about how you might generate evidence during your placement.

DIRECT OBSERVATIONS

Universities typically expect students to be observed by their practice educator and/or on-site supervisor several times during the course of the placement. These observations are likely to illuminate the student's progression and development throughout the placement experience. A written summary of direct observations usually forms part of the practice placement portfolio that students submit to their university at the end of placement. The standards issued by TCSW require practice educators to use direct observation as a method of assessment with social work students (TCSW, 2012e), and upon qualification social workers can expect further observations of practice during the Assessed and Supported Year in Employment (ASYE) (Skills for Care and Department for Education, undated (a)). Observation of practice is also a characteristic of many vocational courses that leads to professional qualification (Keady and Thompson, 2009; Murdoch-Eaton and Roberts, 2009; Rowan and Alsop, 2009), probably because it provides an opportunity for accurate and first-hand assessment of the student's skills (Williams and Rutter, 2010) as well as ensuring that the student is competent to practise.

Formal direct observations of your practice will be undertaken on a number of occasions during the placement by the practice educator, on-site supervisor or another suitably qualified and experienced practitioner. Observations of practice provide first-hand evidence of your capability in real practice and are therefore a crucial part of the assessment process (Williams and Rutter, 2010). Direct observations usually involve observations of practice with service users although they can include other situations such as delivering a presentation or training event. Whichever type of practice is chosen, it is vital that you undertake careful preparation to ensure you are ready for being observed. When planning your direct observation, you need to consider several things. Most importantly, you need to ensure that the service users or people you will be working with give informed consent to the observation in advance of the event. You will therefore need to explain why you are being observed, who the observer will be and how the evidence will be used. Remember that interactions with service users inevitably involve power imbalances and you need to give people a real choice in whether they participate. Ideally, you should give the service user(s) time to think through whether they are prepared to take part and provide them with an opportunity to ask questions about the process. Having obtained this permission, you will then be able to plan other aspects of the direct observation, including the objectives of the session, skills you might want to evidence, the theoretical approach that will be used or which will underpin the observation and which domains of the PCF you anticipate providing evidence for.

In order to maximise learning from observations, you should aim to space your direct observations evenly across the placement period. This will allow you to demonstrate increasing confidence and competence in your skills and knowledge. You may be inclined to choose a piece of work that shows how effective your practice has been or how well you are working with a particular service user. Remember, however, that learning can also arise from situations that you find challenging or difficult. Do not worry if the observation does not go as planned as social work can be unpredictable and much can be learned from unexpected situations.

The thought of being assessed in practice can be nerve wracking for students (Williams and Rutter, 2010), but rest assured that your practice educator will give you balanced feedback. Observations therefore are an opportunity for you to show how well you are doing in practice and to receive positive feedback about this, as well as being given some constructive developmental feedback that will help you improve your practice. Also, the more you are observed, the less anxiety provoking it becomes, so try to build in other (informal) observation opportunities; co-working is a good way to achieve this. You might also like to observe your practice educator and on-site supervisor and discuss their practice with them (Doel et al., 1996).

Top tips – Direct observations

- In order to calm your nerves, undertake a number of observations of your practice before doing one that is formally assessed

- Obtain voluntary informed consent from the service user – consider power differentials and do not ask service users to give you an immediate answer

- Explain why you are being observed and what will happen to the written documentation that is produced

- Spread direct observations evenly across the placement to show your development over time

- Consider what aspects of the PCF you hope to evidence

- Outline what skills you intend to demonstrate

- Identify what theories you will be using within the direct observation

- Avoid using pieces of observed practice where pre-observation planning has not taken place

- Allow some time immediately after the observation for verbal feedback from the person who observed you

RECEIVING FEEDBACK FROM OTHERS

Receiving feedback from others is another core element of being assessed whilst on placement. Universities usually require students to seek and reflect on service user and carer feedback whilst on placement, sometimes appending this to their portfolio. You may be required to develop a method for gathering service user and carer feedback. Whilst this might seem straightforward, obtaining meaningful feedback can be much more complex and difficult than it first appears. For example, you need to consider issues of power and whether people are giving you feedback voluntarily and without influence. In research terms, this is a risk of 'social desirability' (Bryman, 2008: 211), where people give you the answers that they think you are looking for. You therefore need to be clear that providing feedback is entirely voluntary and the feedback will not affect the service respondents are receiving. You will also need to consider how you collect feedback. You will need to devise a method that is appropriate for the service users you work with. For example, you might generate feedback yourself with service users, or ask your practice educator to obtain this for you, or you could even use a questionnaire that the service user could self-complete. Guidance on obtaining service user and carer feedback has been produced by The College of Social Work (TCSW, undated (b)); this will help you think through how to obtain this type of feedback.

In the following extract, student social worker Jasmine provides an example of obtaining service user feedback from a child she was working with in a domestic abuse project.

Student voice – Jasmine

I chose to obtain feedback from a young boy who had witnessed his mum being subject to severe and enduring domestic abuse over many years. As a result of this his life had been very chaotic with him being afforded limited (if any) control over every aspect of his life; it seemed his wishes and feelings had never been sought. In addition to this he had 'moderate' learning disabilities. I therefore wished the feedback to achieve two functions. The first of which was to obtain meaningful and honest feedback on my practice in order to promote my own learning. Secondly I wanted to place emphasis on the process of obtaining this feedback as well as the outcomes of it; to endeavour to create an environment where this young boy could feel empowered, hopefully having a positive effect on his sense of self.

In order to achieve this I chose to gain feedback through the medium of puppets. Although there is much literature about the therapeutic nature of play with puppets and the way they create a less intrusive environment by externalising thoughts and feelings; this decision was informed primarily by the boy himself, who had often used these puppets in play sessions with myself, something he enjoyed and that he found very useful. I believe that in taking a child-centred approach and aiming to work within Vygotsky's 'zone of proximal development', I could fully maximise this boy's capacity in order to be able to express himself fully and truthfully.

(Continued)

(Continued)

During the session I realised that there was beginning to be a conflict between my own agenda for the session and the boy's agenda in what he needed from it. In order to take as much as a child-centred, non-directive approach as possible, I felt that it was important to forgo my own agenda to some extend to fully facilitate the service user's agenda, which was much more important. As a result the feedback I received was a little limited; however, overall I felt that the session was a success relating to the second function I wanted it to fulfil: that of making the service user feel empowered enough to express himself and giving the indication that his thoughts and feelings were important and needed to be listened to and acted upon.

We have worked with service users to develop some 'top tips' about obtaining the views of service users and/or carers, which are presented below.

Top tips – Obtaining service user and career feedback

- Be creative (e.g. drawings and puppets)
- Ask someone who is independent of the situation to obtain feedback
- Make sure service users know the provision of services will not be affected by the feedback they give
- Use anonymous feedback methods
- If using a questionnaire, make the questions clear and simple
- Seek continual feedback – not just a one-off event
- Persevere in seeking feedback – do not give up
- Use a suggestion box
- Make sure the method chosen is appropriate to the person you are working with
- If appropriate, use group feedback
- Think about and reflect on the feedback you have received and consider what you might do differently and how you might improve your practice

You may also be given feedback from colleagues within the team or perhaps even professionals from other agencies. Your practice educator and/or on-site supervisor will probably give you feedback on a regular basis throughout your placement. Feedback, whether positive or negative, can sometimes be difficult to hear or receive. The Open University has produced advice about giving and receiving feedback as a fundamental social work skill (Open University, undated) and advises that when receiving feedback, you should listen to it without disagreeing or challenging, be receptive to trying new approaches and, if you are unsure, ask for further information.

SUPERVISION DISCUSSIONS

As discussed in Chapter 3, during placement you will have regular supervision with your practice educator and/or on-site supervisor. Supervision will provide a protected space for you to reflect on your practice and learn about social work. Supervision discussions about pieces of work you have done and about theory and values will therefore be able to provide evidence of your capabilities in relation to the PCF domains. It might be a good idea to have evidence as a standing agenda item for your supervision as this would give you a way to track evidence that has been agreed.

PROJECT ACTIVITIES

Project activities relate to discrete tasks or projects given to you by your practice educator that will help you collate evidence, which may be for a specific capability domain in the PCF. Projects are usually time-limited activities and the end product will often be something that will support future practice within your placement. For example, you might be asked to run a group or collect information about local services or a specific aspect of practice relevant to your placement setting.

SIMULATED PRACTICE

You might find that your practice educator and/or on-site supervisor use case studies to discuss 'what if' scenarios and explore what your reactions would be in particular situations. Similarly, they may also ask you to role play a scenario. Role plays help you practise skills in a safe environment and may be particularly useful when using a new technique or in helping you prepare for a challenging situation.

REFLECTIVE WRITING

We have discussed reflective practice in Chapters 2 and 3 at some length and, given the perceived benefits of reflection for professional practice, it is highly likely that your university will require you to submit a piece of reflective writing within your portfolio. By the end of the first placement, the 'Critical reflection and analysis' domain requires you to demonstrate that you can 'with guidance, use reflection and analysis in practice' (TCSW, 2012g). By the end of the final placement, the requirement increases to demonstrating a more sophisticated level of reflection and 'apply the theories and techniques of reflective practice' (TCSW, 2012f).

Referring back to Jessica you will see that she was able to reflect on her own personal circumstances about her daughter starting school and the effect this had on her as well as professional practice within the placement. She was able to articulate how aspects of her personal and professional lives were co-dependent, but understood the need for professional boundaries. Jessica also critically appraised the responses of the placement setting and contrasted this with her understanding of the social work role.

CO-WORKING OR SHADOWING

Working with others can provide a significant amount of evidence during the placement. You may begin by shadowing other practitioners and simply observing what they do. This will give you the opportunity to critically appraise practice and demonstrate your understanding of situations through the application of knowledge, values and skills. You may also be given the chance to co-work or joint work with other practitioners, possibly even your practice educator and/or on-site supervisor. In planning and delivering the work together, you should be able to evidence your learning and skills and relate these to the PCF. Moreover, co-working allows opportunity for informal observations of practice.

WORK PRODUCTS

During the course of your work on placement, you will produce products. Often these relate to recording the work you have undertaken (Williams and Rutter, 2010) (e.g. emails, letters, case recording) but may also be generated in direct work with service users (e.g. pictures and drawings, life-story books). Your university may ask you to identify some products which are left in the agency or perhaps even include some anonymised examples in your portfolio; practice varies from university to university, so you need to check what your university requirements are.

UNDERTAKING SOCIAL WORK WITH SERVICE USERS

An important part of becoming a social worker is the experience gained from working with service users and, where relevant, their families and carers. Central to working effectively with service users and carers is the ability to form working relationships and to communicate, often in difficult or stressful circumstances (Riggall, 2012; Wilson et al., 2011). The PCF domain 'Intervention and skills' requires you to show verbal and written communication skills and aptitude in forming relationships with others, demonstrating increasing sophistication, knowledge and skills as you progress through the domain levels (TCSW, 2012d, 2012f, 2012g).

The nature of the relationship you build with a service user and/or their carers makes a significant difference to the outcomes of intervention (Koprowska, 2005; Riggall, 2012) and values the contribution service users can make to their own lives (Wilson et al., 2011). However, some students may feel nervous about their ability to forge effective working relationships with people. Such relationships necessitate that you draw together knowledge (e.g. about communication or partnership working or knowledge specific to the service user's circumstances), values and attitudes (e.g. about the value of working with service users and a commitment to work in an anti-oppressive manner), skills (e.g. in asking questions or building rapport) and your use of self (being able to use yourself as a resource, which means that you need to be aware of your own responses to situations, what scenarios might be challenging for you, being able to show empathy and to know when you are not functioning at full capacity) (Riggall, 2012; Wilson et al., 2011).

However, working with people, no matter how well intentioned you might be, can sometimes be problematic. For instance, you might find that service users ask intrusive or challenging questions, make statements or display behaviours that you find difficult. You might also be asked whether you have children, or people may challenge your knowledge about the problems they are experiencing, or be reluctant to engage. You might want to think through how you will manage questions, statements or behaviours that you find challenging. The following activity allows you to reflect on these circumstances. In particular, self-disclosure is a complex issue to manage which may cause difficulties for service users and other colleagues, so you will need to exercise great care about sharing information about yourself (Cooper, 2012). A sound understanding of professional boundaries will also allow you to navigate your way through issues relating to self-disclosure.

The General Social Care Council put forward the following questions to enable you to audit whether your professional boundaries are appropriate:

- Would you be comfortable discussing all of your actions, and the rationale for those actions, in a supervision session with your manager?

- Would you be uncomfortable about a colleague or your manager observing your behaviour?

- If challenged, could you give an explanation as to how your actions are grounded in social work values?

- Do your actions comply with the relevant policies of your employer? (GSCC, 2011: 7)

Activity 5.3

Preparing for difficult questions or comments

Using the grid below, note down any questions, comments or behaviours from service users that you might find challenging or difficult and your thoughts about how you might respond to this situation. You will find it useful to discuss this activity with your practice educator.

The question, behaviour or comment that you might find difficult	How you might respond

COMMENT

Through this activity you may have identified a range of issues and thought through possible pre-set responses that you could use. However, there will always be situations that you did not predict or which catch you 'off guard', so you will need to develop a way of dealing with the unanticipated. Additionally, the ability to manage challenging situations is, to some degree, dependent upon your own level of emotional resilience (see PCF domain 'Professionalism'), which will inevitably fluctuate from week to week dependent upon your own health and the pressures you are under.

TAKING CARE OF YOURSELF

As discussed in Chapter 1, as a beginning practitioner, you need to take responsibility for your health and wellbeing and to recognise when you are not fit for practice (HCPC, 2012a). Social work is a profession where you will work with some vulnerable and disadvantaged service users and the emotional component of social work can cause stress for practitioners (Morrison, 2007). Indeed, Morrison (2007: 259) argues that emotional intelligence is a 'central concern' for social work as it is relevant to processes involved in working with service users, managing staff and working with other professionals. Emotional intelligence combines skills in self-awareness, an ability to regulate and manage one's emotions and behaviours, along with the capacity to work with, understand and engage others (Consortium for Research on Emotional Intelligence in Organizations, 1998; Goleman, 1998). Having emotional intelligence has beneficial outcomes for service provision and practitioner competence and is therefore a salient issue in the helping professions (Hurley, 2012; Hurley et al., 2012). Five areas are proposed within the Emotional Competence Framework (Consortium for Research on Emotional Intelligence in Organizations, 1998; Goleman, 1998) which we outline in Table 5.2, showing the connections to the requirements of the PCF.

Table 5.2   The Emotional Competence Framework and its application to social work practice (adapted from Goleman [1998]) and Consortium for Research on Emotional Intelligence in Organizations (1998)

Emotional competence	Description	Link to the PCF end of first placement (TCSW, 2012g)	Link to the PCF end of final placement (TCSW, 2012f)
Self-awareness	This includes: • The ability to recognise emotions and responses • The capacity to self-appraise and reflect • Self-efficacy	**Professionalism:** • Show awareness of personal and professional boundaries • With guidance, recognise your limitations • Show awareness of own health, safety, wellbeing and emotional resilience and seek advice as necessary	**Professionalism:** • Be able to explain the role of the social worker • Demonstrate professionalism in terms of presentation, demeanour, reliability, honesty and respectfulness • Recognise the impact of self in interactions with others • Maintain personal and professional boundaries • Recognise professional limitations • With support manage and promote own safety, health, wellbeing and emotional resilience

Emotional competence	Description	Link to the PCF end of first placement (TCSW, 2012g)	Link to the PCF end of final placement (TCSW, 2012f)
		Values and ethics:	**Values and ethics:**
		• Recognise and with support manage the impact of own values on professional practice • Identify, and with guidance, manage potentially conflicting values and ethical dilemmas	• Recognise and, with support, manage the impact of own values on professional practice • Manage potentially conflicting or competing values
		Critical reflection and analysis:	**Critical reflection and analysis:**
		• With guidance use reflection and analysis in practice	• Demonstrate a capacity for logical systematic, critical and reflective reasoning and apply the theories and techniques of reflective practice
		Intervention and skills:	**Intervention and skills:**
		• With guidance, understand the authority of the social work role	• Understand the authority of the social work role and begin to use this appropriately
Self-regulation	The ability to manage thoughts, feelings and behaviours. Being reliable and trustworthy.	**Professionalism:**	**Professionalism:**
		• Recognise the role of the professional social worker in a range of contexts • Demonstrate professionalism in terms of presentation, demeanour, reliability, honesty and respectfulness • With guidance take responsibility for managing your time and workload effectively • Recognise and act on own learning needs in response to practice experience	• Be able to meet the requirements of the professional regulator • Be able to explain the role of the social worker in a range of contexts and uphold the reputation of the profession • Demonstrate an effective and active use of supervision for accountability, professional reflection and development • Demonstrate professionalism in terms of presentation, demeanour, reliability, honesty and respectfulness • Take responsibility for managing your time and workload effectively, and begin to prioritise your activity including supervision time
		Values and ethics:	**Values and ethics:**
		• Understand and with support, apply the profession's ethical principles	• Understand and apply the profession's ethical principles and legislation, taking account of these in reaching decisions

(Continued)

Table 5.2 (Continued)

Emotional competence Description	Link to the PCF end of first placement (TCSW, 2012g)	Link to the PCF end of final placement (TCSW, 2012f)
	Diversity:	**Diversity:**
	• Recognise and, with support, manage the impact on people of the power invested in your role	• Recognise and manage the impact on people of the power invested in you role
	Rights, justice and economic wellbeing:	**Rights, justice and economic wellbeing:**
	• Understand and, with support, apply in practice the principles of social justice, inclusion and equality • Work within the principles of human and civil rights and equalities legislation	• Understand, identify and apply in practice the principles of social justice, inclusion and equality • Work within the principles of human and civil rights and equalities legislation, differentiating and beginning to work with absolute, qualified and competing rights and differing needs and perspectives
	Knowledge:	**Knowledge:**
	• With guidance, apply research theory and knowledge • Understand the legal and policy frameworks and guidance that inform and mandate social work practice	• Demonstrate a critical understanding of the application to social work of research, theory and knowledge • Demonstrate a critical understanding of the legal and policy frameworks
	Critical reflection and analysis:	**Critical reflection and analysis:**
	• Recognise the importance of applying imagination, creativity and curiosity to practice	• Apply imagination, creativity and curiosity to practice
	Contexts and organisations:	**Contexts and organisations:**
	• With guidance work within the organisational context of your placement setting	• Be able to work within an organisation's remit and contribute to its evaluation and developments • Take responsibility for your role and impact within teams and be able to contribute positively to effective team working

Emotional competence	Description	Link to the PCF end of first placement (TCSW, 2012g)	Link to the PCF end of final placement (TCSW, 2012f)
		• Take responsibility for your role and impact within teams and with guidance contribute positively to team working • With guidance understand the changing economic, social, political and organisational contexts • Understand inter-agency, multidisciplinary and interprofessional dimensions to practice and with guidance, demonstrate effective partnership working	• Recognise the changing economic, social, political and organisational contexts • Understand multi-agency, multidisciplinary and interprofessional dimensions to practice and demonstrate effective partnership working
Motivation	Being tenacious in attempts to achieve goals.		**Professionalism:** • Demonstrate a commitment to your continuing learning and development
Empathy	Being sensitive and responsive to the needs of others and being able to understand others' points of view.		**Professionalism:** • Recognise the impact of self in interactions with others, making appropriate use of personal experience
		Values and ethics: • Elicit and respect the needs and views of service users and carers • Recognise and, with support, promote individuals' rights to autonomy and self-determination • Promote and protect the privacy of individuals	**Values and ethics:** • Demonstrate respectful partnership work with service users and carers, eliciting and respecting their needs and views, and promoting their participation in decision making • Recognise and promote individuals' rights to autonomy and self-determination • Promote and protect the privacy of individuals

(Continued)

Table 5.2　(Continued)

Emotional competence	Description	Link to the PCF end of first placement (TCSW, 2012g)	Link to the PCF end of final placement (TCSW, 2012f)
		Diversity:	**Diversity:**
		• Recognise personal and organisational discrimination and oppression and identify ways in which they might be challenged	• Recognise personal and organisational discrimination and oppression and with guidance make use of a range of approaches to challenge them
		Rights, justice and economic wellbeing:	**Rights, justice and economic wellbeing:**
		• Understand how legislation and guidance can advance or constrain people's rights • Recognise the impact of poverty and social exclusion and promote enhanced economic status • Recognise the value of independent advocacy	• Understand how legislation and guidance can advance or constrain people's rights and recognise how the law may be used to protect or advance their rights and entitlements • Recognise the impact of poverty and social exclusion and promote enhanced economic status • Recognise the value of, and aid access to, independent advocacy
		Intervention and skills: • Demonstrate an awareness of the impact of multiple factors, changing circumstances and uncertainty in people's lives • With guidance, demonstrate a holistic approach to the identification of needs, circumstances, rights, strengths and risks • Recognise the importance of community resources, groups and networks for individuals • With guidance, demonstrate skills in sharing information appropriately and effectively	**Intervention and skills:** • Recognise complexity, multiple factors, changing circumstances and uncertainty in people's lives, to be able to prioritise your intervention • Demonstrate an holistic approach to the identification of needs, circumstances, rights, strengths and risks • Recognise how the development of community resources, groups and networks enhances outcomes for individuals • Demonstrate skills in sharing information appropriately and respectfully

Emotional competence	Description	Link to the PCF end of first placement (TCSW, 2012g)	Link to the PCF end of final placement (TCSW, 2012f)
Social skills	This includes: • The ability to effectively communicate with others, resolving any differences that arise • Being able to work in a team • Demonstrating professional leadership	**Intervention and skills:** • With guidance use a range of verbal, non-verbal and written methods of communication relevant to the placement • With guidance, communicate information, advice, instruction and opinion so as to advocate, influence and persuade • Demonstrate the ability to build and conclude compassionate and effective relationships appropriate to the placement setting • Demonstrate skills in recording and report writing appropriate to the setting • With guidance, demonstrate skills in sharing information appropriately and respectfully **Contexts and organisations:** • Understand and respect the role of others within the organisation and work effectively with them • Take responsibility for your role and impact within teams and with guidance contribute positively to team working	**Intervention and skills:** • Identify and apply a range of verbal, non-verbal and written methods of communication and adapt them in line with people's age, comprehension and culture • Be able to communicate information, advice, instruction and opinion so as to advocate, influence and persuade • Demonstrate the ability to engage with people, and build, manage, sustain and conclude compassionate and effective relationships • Demonstrate skills in sharing information appropriately and respectfully **Contexts and organisations:** • Understand and respect the role of others within the organisation and work effectively with them • Take responsibility for your role and impact within teams and with guidance contribute positively to team working

(Continued)

Table 5.2   (Continued)

Emotional competence Description	Link to the PCF end of first placement (TCSW, 2012g)	Link to the PCF end of final placement (TCSW, 2012f)
	Professional leadership:	**Professional Leadership:**
	• Identify how professional leadership in social work can enhance practice • Recognise the value of sharing and supporting the learning and development of others	• Recognise the importance of, and begin to demonstrate, professional leadership as a social worker • Recognise the value of, and contribute to, supporting the learning and development of others

COMMENT

As you will see, the domains of the PCF are easily matched against the areas of competence in relation to emotional intelligence, situating it as a theme and requisite skill in many aspects of social work practice. Research indicates that social work students are likely to experience stress within their qualifying training, but this can be mitigated by the possession of emotional intelligence (Kinman and Grant, 2011).

RESEARCH SUMMARY – SOCIAL WORK STUDENTS AND EMOTIONAL RESILIENCE

Kinman and Grant's (2011) study with 240 social work students identified that students who were able to demonstrate emotional resilience and social competence were better placed to handle the stresses associated with social work practice. Resilience was enhanced by:

• The ability to show empathy without being overwhelmed by the needs of others

• The ability to see situations from differing points of view

• The ability to reflect on practice

• Awareness of your own and others' emotional responses (i.e. emotional intelligence)

- The possession of social skills and the ability to relate to people
- Having a supportive network

It is possible to relate the aspects of emotional intelligence and resilience identified by Kinman and Grant (2011) to Jessica (student voice), who we discussed earlier in this chapter. Jessica was able to show empathy for the young person and had personal insight into the potential for the young person's needs to overwhelm her. Jessica sought advice and supervision, thus creating a supportive network for her practice and providing a source of support to boost resilience.

You will therefore need to be able to recognise situations and sources of stress and think through how you will look after yourself whilst on placement and also during your social work career. That is, you will need to be emotionally resilient (which is explicitly mentioned in the PCF domain 'Professionalism'). Emotional resilience is the capacity to employ a range of strategies to effectively manage stressors (Klohen, 1996). In relation to social work, being emotionally resilient includes the ability to (Collins, 2007, 2008):

- Actively and creatively solve challenges;
- Have a positive outlook when stressed and be able to see the opportunities and benefits as well as obstacles;
- Derive pleasure from the social work task;
- Develop and maintain supportive relationships and networks, including use of supervision.

Activity 5.4

Recognising the warning signs of stress and identifying coping strategies

For the first part of this activity, make a note of all the indicators and signs that will tell you when you are stressed.

(Continued)

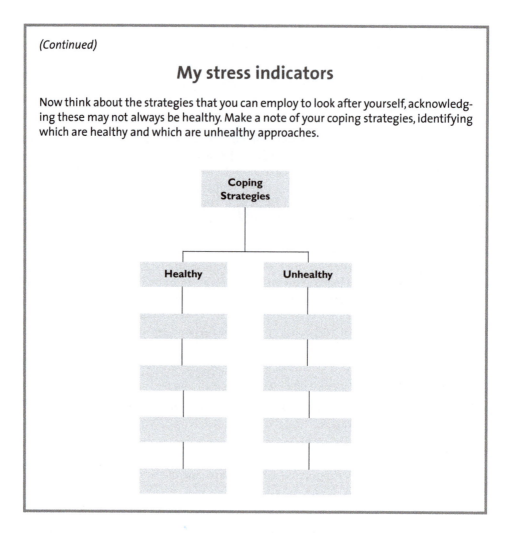

(Continued)

My stress indicators

Now think about the strategies that you can employ to look after yourself, acknowledging these may not always be healthy. Make a note of your coping strategies, identifying which are healthy and which are unhealthy approaches.

COMMENT

Recognising when you are stressed is commendable, but in order to develop your resilience, you also need to know how to manage your stress and you need to try to make sure the healthy strategies outweigh the unhealthy ones. Hopefully you will have identified a range of coping strategies for dealing with the times when you feel stressed or when you find placement challenging. Whilst you have responsibility for taking care of yourself, do not forget that your placement will also have a duty of care to you. Speaking to your practice educator or on-site supervisor can be helpful both in sharing your concerns and also in providing ideas about how to manage the stresses and demands of placement. As we have already suggested, coping strategies may be healthy or unhealthy, or indeed both (for example, having a glass of wine may be a healthy way to unwind, but this becomes problematic if alcohol consumption exceeds recommended levels). Collins (2008: 1178) identifies problematic ways of coping which are those that rely on avoidance or 'behavioural disengagement' (e.g. substance use or disengagement from the workplace or home life).

Student voice – David

You might recall David from Chapter 1; here he discusses how he manages the challenges and stresses of placement.

I think for me the best way of switching off or dealing with the high emotions involved has been on the drive home trying to concentrate on reflecting on the case in question and trying to place theories to it. This seemed to make the cases less real and more of an academic practice so it removes the emotion from it by the time you get home. I also found this helps the service user as you better understand the case. It's exceptionally important not to take anything home with you. Sometimes it can't be avoided, you do sit and mull it over and this is when, for me, it's back to basics, things like playing with my daughter, reading a sci-fi book, playing computer games – any form of escapism, forget the placement, forget uni and have a night off.

PROCESSES AND PRACTICALITIES

Having settled into placement, you will probably find that you become very busy in placement and the expectations placed upon you increase. We now discuss some of the processes and practicalities associated with this stage of the placement.

MID-POINT REVIEWS

Most universities will have a mid-point review or a process to review your progress and plan the remaining placement days. Some universities will ask a tutor to visit you, your practice educator and/or on-site supervisor in placement, but others will not. It is likely that you and your practice educator and, where applicable, on-site supervisor, will need to produce mid-point reports for your portfolio. These do not have to be very long but they do need to give a snapshot of your progress, any concerns or problems and the plans for the rest of the placement time. Your university portfolio will provide guidance on what is required.

LONE WORKING

As your confidence and skills increase, you will be given increasing responsibility for pieces of work. This may include working on your own, which is something that students may find daunting but is part of becoming an autonomous social work professional. If you do not feel ready to be working without direct supervision or support, please discuss this with your practice educator. If you do feel ready to work autonomously, the following tips may help you practise safely and effectively.

Top tips – Lone working

- Make sure you are clear about what you are being asked to do

- Plan your work to avoid forgetting key aspects that you need to cover – but be prepared to be flexible

- Make sure you are familiar with and comply with the placement's lone working policy

- If leaving the placement building, make sure you sign out, that colleagues know where you are going and when you will return

- Make your recording of the piece of work as soon after the event as you can

---

TIME MANAGEMENT

As the pace and amount of work increases, it is likely that you will need to consider carefully how you manage your time and workload, particularly when also trying to meet the demands of academic work. You will need to find a time management system that works for you. In Chapter 1, David spoke about allocating time for all aspects of your life – placement, family and university. It might also be useful to identify what your most productive times of day are and to leave more complex tasks until that time. The Open University (Cooper and Rai, 2011) has developed an online resource simulating the day in the life of a child care social worker, where you have to manage the demands on your time and interact with service users (available from: www.open.edu/openlearn/body-mind/social-care/social-work/day-the-life). This resource is supported by additional materials, including written documents and video clips of actual social workers and managers, some of which consider caseload and diary management and recognising signs of stress.

IF THINGS DO NOT GO AS PLANNED

Social work placements can be unpredictable and you may find that you face some unanticipated obstacles or problems. These can include illness (yourself or your practice educator), changes to service provision, lack of learning opportunities, problems caused by bad weather, the relationship between yourself and practice educator, undiagnosed or recently diagnosed learning needs or not liking the practice placement experience. Some students commence placement and then realise that this is not what they thought social work would be and they feel this is not the right career for them. It is not possible to plan for all eventualities, or to predict whether placement will confirm your aspirations to be a social worker, but if something occurs unexpectedly that might throw your placement off track, we strongly advise you to speak with your practice educator and/or on-site supervisor and if necessary contact your university tutor or link person. Quite often, problems can be resolved quickly through informal negotiations and the placement will continue successfully.

However, some issues may arise that necessitate a response under your university's formal concerns process. You will have been provided with documentation about concerns and if you find yourself in this process, it is advisable to re-read the guidance. The response of your university will be determined by the nature of the concerns which will also influence whether your placement is allowed to continue. Not all concerns relate to the performance of the student, it is possible to invoke this process because of concerns about the placement. In some circumstances the concerns may be sufficiently serious for your placement to be suspended or even terminated and perhaps your fitness to practise re-assessed. If you find yourself subject to concerns procedures or re-assessment of fitness to practise, you might need to seek formal support for yourself. This might be from the students' union, your personal/academic tutor or the university's counselling and wellbeing services. Concerns processes do not necessarily have to be a negative experience. Where concerns meetings are held, it is likely that everyone will be hoping to resolve the problem and will actively engage in developing an action plan to address specific concerns or issues.

The prospect of failing a placement generates stress and difficult emotions for everyone involved with placements (Barlow and Hall, 2007; Parker, 2010b) although there is only limited research about student experiences (Parker, 2010b). Even if you fail a placement, you may be offered a further re-sit opportunity, but future options will be determined by the nature of the concerns and the decisions of the examination board. When concerns arise, it is important to express your views (Parker, 2010b) and it might be wise to talk to the placement team, university tutor or module coordinators to ensure this occurs.

Student voice – Debbie

Debbie describes her experiences of concerns about her first placement which ultimately had a positive resolution:

It wasn't long after I started the placement that I started to notice small things which I was slightly concerned with, like not having regular supervisions and some days not being given anything to do. I was new to placement as this was my first one so I didn't know if this was normal or not.

It was when I was on the university recall day that I decided to mention this to my contact tutor. I liked my placement because it was quite close to home and I felt that I had settled in well so I did want it to work because I personally only had small concerns. Unfortunately other issues had occurred with another student who was at the same placement as me which were highly important concerns. After the recall day it was decided that the placement would be suspended with immediate effect. I received a telephone call and it was explained to me clearly and in detail and I understood why this had to happen.

Very soon after we were invited to attend a meeting at the university where we were informed of all the decisions made and offered support and advice. The tutors were great and very understanding, we were treated very respectfully and I felt supported in every way, e.g. with advice regarding an extension to the portfolio … At the meeting our opinions were given and minutes were taken and sent to us so we had a record of what was discussed and decisions made.

I was found a new placement very quickly in a very similar setting to the one I was in. I have settled in really well and have no issues with the placement or the portfolio, which is progressing very well. What happened to me has made me feel more comfortable about identifying any concerns when they arise if they should arise in the future because I received a lot of support with this placement.

CONCLUSION

This chapter has provided an overview of topics pertinent to the middle part of your placement particularly about evidence gathering, how you might establish yourself as a beginning social work practitioner and issues of emotional resilience. The middle section of the placement is crucial for locating evidence in relation to the PCF, but it is also where you might encounter challenges and problems and we have provided some advice and guidance about how to manage difficulties that typically arise during placement.

FURTHER READING

Hurley, J. and Linsley, P. (eds) (2012) *Emotional Intelligence in Health and Social Care.* London: Radcliffe Publishing.
Hurley and Linsley's edited text provides a range of chapters about the applicability of emotional intelligence to health and social care practice. Chapters are supported by activities to help the reader think through issues relating to emotional intelligence.

Riggall, S. (2012) *Using Counselling Skills in Social Work.* London: Sage/Learning Matters.
This book discusses how counselling skills and theory can be used in social work practice. There is a helpful chapter on how to build relationships with service users.

INTERNET RESOURCES

Cooper, B. and Rai, L. (2011) *Try a Day in the Life of a Social Worker.*

This is a creative online activity that allows you to try a day in the life of a social worker. This activity will test your time management skills and has lots of additional resources to support your learning, including video clips of real social workers. This resource can be accessed at: www.open.edu/openlearn/body-mind/social-care/social-work/day-the-life

Open University – *Introducing Social Work*

The Open University has uploaded materials entitled *Introducing Social Work* onto JORUM, a website for Open Educational Materials. *Introducing Social Work* is available at: http://dspace.jorum.ac.uk/xmlui/handle/123456789/791

One of their practice cards contains information about giving and receiving feedback, and can be accessed at: http://dspace.jorum.ac.uk/xmlui/bitstream/handle/123456789/791/Items/K113_1_PracticeCards_p65-78.pdf?sequence=77

The College of Social Work – *Principles for Service User and Carer Feedback*

This TCSW resource provides some thought-provoking principles about how to effectively seek feedback from people who use social work services. This document is available from: www.collegeofsocialwork.org/uploadedFiles/TheCollege/Media_centre/SUandCarerFeedbackPCF20.pdf

6

KNOWLEDGE, SKILLS AND VALUES

Chapter summary

When you have worked through this chapter, you will be able to:

- Understand and analyse the complexities of power;

- Relate the concept of power to anti-oppressive practice;

- Identify personal, cultural and structural aspects of oppression;

- Appreciate the need to exercise appropriate professional power in practice;

- Analyse the complexities of decision making in professional practice;

- Recognise the importance of multi-agency, interprofessional approaches to decision making.

INTRODUCTION

In Chapter 2 we introduced the concepts of power and anti-oppressive practice. Now that you have reached the middle part of your placement and will be developing your own body of work, we will re-visit these important concepts and help you relate them to your practice. Through the chapter you will develop your understanding of the use of power and authority in social work practice and how the Professional Capabilities Framework addresses these concepts. Within this the chapter also explores the issue of diversity and draws on a model for understanding oppression. In the latter part of the chapter you will learn about the importance of these ideas in relation to decision making in practice and multi-agency and interprofessional practice. Throughout the chapter, you will be given guidance and encouraged to consider how you will draw on your learning about these concepts as part of your practice placement and how you will integrate them into your assessed work for practice learning.

THE NATURE OF POWER

'Power' is a difficult and complex word which, like a number of terms you may encounter in this book, is open to a range of meanings. Smith (2008: 23–38) suggests that power can be perceived and applied in a number of interconnected ways. Whilst his argument is complex, it is helpful as it encourages us to think more broadly about the nature and exercise of power and how it may be seen in operation. He divides his analysis into four ways in which power can be demonstrated.

Power as potential – this idea draws on the work of sociologists such as Talcott Parsons (1902–79) who view power as a form of currency which facilitates and maintains order across structures within society. This type of power is often demonstrated by people who have a specific function within society such as police officers, teachers, magistrates or social workers. In order for this type of power to be exercised certain social arrangements need to be in place and the authority of people exercising power needs to be widely recognised and supported. This is a straightforward view of how power operates in society and is especially relevant to the way that our communities and roles are organised in western countries.

Power as a possession – this understanding moves away from seeing power as being vested in the individual and the position they have within society, to seeing power as being possessed and exercised by institutions and the people within them. This view corresponds with a Marxist interpretation which would see prominent social institutions in capitalist societies such as schools, the church, and even the family, as owning and exercising power as a means of protecting and enhancing their own privileged position.

Power as a process – in simple terms, this understanding concentrates on the processes and relationships that enable power to be used or revealed. This view reflects the fluidity of contemporary power dynamics where traditionally powerful institutions such as the church, politicians, or bankers have been undermined by changing social and political views, and on occasions even replaced. Smith (2008) suggests that in order to exert power organisations and individuals need to compete and negotiate with one another according to a complex set of rules and norms devised by society. This understanding of power helps to explain the organisational clashes that often occur in social work practice (for example, arguments between statutory health and social care organisations) and also reflects a contemporary view of British society where traditional sources of power and respect have been eroded by social changes or scandal.

Power as a product – in this final view, power is a seen as being the product of interaction between people and social systems. Powerful social systems, such as governments, retain power over the individual through the reproduction of structures which assist them to dominate; for example, the control of resources and the way in which society is organised. Smith (2008) helpfully uses an example from practice to illustrate this point. He suggests that the way in which information about service users is used sustains organisational power as the practitioner has control over the detail of the record, how it is stored and how it is reproduced and passed on to other professionals. You may remember this dynamic from the example of Katie we used in Chapter 4, where following a visit her practice educator recorded that the service user they had seen was 'sullen and rude' – a description which now becomes an integral part of the information collated by the agency.

This theoretical discussion provides a useful contextual backdrop to our work in this chapter and we hope that you can see that, despite the complexity of Smith's analysis, it is useful to explore ideas like power. This analysis is particularly important when you complete written work within your portfolio as often we read statements where important ideas and concepts, such as power, are uncritically used. It is important that you take care to 'showcase' your work and offer a thoughtful account of how you have applied theory and knowledge to your work.

'POWER' AND THE PROFESSIONAL CAPABILITIES FRAMEWORK

Interestingly, despite its clear relevance to social work practice, the word 'power' is mentioned only twice in the nine domains of the PCF (TCSW, 2012c). It first occurs as part of the requirements about difference and diversity:

> Diversity – Recognise diversity and apply anti-discriminatory and anti-oppressive principles in practice

> Social workers understand that diversity characterises and shapes human experience and is critical to the formation of identity. Diversity is multi-dimensional and includes race, disability, class, economic status, age, sexuality, gender and transgender, faith and belief. Social workers appreciate that, as a consequence of difference, a person's life experience may include oppression, marginalisation and alienation as well as privilege, **power** and acclaim, and are able to challenge appropriately. (TCSW, 2012c)

This particular reference is readily understandable and locates power within a general discussion of the need to acknowledge the significance of diversity. As this statement makes clear, social workers and students on placement encounter a wide range of people in their day-to-day professional work. Many of the service users and carers we work with have limited power, although this is not always the case. Consequently, the recognition of difference, and differences in power, is central to social work practice and again needs to be clearly evident within your portfolio.

Activity 6.1

Demonstrating your understanding of diversity

Think specifically about this section of the PCF. Make some notes about how you might demonstrate your understanding of diversity through your learning on placement.

You might find it helpful to look back at Chapter 5 where you learnt about the different sources of evidence that you could draw on to demonstrate learning and meeting the PCF.

COMMENT

There are numerous ways in which you might meet this element of the PCF. For example, many students complete a reflective log or journal which is principally used in supervision, but also forms an integral part of the portfolio. Within your reflection you could comment on how you identified, understood and worked with the elements of difference which are mentioned in the PCF – race, disability, class, economic status, age, sexuality, gender and transgender, faith and belief. Crucially, you need to say what difference an understanding of diversity has made to your practice. For example, if you are a young, white, female student who is working with an older black male service user, how would you recognise and articulate the differences (and of course commonalities) that exist between you and your service user?

The second reference to power within the PCF occurs in the requirements regarding social work intervention:

> Intervention and skills – Use judgement and authority to intervene with individuals, families and communities to promote independence, provide support and prevent harm, neglect and abuse. Social workers engage with individuals, families, groups and communities, working alongside people to assess and intervene. They enable effective relationships and are effective communicators, using appropriate skills. Using their professional judgement, they employ a range of interventions: promoting independence, providing support and protection, taking preventative action and ensuring safety whilst balancing rights and risks. They understand and take account of differentials in **power**, and are able to use authority appropriately. They evaluate their own practice and the outcomes for those they work with. (TCSW, 2012c)

This second reference, whilst clearly related to the need to acknowledge diversity, is perhaps more complex and requires consideration.

Activity 6.2

Understanding differentials in power

The extract above from the PCF refers to 'differentials in power'. Write an explanation of what you think is the meaning of the phrase 'They understand and take account of differentials in power'. It would be interesting to discuss your thoughts with other students, or perhaps with colleagues in your placement setting.

COMMENT

First, you might think that this statement refers to the disparities that exist in power between and within a number of relationships and the fact that social workers need to demonstrate an awareness of them; for example, power differentials in families, or the disparity in power between abusers and their victims, or social workers and service users. Whilst an understanding of these individual relationships is helpful, you also need to develop an appreciation of wider structural issues which relate to the exercise of power. An integral part of this analysis is developing an understanding of the way in which powerful groups within society, such as governments, organisations and the media, generate, maintain and exercise power. To return to Smith (2008) and his analysis, this thinking corresponds to his concept of 'power as a product' where powerful social systems, such as governments, exercise power through the maintenance of social structures which assist them to dominate.

In order to explore these wider issues in more detail, let us re-visit the example of Jasveer, the social work student we met in Chapter 2. You will recall that Jasveer, who is on placement in a school for children with special needs, overhears a teaching assistant making racist and disablist remarks about a child from a travelling family who has significant learning difficulties, and decides to challenge her colleague about their views. Jasveer needs to recognise that the offensive remarks of her colleague are in part created and supported by a range of assumptions and positions common within wider society. For example, the fact that travelling families are often portrayed negatively in the media, inadequately provided for by local councils, stereotyped in literature and disliked by the general public. In other words, the way that they are portrayed, viewed and stereotyped permits, even encourages, people to make oppressive remarks and, of course, adversely affects their day-to-day lives.

THE PCS MODEL

There are a number of theoretical models which help to explain the connections between these different dynamics we have identified. One of the most helpful is provided by Thompson (2006), who over a number of years has developed a well-known model which considers how power and oppression manifests itself in different areas of society.

Thompson divides his analysis into a consideration of three interlocking levels of oppression. The first is situated at the *personal* level where individual behaviours, actions and attitudes are used to oppress and disempower another person. This individualised oppression can be either consciously or unconsciously done by one person to another. The second tier of oppression identified by Thompson (2006) is positioned at the *cultural* level. In this part of the model the focus is on how powerful groups reach an agreement concerning what is 'normal' or 'abnormal'. People or groups who are considered not to be normal are then dealt with in a range of adverse ways by the dominant group. For example, they are shunned or segregated, or openly oppressed, sometimes through the use of 'jokes' and comedy. You may remember over the years how various groups of disadvantaged people, for example black people and gay people, have often been the butt of jokes and stories. This common and casual use of 'humour' in society has often reinforced the 'otherness' and 'abnormality' of oppressed groups leading to increasing exclusion and marginalisation. Equally, you may be aware of how certain oppressive cultures form and develop where people live and work in close proximity, for example in school staff rooms or in social work teams.

The final level in Thompson's analysis is where oppression and the misuse of power are *structural*. By this he means that major institutions in society, such as the police, government or the educational system, are inherently oppressive towards some groups or individuals in the way that they exercise their power. This corresponds to Smith (2008) and his comments about 'power as a possession'. Both writers note that society is inherently unequal and that power is achieved and maintained through the use of social structures which oppress and dominate whole groups within society.

CASE STUDY

Institutional racism: an example of structural oppression

Institutional racism is a relatively new term but has particular relevance to the murder of Stephen Lawrence and the subsequent investigation of his murder by the Metropolitan Police in London.

Stephen Lawrence was a young black man who was murdered in a racist attack in London in April 1993. In 1997 the then Home Secretary Jack Straw ordered a public inquiry into the Metropolitan Police Service's investigation into Stephen's murder which was conducted by Sir William Macpherson, who concluded that the police were 'institutionally racist'. He defined this as 'the collective failure of an organisation to provide an appropriate and professional service to people because of their colour, culture or ethnic origin', which 'can be seen or detected in processes, attitudes, and behaviour, which amount to discrimination through unwitting prejudice, ignorance, thoughtlessness, and racist stereotyping, which disadvantages minority ethnic people' (Home Office, 1998: section 6:34). Whilst this concept was not new and had been previously articulated by a number of black commentators, such as American civil rights leader Stokeley Carmichael in the 1960s, it represents the first time that a major British institution had been publicly accused of being fundamentally racist in its outlook and practice. Since the Macpherson Report other institutions in the UK, such as the NHS and the psychiatric system, have also been branded as 'institutionally racist' or 'colour blind' in their approach to black and ethnic minority people (Campbell and Maclean, 2002; Fernando, 2010).

As you can see from this definition of institutional racism provided by the Macpherson Report (Home Office, 1998), often oppression by groups, individuals and organisations is unconscious and not done deliberately but is 'sewn into the fabric' of the organisation. This is an important practice point as often people from a black or ethnic minority background feel that professional social work ignores their needs and oppresses them through the lack of culturally appropriate service provision, an inadequate recognition of cultural differences and an assumption of homogeneity (Butt, 2006). As a student you need to be aware of these issues especially in a rapidly changing society. For example, you may like to consider how your placement organisation meets the needs of newer immigrants to the United Kingdom, many of whom are white, Christian and European. Are they too victims of 'institutional racism'?

Activity 6.3

Using Thompson's PCS model

Having read about Thompson's model, how helpful do you think it is in explaining and contextualising the incident that Jasveer witnessed?

Write some notes on how the model can be used with regard to this incident. Within your notes attempt to identify the personal, structural and cultural aspects of oppression within the case study.

COMMENT

Thompson's understanding of how oppression operates at the *personal* level is clearly applicable as the person makes a racist and disablist comment in the hearing of the child and Jasveer. At a *cultural* level oppression could occur through disparaging conversations and jokes made in the staff room about children from travelling communities. In turn, these group conversations and the confirmation of discriminatory views may encourage individual staff to act and behave in oppressive ways. Finally, at a *structural* level some commentators argue that the educational system within the UK is institutionally racist and often reflects oppressive views and attitudes that are prevalent in wider society (Ross, 2002; Siraj-Blatchford, 1991). Consequently, the person was merely reflecting in everyday conversation elements of oppression that are articulated and supported in wider society.

We have implied that 'institutional racism' is commonplace in British society and have used the example of the police to argue our point. As social work practitioners, however, we cannot afford to be complacent and assume that institutional racism or oppression does not occur in social care organisations. In 2006 the Social Care Institute for Excellence (SCIE) published a discussion paper on race inequality within social care organisations (Butt, 2006). The paper highlighted a number of obstacles to promoting diversity within social care organisations, which included:

- A lack of knowledge amongst black and ethnic minority communities about what support was available to them from social care agencies;

- A lack of appropriate services for black and ethnic minority groups in the community;

- Workers who did not possess effective communication skills;
- Workers without the skills and experience to work with racially and culturally diverse communities. (Butt, 2006)

These barriers or obstacles are worrying and are a forceful reminder that social workers need to keep anti-oppressive practice in mind at all times and not be reticent to challenge oppressive behaviour, cultures or services which may be evident in social care agencies.

THE APPROPRIATE USE OF POWER IN SOCIAL WORK

You may remember that the second reference to power we highlighted from the PCF concluded with the phrase that social workers need to know how to 'use authority appropriately'. Clearly, there are a number of obvious examples which could be used to demonstrate the appropriate use of authority in practice; for example, where a social worker uses legal powers to protect a child or a vulnerable adult from harm. What we want you to note, however, is that the use of power and authority is an expectation and requirement of the social work role and that it must be appropriately, consistently and professionally exercised if practice is to be effective. There may well be occasions on placement when you have to use your authority to take difficult decisions; tell a service user news that they do not want to hear; or to argue your case with your manager or an outside agency. All of these examples require you to exercise the authority that comes with your professional role.

Fauth et al. (2010) in their review of effective practice in protecting children living in what they term 'highly resistant' families, those families who do not cooperate with any form of authority and are often difficult to engage with, identified a range of practice issues which hamper the protection of vulnerable children. These included:

1. The complexities of the adults' problems within the family were often allowed to overshadow the needs of the child;
2. A lack of timely and consistent service provision was associated with repeated maltreatment or serious injury or death of children;
3. Practitioners were often misled by 'false compliance'. This is where families make a show of cooperating or engaging with intervention, but have no intention of changing their abusive behaviour;
4. Practitioners became overly optimistic, focusing too much on small improvements made by families rather than keeping the family's full history in mind;
5. Assessment information needs to be organised and analysed and information from a range of sources must be included;
6. Direct observation of the parent–child interaction is essential in complex cases;
7. A more concerted effort to ensure children's voices are captured is also needed. (Fauth et al., 2010)

Activity 6.4

Exercising power and authority

Consider the issues identified by Fauth et al. (2010) and note those areas where practitioners need to exercise professional power and authority in order to ensure that their practice is effective.

COMMENT

Let us consider the first three practice issues identified by Fauth et al. (2010):

The complexities of the adults' problems within the family were often allowed to overshadow the needs of the child. On placement you may encounter dysfunctional families where the needs of the parents appear to take precedence over the care of the children in the household. It could be necessary to use your professional power and authority to challenge the adults' understanding of their role and responsibilities. It may even be necessary to take further steps to safeguard the children such as instigating formal child protection proceedings or compelling the adults to attend a parenting class.

A lack of timely and consistent service provision was associated with repeated maltreatment or serious injury or death of children. Service provision is a scarce resource and many organisations have to make difficult decisions in terms of rationing services and prioritising those families who are in the greatest need. On placement it may be necessary to challenge decisions made by your manager or agency or an outside agency where you feel that the provision of a service is essential. Challenging organisational power is not always easy, but advocating on behalf of your service users with those in positions of power is a key component of effective practice. On occasions, you will have to appropriately and professionally 'argue your corner'.

Practitioners were often misled by 'false compliance'. This is where families make a show of cooperating or engaging with intervention, but have no intention of changing their abusive behaviour. Working with such families can be very difficult and it is unlikely that you will be working by yourself with such complexity on placement. Nonetheless, many service users can be dishonest and manipulative and refuse to fully and openly engage with practitioners. In such circumstances you will have to use professional power and authority to undertake some potentially difficult tasks. For example, negotiating to interview a child without their parents being present; arranging to visit and gain entry to a property; checking that parents have done what they agreed to do; challenging parents about their behaviour and making agreements that can be readily monitored for compliance.

To summarise, Fauth et al. (2010: 2) argue that practitioners must adopt 'an eyes-wide-open, boundaried, authoritative approach aimed at containing anxiety and ensuring that the child's needs stay in sharp focus'. This is excellent advice as it emphasises the enquiring and authoritative position of professional practice whilst focusing attention clearly on the needs of the child.

TEN PITFALLS AND HOW TO AVOID THEM

The issues identified by Fauth et al. (2010) are echoed in another influential report from Broadhurst et al. (2010) on practice in child protection, which was first published in 1998. The updated version reiterates that failings which were evident in practice over 15 years ago are still observable today.

Broadhurst et al. (2010: 7) identified 10 'pitfalls':

1. 'An initial hypothesis is formulated on the basis of incomplete information, and is assessed and accepted too quickly. Practitioners become committed to this hypothesis and do not seek out information that may disconfirm or refute it;

2. Information taken at the first enquiry is not adequately recorded, facts are not checked and there is a failure to feedback the outcome to the referrer;

3. Attention is focused on the most visible or pressing problems; case history and less 'obvious' details are insufficiently explored;

4. Insufficient weight is given to information from family, friends and neighbours;

5. Insufficient attention is paid to what children say, how they look and how they behave;

6. There is insufficient full engagement with parents (mothers/fathers/other family carers) to assess risk;

7. Initial decisions that are overly focused on age categories of children can result in older children being left in situations of unacceptable risk;

8. There is insufficient support/supervision to enable practitioners to work effectively with service users who are uncooperative, ambivalent, confrontational, avoidant or aggressive;

9. Throughout the initial assessment process, professionals do not clearly check that others have understood their communication. There is an assumption that information shared is information understood;

10. Case responsibility is diluted in the context of multi-agency working, impacting both on referrals and response. The local authority may inappropriately signpost families to other agencies, with no follow-up. (Broadhurst et al., 2010: 7)

As can be seen from this list of potential pitfalls, the gathering, recording and processing of appropriate information is vital to the success of casework. It is likely that practitioners are going to have to be both persistent and thorough in their approach if this is to be achieved. Often referrers, parents and neighbours will give partial or subjective views, particularly if they are worried or afraid about the responses of statutory services; these do not always assist the practitioner to uncover the 'truth' of what has occurred. This is where a range of skills and understandings is important, principally the ability to critically appraise situations and keep the child at the forefront of all interventions. We continue our discussion with an analysis of the key skill of assertiveness.

ASSERTIVENESS

A key skill that you will need to demonstrate in your practice, if you are to appropriately exercise professional power and authority, is that of assertiveness. Being assertive means having the ability to articulate and maintain your own position without violating the rights of other people or stakeholders to hold a different view. This is not always easy, especially as so much of practice involves advocacy, negotiation and conflict resolution sometimes with people or groups who are hostile or entrenched in their views. There are, however, a number of skills which can help you to be assertive in challenging situations. For example, you need to consistently use the skills of communication, such as eye contact and an awareness of the signals your non-verbal communication is portraying, which we discussed in Chapter 4. Communicating in a strong, steady voice (especially when nervous, or on the telephone) is also important as is the ability to give a concise, clear message sometimes more than once in the same conversation. Social workers should not be afraid to say 'no' to service users or carers. Given the increasing financial pressures and the scarcity of resources that all social care organisations face it is sometimes necessary to refuse requests for support and assistance. This is often an uncomfortable position to be in as you are the voice of the organisation you represent and need to be able to respond to the anger or frustration of the person you have disappointed. It is in these situations where the skills of assertion and relationship building, coupled with good supervisory support, are essential if you are to be an effective social worker.

Activity 6.5

Recording the use of power and authority

Sometimes recording how you have used power and authority in your portfolio is difficult. Consider the following extracts from two student portfolios. In the first example, the student is talking to two parents at the outset of a meeting to decide how the agency will work with their daughter. In the second example, a student who is assisting with the delivery of a women's group, challenges a colleague.

(Continued)

(Continued)

Identify where they have appropriately used authority and note how they have written about their experiences in their portfolios.

Example 1

'During the meeting I introduced the service and covered service users' rights to complain, access their records and the limits of confidentiality. I confirmed referral details such as dates of birth, etc. I explained that I was a student and how my practice was supervised. I outlined the work plan and purpose of the therapeutic assessment. I confirmed that we would meet again at the end of the assessment to share the report and look at the recommendations it made.'

Example 2

'I was deeply unhappy about the developing infrastructure of the group which would mean the women's group would have been facilitated by five different workers over a six week programme. I found this hard to comprehend as we had been planning the group since February and we all knew the dates, when the group was due to start and end. On returning to the office after the second session I challenged the absent worker about a number of areas I was unhappy with. These included the change in facilitators, the lack of continuity and as a student I should not be relied upon to take a lead role.'

COMMENT

In the first example, the student clearly introduces and discusses a range of important practical issues. For example:

- The role of the agency;
- The student's position within the service and how he is supervised;
- The rights of service users;
- The accuracy of the referral information;
- The plan and purpose of the work to be undertaken;
- A promise to meet and review the recommendations that flow from the work.

This is a straightforward example which demonstrates how a student has a set of clear objectives and how he articulates those objectives. Whilst it would be unwise to read too much into such a short extract, it could be suggested that the student has appropriately used his authority to establish a purposeful working relationship with the family.

In the second example, the student is unhappy about the lack of commitment from a colleague to a group that has been planned for several months. She directly addresses the situation by talking to the person involved and again has a clear 'agenda' or list of grievances that she wants to address. What neither of these examples shows is how the students communicated their messages and used their authority. Nonetheless, they are good examples of the use of authority on placement and demonstrate that students, who often feel in a powerless position, can appropriately use professional power.

As a conclusion to this section we provide you with some 'top tips' which concentrate on the skills you need to develop when working with challenging situations.

Top tips – Working with challenging situations

- Do not be frightened to rehearse a difficult telephone call or interview with your practice educator, or in your own head. Think about what you might say, the skills you may need to use, and anticipate the responses of the other person.

- Remember that the recording of information and the appropriate sharing of information is crucial. Familiarise yourself with your agency's recording policy and develop your skills in word processing, using the telephone and note taking.

- Try to remain calm and confident when faced with difficult situations. Develop the skill of controlling your anxiety – breathing deeply and rhythmically for example can be a way of relieving stress.

- Concentrate on developing your communication skills such as maintaining eye contact and being aware of non-verbal communication.

- Practise the skills of assertiveness. For example, do not be afraid to be a 'broken record' where you repeat the same information in order to reiterate your position.

- Do not overestimate or underestimate your abilities.

- Learn when to ask for help, who to ask, and how.

DECISION MAKING

We have spent a considerable amount of time in this chapter analysing the use of power and authority as these attributes are central to effective professional practice. They are particularly relevant to a key skill within social work, that of making good, understandable and defendable decisions. On placement you will be expected to make decisions about your work on a regular basis. Some decisions you make will require extensive deliberation on your part and on the part of others, whilst others will be routine and straightforward. Some decisions will have potentially far reaching outcomes for you, your agency or for the service users you work with, whilst others will have only minimal consequences. Some decisions will have a considerable personal impact on you and will cause you considerable distress or anxiety, whilst others will not affect you. As you can see from this brief introduction, decisions are extremely varied in nature, substance and consequence – but they are the building blocks of social work practice.

Decision making, however, is surprisingly difficult to define and is perhaps most helpfully seen as a process which assists us to make choices. The emphasis we have placed on process is deliberate as it highlights the fact that few decisions of any significance have a clear-cut beginning and end. Often a significant decision in professional practice leads to a number of consequences or outcomes, some of which are anticipated or desired whilst others are unexpected or unwanted, which in turn generate another set of choices which require the practitioner to make further decisions. Consequently, the making of a decision can rarely be seen in isolation and needs to be viewed in the context of an ongoing process which is open to change and fluctuation.

MAKING "SOUND" DECISIONS

O'Sullivan (2011) makes a helpful distinction between 'sound' and 'effective' decisions. Sound decision making refers to the process undertaken when making a decision. The outcome of the decision making process, however, cannot be known until the decision has been implemented. It is only at that point that a judgement can be made as to whether or not the decision has been 'effective'. O'Sullivan (2011) suggests that a sound decision-making process is characterised by a number of features which include:

Being critically aware of the practice context – this means having awareness of a range of important factors which give your practice a framework and context. For example, you need to be aware of the knowledge that is required on your placement, the legal context of practice and wider structural issues, such as class, gender and race, which we have already highlighted in this chapter. In other words, decision making needs to be supported by a holistic and well-balanced understanding of all the factors that are likely to contextualise your practice.

The involvement of service users and carers – you will note that this point corresponds with the previous comments from Fauth et al. (2010) and Broadhurst et al. (2010), both of whom identified that social workers in child protection often failed to actively involve the child (the service user) in their decision making. The involvement of service users is clearly crucial to effective and ethical social work practice and there have been several attempts to conceptualise how this can be achieved. Arnstein (1969) viewed the participation of citizens in the making of civic decisions as an eight-staged ladder which rose from tokenistic non-involvement through to full control. This theory has often been related to service user involvement in social work and has been re-worked on a number of occasions. For example, McLaughlin (2007), with specific reference to the involvement of service users in research, suggests that the lowest level of involvement is 'tokenistic', where service users exercise no real influence and are not permitted to make a meaningful contribution. The next stage is that of 'consultation', where the views of service users are sought but can be readily ignored or dismissed by those who hold power. This may lead to 'collaboration', where service users have some limited influence on decisions and processes. The final and most influential level of involvement is that of service user control where users attain full control and responsibility. These sequential models of involvement are open to critique as they implicitly assume that there are clear stages within involvement and that the greater the level of involvement the better the practice or decision. In many cases this may be true, but our previous discussion regarding the appropriate use of professional power and authority clearly articulated that there are occasions when social workers need to take control of a situation and act decisively, sometimes without the express approval of a service user, especially if a vulnerable child or adult is to be protected. Whilst this is not an overly popular view of the role of social work, and tends to diminish the caring aspect of the role that attracts so many students to the profession, we maintain that social workers must appropriately exercise their legal and moral powers.

Using knowledge, thinking clearly and managing emotions – these attributes are central to making sound and defensible decisions. As we argued in Chapter 2, social work practice requires practitioners to know and absorb a breadth of knowledge drawn from a range of disciplines. Knowledge alone is not enough to make a good decision as a practitioner must take a balanced view which is not swayed by anxiety, pressure or the stress of the situation.

Making effective use of supervision – this is crucial if your decision making and practice is to be well informed, appropriately supported and credible. Your practice educator and/or on-site supervisor should be providing you with regular, high-quality supervision. Do not be afraid to seek support, and do not view it as being a sign of weakness, as even the most experienced practitioner will require help and guidance with their decision making.

THE SHARING OF DECISION MAKING – MULTI-AGENCY WORKING

As a social work student on placement you will be required not only to work collaboratively with service users and their carers but also with a range of other professionals such as nurses, teachers and occupational therapists. This ability to work in collaboration with others, and the knowledge and skills that underpin it, are explicit throughout the requirements of the PCF (TCSW, 2012c). For example, at the end of your first practice placement you should be able to demonstrate 'critical reflection and analysis' to the following level:

- Recognise the importance of applying imagination, creativity and curiosity to practice;
- Inform decision-making through the identification and gathering of information from more than one source and, with support, question its reliability and validity;
- With guidance, use reflection and analysis in practice;
- With guidance, understand how to evaluate and review hypotheses in response to information available at the time and apply in practice with support;
- With guidance, use evidence to inform decisions (TCSW, 2012g).

At the conclusion of your final practice placement the expectations have understandably increased and you should be able to demonstrate 'critical reflection and analysis' to the following level:

- Apply imagination, creativity and curiosity to practice;
- Inform decision-making through the identification and gathering of information from multiple sources, actively seeking new sources;
- With support, rigorously question and evaluate the reliability and validity of information from different sources;
- Demonstrate a capacity for logical, systematic, critical and reflective reasoning and apply the theories and techniques of reflective practice;
- Know how to formulate, test, evaluate, and review hypotheses in response to information available at the time and apply in practice;
- Begin to formulate and make explicit, evidence-informed judgments (TCSW, 2012f).

As you can see, and as you would expect, whilst there is a clear difference between the two stages of professional development, there are also commonalities. For example, at both stages work is informed by collaboration and the sharing of knowledge. Implicitly, several sources of information and knowledge are sought and used in practice, and the role of the wider community is acknowledged. What we would like you to see from these references is that social workers do not, cannot, work in isolation. Indeed, it would be dangerous and unwise to do so given the complexity and fluidity of the professional task and the need for personal and organisational accountability.

Social workers then are required to work with other practitioners across organisations, disciplines and professions. Multi-agency, interprofessional working, however, is not necessarily straightforward and sometimes there can be difficulties when working across organisational and professional boundaries (Crawford, 2012). These tensions have been evident in a number of high-profile inquiries established to investigate significant injury or death to a vulnerable child or adult. For example, in adult care the serious case review conducted by the Cornwall Safeguarding Adults Board into the death of Steven Hoskin, a 38-year-old man with learning difficulty who was murdered in 2007, concluded that the housing association, police, health and social care agencies had not communicated effectively and that more could and should have been done to protect Steven (Flynn, 2007). In child care there have been a number of inquiries and reports that have highlighted similar incidences when professionals have failed to work together in an effective and cohesive way. For example, the serious case review into the death of Peter Connelly (Haringey Local Safeguarding Children Board, 2009) identified that a succession of opportunities to intervene had been missed by staff from a range of agencies and that no one professional had an overview of the overall situation. Explicitly, the agencies had failed to share their knowledge of the family with one another and they collectively failed to act in an 'authoritative manner' (Haringey Local Safeguarding Children Board, 2009). Whilst these failings are tragic and have far-reaching consequences, we need to remember that often on a day-to-day basis practitioners from different backgrounds and agencies do work well together. One of the challenges of your placement, but also one of the real opportunities, will be gaining knowledge about the roles, tasks and professional attitudes of those non-social care professionals that you will encounter in your practice

Barrett and Keeping (2005) identify the following factors as being important if collaborative working is to be successful:

Knowledge of professional roles – it is necessary to have a clear understanding not only of your own role and responsibilities but also how, when and where other professionals can make a contribution.

Open and honest communication – this is important especially if there are conflicting views or complex decisions to be made. As can be seen from the two serious case reviews we gave as examples, communication across agencies is vital. You must ensure that all people involved in decision making have the full facts and that you have taken responsibility to accurately and comprehensively record all the information available to you.

Trust and mutual respect – professionals need to be able to trust one another and feel able to support the decisions made by other people.

A recognition of power – a recognition that not all stakeholders in decision making have equal power. Sometimes social care agencies and practitioners need to take a lead role and accept that they have the power and responsibility to make certain decisions. In other cases, it may be that other agencies, such as the NHS, take responsibility for a particular decision, especially if the case involves detailed health concerns. As a student you need to be aware of power differentials in your team. Do some people seem to have more power and influence than others? If so, why might this be the case? It may be that it is due to role or length of experience, or personality or status within the team. Equally, outside of your team you may find that some practitioners (e.g. doctors) tend to expect to lead in decision making due to their inherent status and power (Mathews and Crawford, 2011).

Conflict resolution – sometimes conflict arises over resource allocation, lines of accountability, who will do what, etc. If interprofessional work is to be successful it is necessary to have clear mechanisms to resolve these potential conflicts – otherwise there is a danger that service users and patients will lose out whilst practitioners squabble.

Support at a senior level – there are an increasing number of legal and policy drivers that persuade, even coerce, health and social care organisations to work together. Nonetheless, beyond this formal encouragement managers need to facilitate active partnerships through the provision of resources and role modelling.

A recognition of different professional cultures – each organisation has its own way of working, language, jargon and style. Sometimes there is almost a 'Berlin Wall' that separates organisations from one another. Practitioners need to recognise the validity and strength of their own professional culture and develop ways of working with other cultures.

Student voice – Danielle

Danielle is on her first placement with a voluntary agency which specialises in supporting families and children where substance misuse is evident. Towards the middle of her place-ment her reflective journal contains the following description of her activity during the week:

> I had a meeting with two of the workers offering the internet-based counselling service. It was very interesting reviewing the reasons why children and young people access the service. ... I met with a member of the Domestic Violence Team who informed me about the history of the team and the different types of work they undertake with perpetrators, their partners and children ... I had the opportunity to meet with two external agencies offering different services. One delivering services for young people involved in substance misuse the other providing work, education and training for adults who have been through drug rehabilitation services.

Activity 6.6

Reflecting on working with other professionals

Now that you are mid-way through your placement, like Danielle you may have encountered or worked with a number of other professionals and had contact with a range of different agencies. Think about a specific case example or situation where

(Continued)

(Continued)

another professional has been involved and analyse the differences and commonalities with social work practice that you noticed. For example:

- Were you guided by the same legislation and policy?
- Were your lines of accountability different?
- Did you adopt the same approach to the service user?
- Did you have access to different resources?

You may find it helpful to use this exercise as the basis for a reflective journal, or to take to supervision as a discussion starter.

Top tips – Multi-agency and interprofessional working

- Do not be frightened to seek advice and guidance when faced with difficult decisions.

- Remember to accurately record all the information you know about a case or situation in a timely and appropriate way.

- Appropriately share information with other professionals and agencies. This helps others make sound, effective and defendable decisions.

- Make sure that you are aware of organisational policy regarding information governance. Check with your practice educator if you are unsure about using or sharing information.

- Be clear about the value of your contribution to decision making when working with other professionals. Social work has a distinctive voice and an important contribution to make. Do not be afraid to articulate your view.

- Ensure that your contribution is balanced and well informed. This will ensure that your view is respected and 'heard' by others.

CONCLUSION

In this chapter we have provided an in-depth analysis of the concept of power and have related it to a discussion of anti-oppressive practice. Using this analysis as a platform, you have been able to consider some of the issues relating to the making and taking of decisions in professional practice. Finally, we concluded this chapter with a consideration of how multi-agency, interprofessional collaboration is essential to professional decision making. We feel that there are a number of key messages in this chapter – not least the central message that social workers need not to be afraid of exercising professional power and authority in a purposeful, thoughtful and conscious way. As you progress through your placement you need to be aware of this essential attribute and provide within your practice portfolio a critical analysis that reflects the nuances of power, authority and anti-oppressive practice that we have discussed in this chapter.

FURTHER READING

O'Sullivan, T. (2011) *Decision Making in Social Work,* 2nd edn. Basingstoke: Palgrave Macmillan.
An excellent introductory text which provides a comprehensive analysis of the context and practice of decision making in social work practice.

Crawford, K. (2012) *Interprofessional Collaboration in Social Work Practice.* London: Sage.
This book develops a focus on professional practice in the collaborative environment; for example it explores the importance of contexts, ways to draw on theories and models to help understand interprofessional working, and working with service users and carers in the collaborative environment.

Rutter, L. and Brown, K. (2012) *Critical Thinking and Professional Judgement for Social Work,* 3rd edn. Exeter: Learning Matters.
This book takes a pragmatic look at a range of ideas associated with critical thinking and highlights the importance of taking well-informed and balanced decisions.

Taylor, B.J. (2013) *Professional Decision Making and Risk in Social Work,* 2nd edn. Exeter: Learning Matters.
A comprehensive introduction to a range of important topics relating to risk, consent, professional judgements and safeguarding issues. With an overview of concepts of decision making, this book has chapters on making collaborative decisions, dynamic decision making and the organisational aspects of decision making.

INTERNET RESOURCES

The 'Equality and Human Rights Commission' website contains some interesting (and distressing) analyses of disability related harassment. In particular, it provides detail of 10 serious case reviews (including Steven Hoskin) in adult care where people with disability have suffered extreme harassment. Available from: www.equalityhumanrights.com

The SCIE website contains many useful reports and resources that should inform your practice on placement. In this chapter we have referred to a report for SCIE written by Jabeer Butt, deputy chief executive of the Race Equality Foundation, entitled *Are We There Yet? The Characteristics of Organisations that Successfully Promote Diversity.* This interesting report can be accessed at: www.scie.org.uk/partnerscouncil/assets/files/sep05/diversity.pdf

PART IV

THE END OF THE PLACEMENT

7

PROCESSES AND PRACTICALITIES

Chapter summary

When you have worked through this chapter, you will be able to:

- Reflect upon and plan for the multiple endings associated with placement including identifying ways in which to end your placement and relationships with service users and team members;

- Identify your feelings about placement endings and consider how these might be managed;

- Consider barriers and facilitators to effective endings;

- Review your learning during placement and identify future learning needs;

- Consider placement review processes and how to give effective feedback;

- Consider and plan for the next stage of your professional development.

INTRODUCTION

This chapter takes you through the final stages of your placement, helping you think about managing endings with both service users and your placement, as well as considering aspects of portfolio construction. This chapter considers the processes involved in the review of placement opportunities and how to make best use of this opportunity before finally considering returning to university or entering qualified practice and the requirements of the Assessed and Supported Year in Employment (ASYE).

ENDINGS

Leaving placement necessarily involves a range of endings in relation to your work with service users, other professionals and your colleagues within placement. Endings evoke a range of emotions (Doel and Sawdon, 1999; Lomax et al., 2010; Maclean and Harrison, 2009; Trevithick, 2012); it is therefore vital to consider your feelings about the end of your placement. You may find ending some relationships more difficult than others (Lomax et al., 2010), so it is important to reflect upon the range of endings you will be facing, how you feel about them and what you might do to make this process more effective for all involved. Endings are particularly important given the relationship-based nature of social work practice (Trevithick, 2012; Wilson et al., 2011), the likelihood that attachments may have been formed between you and service users (Wilson et al., 2011) and the possibility that service users may have previous, unsatisfactory or unresolved experiences of endings (Trevithick, 2012; Wilson et al., 2011). Well-managed endings can provide transformative opportunities and therapeutic benefit for service users (Thompson, N., 2002; Trevithick, 2012); they are also important for students, marking the end of an important stage in your journey towards being a qualified practitioner but also embedding a career-long engagement with professional development (Parker, 2010a). Indeed, Doel and Sawdon (1999), in their book about group work, suggest that endings are better understood as transitions where people move on and hopefully sustain progress; this seems an apposite way of thinking about placement endings for student social workers.

The first activity in this chapter aims to help you to begin thinking about the feelings associated with leaving your placement, the source of these feelings and how you might manage. Once complete, this activity might form part of a supervision discussion to help you think about how to effectively end your placement.

Activity 7.1

How do I feel about the ending of my placement?

Use this activity to identify the range of feelings you have about leaving placement and ending your work with service users and colleagues within the placement. For each feeling, try to identify what makes you feel that way (for example, are specific feelings related to specific endings). Next, think about the various ways you might manage these feelings.

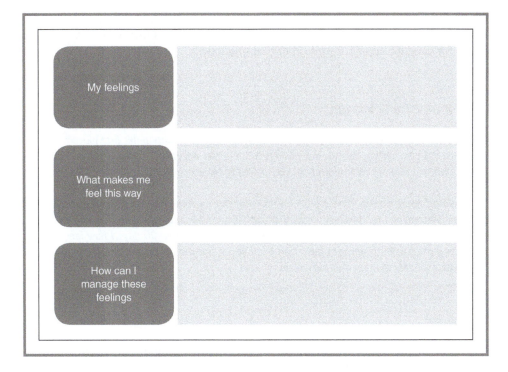

COMMENT

It is likely that you will have a range of emotions including loss of relationships or professional identity, sadness, concerns about abandoning service users, pleasure, relief and anticipation (Coulshed and Orme, 2012; Ford and Jones, 1987; Lomax et al., 2010; Maclean and Harrison, 2009; Walker et al., 2008). Feelings will be determined by the quality of your relationships with the people that you will be leaving behind (Lomax et al., 2010) and your experience of undertaking endings within the placement (Lomax et al., 2010), but they will also be influenced by your own experiences of endings (Doel and Sawdon, 1999). Being aware of how you feel and taking care not to project unhelpful feelings about endings onto service users (Doel and Sawdon, 1999) is therefore an important part of managing feelings. Understanding which relationships may be difficult for you to end can also help you plan how to manage these endings. Supervision may help you identify your feelings about endings and what you might do about them to secure a successful end to your placement. Endings are commonplace within social work practice (Coulshed and Orme, 2012), although this does not mean that you should not pay them careful attention. Each interview, contact or visit with a service user has an ending (Coulshed and Orme, 2012) and therefore in thinking about the end of your placement, you will have already practised skills in managing endings that you will be able to utilise. These skills and approaches can be applied to your placement setting, not only in working with service users, but also within your supervisory relationship with your practice educator and other team members.

Student voice – Safiyah

Following a service user event held at university, Safiyah reflects upon her first placement in an adult care setting, relating her feelings to the experiences that service users reported and making comment about the ending of her placement.

What I heard on the Service User Involvement day mirrored how I felt when ending my placement. I felt privileged that they had allowed me into, and shared, their lives with me. Although we all knew I would be only be around for 100 days, I now feel like the service users when they described what social workers always did and that I too was abandoning them and moving on.

COMMENT

Being able to manage endings with service users and colleagues is a requirement of the 'Intervention and skills' domain of the PCF. The end of first placement requirement is to 'demonstrate the ability to build and conclude compassionate and effective relationships appropriate to the placement setting' (TCSW, 2012g), whereas there is additional complexity in the requirement for the end of final placement which requires students to be able to 'demonstrate the ability to engage with people, and build, manage, sustain and conclude compassionate and effective relationships' (TCSW, 2012f). Safiyah reflects on the relationships she has built, referring to service users having 'shared their lives' with her, perhaps revealing a level of intensity in the relationships she has built with service users. Safiyah's concern that she is abandoning the service users possibly indicates that she has not yet worked out how she will effectively close her relationships with service users and/or how she will manage her own feelings about endings. Supervision may be a useful forum for Safiyah to share her feelings about endings and to produce ideas about how she may approach them. Additionally, reminding service users of the impending end of placement and exploring ideas with them about how to end interventions may also assist Safiyah in leaving her placement without service users feeling abandoned. The placement end is also a transition point for Safiyah as she talks about 'moving on,' presumably onto the next step towards becoming a qualified social worker.

Exploring what a good ending might look like will also help you plan and prepare for leaving your placement. The next activity in this chapter asks you to think about not only what constitutes a good ending, but also the barriers to effective endings. In thinking about what facilitates or hinders endings, you will be able to plan the various endings that you will encounter towards the end of your placement.

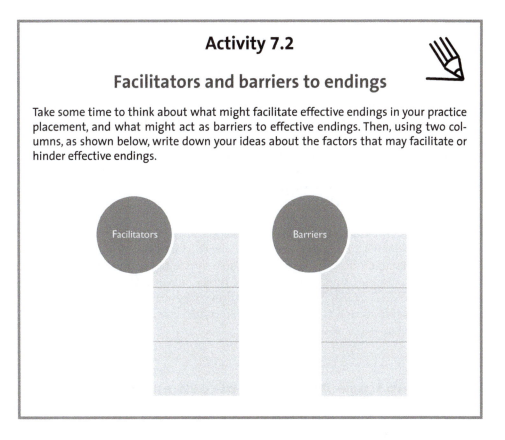

COMMENT

Neil Thompson (2002) identifies a number of barriers to endings that are also pertinent to placement endings. These include feelings (from students and service users) about endings, fear of the future, lack of resources to re-allocate work or meet need, lack of clarity about professional boundaries, concerns that progress may not be sustained without ongoing support, interactions with service users that have created dependency rather than autonomy and weak case management in relation to planning, goal setting and review (Thompson, N., 2002). Conversely, evidence about what constitutes a good ending can also be applied to leaving placement. There is agreement, for example, that managing endings (and therefore the feelings they evoke) begins at the outset of any contact with a service user and continues throughout intervention (Doel and Sawdon, 1999; Koprowska, 2005; Trevithick, 2012; Wilson et al., 2011). Endings can be facilitated by careful planning, reviews of progress towards agreed goals, setting time aside to discuss endings, phased withdrawal of services, introducing new practitioners if the case/work is to be transferred, ensuring service users are aware of the timescales involved and completing written documentation either to close or transfer the work (Coulshed and Orme, 2012; Koprowska, 2005; Trevithick, 2012).

Setting time aside to complete recording about service users (Ford and Jones, 1987; Walker et al., 2008), compile academic work relating to your placement, see and comment upon the report written about you by your practice educator and/or on-site supervisor (Ford and Jones, 1987) and to withdraw from the day-to-day practice of the placement, will also help you manage the feelings about the endings and work towards a successful placement end. There are also likely to be placement ending 'rituals' (Ford and Jones, 1987; Lomax et al., 2010; Walker et al., 2008) either developed specifically for you or which are part of the team's customs for celebrating the end of a student placement. This might include a celebratory lunch or provision of a farewell gift or card. Not every student will be at ease with formal celebrations or ceremonies, but they are an important landmark or transition in your professional development and help everyone to manage the change and loss associated with leaving placement. You must also return any equipment belonging to the placement along with key or access cards and ID cards; typically this is done on your last day.

To conclude this section we provide some 'top tips' advice for managing the end of your placement.

Top tips – Managing placement endings

- Consider endings from the start of your placement

- Remind people of the timescales, especially as your leaving date approaches

- Use case management processes to plan, review and evaluate your work with service users

- If applicable, leave enough time to introduce new workers

- Plan endings with service users

- Make sure case recording is up to date

- Be clear about what you need to do to complete your work within the placement

- Use supervision to consider how best to manage endings and to discuss how you feel about leaving

- Return placement equipment (e.g. laptops, phones, ID badges, access cards, keys)

ACADEMIC WORK — CONSTRUCTING YOUR PORTFOLIO

It is likely that your university will want you to produce academic work during your placement. The format and structure of what you are required to produce will vary from university to university but often this will be a portfolio of evidence relating to your practice. Portfolios tend to include a range of evidence and critical reflection about your performance in placement, linking this to the value base of social work and the PCF domain levels appropriate to either first or final placement. Typical portfolio components include:

- Documentation relating directly to placement such as learning agreements, midpoint reviews of placement and an outline of the placement setting;

- Pieces of reflective writing about practice (e.g. reflective journals);

- Direct observations of practice;

- Service user and carer feedback;

- Written work demonstrating analysis of practice;

- A final student summary or evaluation;

- Final reports from the practice educator and, if applicable, on-site supervisor.

The best advice we can give you is to work on your portfolio regularly and to keep up to date with the tasks within it. Your university might set indicative timescales for the completion of work and, whilst it may be tempting to ignore them, they are designed to help you manage your work. Even if you have sustained effort on your portfolio, it is likely that you will need to set some time aside towards the end of placement to bring this all together. Your practice educator will want to see your completed portfolio, usually to inform their report writing and so that they can address any obvious gaps in your work. You might find that your practice educator asks for your completed portfolio a few weeks before the end of the placement in order to help them to write their final report; you will therefore have to be disciplined about completing the work relating to your portfolio. There should not be any surprises in the practice educator's and, if applicable, the on-site supervisor's final reports as you should have received feedback on your performance throughout the placement. One exception would be if significant issues about your performance arose after the end of your placement and the practice educator submitted an addendum to their original report; however, such circumstances tend to be rare and you will be contacted by your university if this happens to you.

A completed portfolio can become a large and unwieldy document, particularly if you have to submit a paper copy. Presentation and organisation of the portfolio can make all the difference to the person who has to review or grade your portfolio. In the following 'top tips' we provide some ideas to help you construct a portfolio that will be easy to navigate.

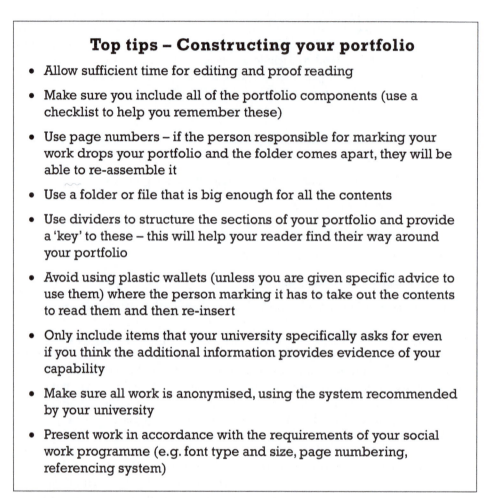

Top tips – Constructing your portfolio

- Allow sufficient time for editing and proof reading

- Make sure you include all of the portfolio components (use a checklist to help you remember these)

- Use page numbers – if the person responsible for marking your work drops your portfolio and the folder comes apart, they will be able to re-assemble it

- Use a folder or file that is big enough for all the contents

- Use dividers to structure the sections of your portfolio and provide a 'key' to these – this will help your reader find their way around your portfolio

- Avoid using plastic wallets (unless you are given specific advice to use them) where the person marking it has to take out the contents to read them and then re-insert

- Only include items that your university specifically asks for even if you think the additional information provides evidence of your capability

- Make sure all work is anonymised, using the system recommended by your university

- Present work in accordance with the requirements of your social work programme (e.g. font type and size, page numbering, referencing system)

REVIEWING YOUR LEARNING

A crucial aspect of your portfolio/academic work is an appraisal of your learning and development during placement, leading on to planning future learning and development needs (Fanthome, 2004). In Chapters 2 and 3 we considered reflective practice and provided ideas on how you might critically reflect upon your developing professional practice. You will have received verbal feedback from your practice educator and/or on-site supervisor during placement and they will also prepare written reports about your performance at the end of placement which will help you think about your future development. Hopefully, you will have kept some sort of record or journal about your progress which will also help you review your learning (pieces of work for your portfolio completed at different stages of the placement should help you with this). It would be worth reading over the work you have completed and making a note of your key learning during placement as well as measuring the learning needs identified prior to placement against the learning you have documented during placement. This will then enable you to consider whether there are any themes arising from your learning, whether you successfully met the learning needs identified at the outset of placement and what else you need to develop.

Activity 7.3

Reviewing learning and identifying future learning needs

In Chapter 1, Activity 1.3 asked you to think about your abilities in relation to the PCF domains; you will be able to use this information to review your learning during placement and plan for the next stage of your development. This activity builds on this, helping you to bring this information together and to consider what this might mean for future development.

1. First, go back to Activity 1.3 and complete the first column in the grid below re-stating the learning needs identified in Activity 1.3 prior to placement.
2. Review these as you complete the second column, thinking about your learning during placement.
3. In the comments section draw out themes or things that strike you about your learning and development.
4. Finally, in the last column identify your future learning needs to address during return to university, final placement or your first year of practice.

As well as identifying gaps or deficits in your learning or skills, this activity can also help you identify strengths and what you can offer either to another placement or to an employer.

Learning needs identified in Activity 1.3	Review of learning during placement	Comments	Future learning needs

---

In Chapter 1, we introduced you to social work student Gulshan, and the identification of his learning needs in relation to the PCF. We now return to Gulshan, reviewing the learning needs identified prior to placement, setting this alongside his work during the placement in order to reach some conclusions about future learning needs. Gulshan was in a voluntary placement working with excluded and marginalised young people.

COMMENT

Gulshan's placement has afforded opportunities to meet the learning needs that he identified at the beginning of his placement. Gulshan's review of his learning during placement indicates that he has developed a greater understanding of the requirements of the

Table 7.1 Reviewing Gulshan's learning and identifying future learning needs

Learning needs in relation to the PCF identified in Activity 1.3	Review of learning during placement	Comments	Future learning needs
Professionalism: I need to work on how to present myself in meetings with other professionals.	I had the opportunity to attend multi-agency CAF meetings but I have struggled to be 'heard' in these meetings and have not had the confidence to express views. I have a much better grasp of the role of a social worker and I am looking forward to having a statutory final placement.		I need to become more assertive. I will practise 'I' statements and try to contain the feeling of panic when I am trying to speak in a group. I thought I might write down all the things I want to say to help me focus.
Values and ethics: I need to learn how to challenge people effectively. I would like to learn how to manage information in accordance with the Data Protection Act 1998.	I used the organisation's procedures for recording information, storing records safely in accordance with the Data Protection Act 1998. Challenging people remains a problem – I need to be able to express my view in a way that other people will be willing to listen to me. Placement also allowed me to explore my values and to understand the tensions between personal and professional values, using supervision to explore dilemmas and conflicts.	There is a theme emerging about developing assertiveness skills. I need to be more autonomous in my exploration of values as much of the discussion occurred in supervision.	I need to make time to think through ethical issues and also to be able to more clearly demonstrate that my practice is in line with the HCPC Guidance on Conduct and Ethics for Students. I need to be constantly in touch with my thoughts and feelings about situations and to be able to dissect these.

Learning needs in relation to the PCF identified in Activity 1.3	Review of learning during placement	Comments	Future learning needs
Diversity: I need to develop skills in discussing issues of discrimination and oppression with service users in a clear and understandable way. I need to keep reflecting on my own perceptions and prejudices to make sure they don't interfere with the work on placement.	My practice educator has helped me think through issues of discrimination and how I might tackle this. It was difficult to discuss concepts of discrimination with service users and I have tried to use different terms such as 'unfairness' and 'prejudice'. Many of the young people told me about how they are stereotyped and that people make assumptions about them.		For the next placement in a statutory setting, I would like to develop my ability to manage aspects of power and authority.
Rights, justice and economic wellbeing: I need to know how legislation is applied in real practice.	I did not realise how much legislation there was relating to my placement. By the end of my placement, I was much more familiar with legislation relating to children and young people but I realise that I know very little about law relating to adults.		I would like to compare issues of exclusion regarding older people against the experiences of younger people.
Knowledge: I am struggling to understand how to apply theory into practice.	I now realise the importance of some of the modules we were taught at university. Understanding theories and methods has helped me to think about people's circumstances and also to develop action plans. I have been drawn to task-centred practice but I am concerned that this is because it seems a straightforward and common-sense method and that perhaps I need to look at other theories. I have learnt a lot from the experiences of service users and have a better understanding of knowledge created by service users.	I am particularly adept at using theoretical approaches that promote practical strategies. However, I realise that not all difficulties or challenges are amenable to this type of intervention.	I need to develop proficiency in using theories that do not focus on practical solutions – for example, counselling skills or attachment theory.

(Continued)

Table 7.1   (Continued)

Learning needs in relation to the PCF identified in Activity 1.3	Review of learning during placement	Comments	Future learning needs
Critical reflection and analysis: I need to develop skills in working with real service users and analysing information.	My practice skills have certainly developed and I have a fairly sound grasp of how to conduct an interview and to collate information. I would like to be more analytical about the information once I have it – how do you weigh up what is important?	My practice educator continually asked me to think about evidence-based practice which was a useful way of making sense of the information gathered during assessment – for example what do we know about this particular issue and what interventions work?	I need to consolidate my understanding and use of evidence-based practice. Extend my ability to analyse information and appropriately assign weight to this, using knowledge and evidence to underpin decision making.
Intervention and skills: I am concerned about how to write things for service users' files.	I was able to make some effective and supportive relationships with the young people although they were initially wary because I was a social work student.	I wondered how we might improve the public perception of social work.	To develop my assessment skills, particularly in relation to risk.
	I was able to forge some really good working relationships with the young people, particularly helped by being similar in age and also because we had similar interests. I was then able to use some of the interpersonal skills that we had studied at university to communicate effectively with the young people.		To develop my understanding of safeguarding processes.
	I was also involved in undertaking assessments and had to consider factors that might elevate risk.		
Contexts and organisations: I do not have any experience of inter-agency or interdisciplinary work.	I have been able to work with a range of different professionals during this placement but have encountered some unexpected barriers to collaborative practice which has surprised me.		To ensure I am familiar with the policies and procedures in my next placement and use time during the induction period to read the necessary procedures.

Learning needs in relation to the PCF identified in Activity 1.3	Review of learning during placement	Comments	Future learning needs
	I spent much of my first two weeks in placement reading agency policies and procedures which gave me a clear understanding of the expectations placement have of staff and students.		To build upon my team working skills.
	I also developed my team or group work skills.		
	There were also budgetary pressures during placement and I was conscious of how the wider economic situation can affect small voluntary organisations.		
Professional leadership: I would like to work on my confidence in presenting information in formal settings.	I was able to give a presentation to the team about substance misuse following some training I had attended.		I will join The College of Social Work and thought this might be a good way to contribute to changes to the media perception of social work.

PCF, using this to inform his learning needs for the next placement. By re-visiting his initial learning needs and considering his development during placement, Gulshan has been able to think about his learning needs for his final placement which include a mixture of consolidation of existing skills or knowledge as well as developing new ones. He therefore has a clear starting point for the final placement. However, he might also have used the comments section to consider what his skills and strengths are as it is important to have clarity about these for employment or your next placement.

REVIEWING YOUR PLACEMENT

Placements are often keen to receive feedback about what was offered and how this can be improved. In England, universities also have to formally collect and collate feedback about placements using the Quality Assurance in Practice Learning (QAPL) process (TCSW and Skills for Care, 2012), which we mentioned in Chapter 1. This form enables universities to measure, review and support the placements they work with, so your feedback is essential. It is, however, important to make sure that you manage feedback professionally and sensitively. Consider how you write your feedback, the language you use and how you might feel if you were receiving that feedback. If you have concerns about the placement and what it can offer, please voice your concerns whilst the placement is taking place so that, if necessary, changes can be made. However, please also mention the concerns within the QAPL form and what action was taken to address them. It is also important to make sure you are specific about feedback points, providing evidence where necessary, as general sweeping statements can be problematic (e.g. 'this was a fantastic placement' – you need to explain why you reached that conclusion).

MOVING ON AND FUTURE PROFESSIONAL DEVELOPMENT

At the end of your placement, you will either be returning to your studies at university or making the transition into qualified practice. This final section considers the next steps in your journey by looking at each of these options.

RETURNING TO UNIVERSITY

Resuming studies after the excitement and challenge of placement may seem like an unattractive undertaking. However, there is still much to be learnt and returning to university gives you the opportunity to address the learning needs identified at the end of placement (Fanthome, 2004), rather than leaving this development until your final placement. In Table 7.1 the review of Gulshan's learning resulted in the identification of several future learning needs, some of which can begin to be addressed upon return to university. In Table 7.2, we make some suggestions about how Gulshan might be able to start work on his developmental needs.

You will be able to see from Gulshan's example that addressing future learning needs can commence prior to the final placement although this may continue and be consolidated in the final practice learning opportunity. There are various ways in which Gulshan might develop his practice, from participating within formal taught elements

Table 7.2 Meeting Gulshan's future learning needs on his return to university

Future learning need	Meeting learning needs at university
I need to become more assertive. I will practise 'I' statements and try to contain the feeling of panic when I am trying to speak in a group. I thought I might write down all the things I want to say to help me focus.	Gulshan could begin to develop his assertiveness skills: • By speaking during group presentations within modules • Active engagement with learning opportunities and practising giving his opinion • By taking on the role of student representative or being involved in a university committee
I need to make time to think through ethical issues and also to be able to more clearly demonstrate that my practice is in line with the HCPC Guidance on Conduct and Ethics for Students.	On his return to university, there are some further days set aside as part of the 30 days allocated for readiness to practise which uses problem-based learning and asks students to discuss case studies, identifying practice issues and responses, which will include identifying ethical issues.

Future learning need	Meeting learning needs at university
I need to be constantly in touch with my thoughts and feelings about situations and to be able to dissect these.	Gulshan might address this learning need in the following ways: • Contributing to online discussion groups on the university's virtual learning environment • Through in-class group discussions • Using tutorials with his academic tutor • Keeping a journal or diary • Using assignment opportunities to reflect on use of self
To develop proficiency in using theories that do not focus on practical solutions – for example, counselling skills, attachment theory, psycho-dynamic theory.	Opportunities to develop in this area at university include: • Classroom activities based around case studies would give Gulshan the chance to explain why a particular theory might be applicable and how this might be used • Skills development sessions as part of the 30-day readiness to practice would allow Gulshan to rehearse skills
I need to consolidate my understanding and use of evidence-based practice.	Gulshan could develop his understanding of evidence-based practice by: • Undertaking self-directed study • Using assignments to discuss interventions that are known to be effective • Using assignments to identify a range of types of knowledge
Extend my ability to analyse information and appropriately assign weight to information, using knowledge and evidence to underpin decision making.	Gulshan could develop his decision-making skills through: • Engagement with readiness to practise skills development sessions • Assignment writing where risk is analysed and intervention options identified • Group discussions within modules
To develop my assessment skills, particularly in relation to risk.	Gulshan could address this learning need by: • Engagement with academic modules • Participation in readiness to practise modules • Independent research about particular issues
To develop my understanding of safeguarding processes.	Gulshan could address this learning need at university through: • His engagement with academic modules about children and families and also vulnerable adults • Independent research – for example, by accessing the Department for Health or NSPCC websites
To build upon my team working skills.	Gulshan's team working skills can be enhanced by: • Active participation in group activities • Engagement with volunteering or other extra-curricular activities that require him to work in a team (e.g. sports)
I will join The College of Social Work and thought this might be a good way to contribute to changes to the media perception of social work.	Gulshan could join TCSW as an Affiliate Member. He can also receive the TCSW monthly magazine. There are also blogs on TCSW website that Gulshan could take part in.

of the social work degree through to self-directed study and engagement with online discussions. It is likely that using various methods will enable Gulshan to develop and practise the skills and knowledge required in several different settings, thus embedding his learning. Universities are able to use some of the 30 days' readiness for practice for advanced skills development prior to the final placement (TCSW, undated (c)) and you can see that Gulshan's engagement with this component of his degree will enable him to develop specific skills and knowledge in relation to the PCF.

If applicable to your stage of development, use the same format and heading from Table 7.2, to make a note of how you might address your learning needs on your return to university prior to the final practice placement.

BECOMING A QUALIFIED SOCIAL WORKER

Of course, the conclusion of your placement might mean that your programme is at an end and you are about to qualify as a social worker. We concentrate now on getting your social work career started, including the Assessed and Supported Year in Employment (ASYE).

PROFESSIONAL REGISTRATION

As soon as you receive confirmation from your university's examination board that you have passed your social work programme, you will be a qualified social worker. In order to legally call yourself a social worker, you will need to register with the relevant regulatory body. In England, this is the Health and Care Professions Council; in Wales, the Care Council for Wales; in Scotland, the Scottish Social Services Council; and in Northern Ireland, the Northern Ireland Social Care Council. Application forms for professional registration are available online and will need to be endorsed by someone from your social work programme – this might be your academic tutor or a nominated member of staff, so you will need to check with your university. You will also need to pay a registration fee, the cost of which varies across the regulatory bodies, so make sure you know how much this will cost and have the funds available for this expense, although some employers might be willing to reimburse the cost of registration.

APPLYING FOR JOBS

During your final placement, you will probably want to start thinking about applying for jobs. It is not unusual for some students to have secured their first social work post whilst still on placement. Graduate employability is a key concern for universities (Higher Education Funding Council for England, 2010) and you might find that your university provides specific advice or support about applying for jobs, which often can continue after graduation. Finding a job has become more challenging for newly qualified social workers (NQSWs) in recent years (BASW, undated), so it is important to do all that you can to increase your chances of success.

The first hurdle is to find a job you wish to apply for and complete the application form. You might know which area or organisation you wish to work for, so you could search their job opportunities online. Alternatively, you may be more flexible about where and for whom you wish to work; websites such as Community Care (www.communitycare.co.uk), the *Guardian* (http://jobs.guardian.co.uk/) or British Association of Social Workers (BASW) (www.basw.co.uk/jobs) provide lists of social work vacancies.

If you manage to secure a job interview, you will need to try to maximise your chances of being offered the job. The BASW provides some useful guidance about finding employment (BASW, 2013) including some very helpful advice about interview etiquette and presentation. Additionally, the BASW has also produced materials for newly qualified social workers looking for employment (BASW, undated).

ASSESSED AND SUPPORTED YEAR IN EMPLOYMENT (ASYE)

Assuming you have been able to find employment, you will need to undertake the ASYE during the first year of your qualified practice (or pro-rata equivalent if you work part-time). The ASYE was introduced in September 2012, replacing the Newly Qualified Social Worker (NQSW) framework. The ASYE provides an opportunity for you to consolidate and extend your skills and knowledge, supported by increased levels of supervision and a reduced workload whilst being supervised and assessed by a qualified and registered social worker (Skills for Care and Department for Education, undated (a), undated (c)). In many ways, the ASYE will mirror your experiences of being on placement as there will be a learning agreement, ongoing assessment of your practice in relation to the PCF domain levels for ASYE using multiple sources of evidence, direct observations of your practice, a requirement for obtaining service user and carer feedback and the expectation that you will critically reflect upon your practice and present written evidence of reflective practice (Skills for Care and Department for Education, undated (a)). You can see therefore that having a clear understanding of your learning needs from your final placement will help you plan your professional development during your first year of qualified practice. Successful completion of the ASYE will be formally recognised and certified by TCSW (Skills for Care and Department for Education, undated (b)).

CONCLUSION

Leaving your placement can be a difficult process and it is important to think about how you might manage endings in a way that enables you and service users to move forward. The end of your placement signals the next stage in your learning and development, either in your final placement or during the ASYE and you will therefore need to have clarity about your learning needs. You might of course keep in contact with staff you have met in placement, including your practice educator, but their formal role in assessing your capabilities in relation to the PCF is at an end and your future relationship will therefore be re-defined. You will also need to pay particular attention to the academic requirements of your programme which is typically evidenced through the submission of a portfolio. Do not underestimate the effort and time needed to complete a satisfactory portfolio and remember that this task will be much easier if you keep up to date with the requirements of the portfolio during placement. If you have successfully completed your social work degree, then your next steps will be to obtain professional registration, find suitable employment and complete the ASYE.

FURTHER READING

Trevithick, P. (2012) *Social Work Skills and Knowledge: A Practice Handbook*, 3rd edn. Maidenhead: Open University Press/McGraw-Hill.

This book provides underpinning knowledge of social work in an accessible manner. We particularly like the short appendices which outline and critique theoretical approaches. These concise appendices are useful for when you are in busy practice settings and need 'bite sized' information which includes some critical appraisal. Two of Trevithick's 80 skills and interventions relate to ending interventions with service users which will be useful in helping your organise endings with service users.

Fenge, L.A., Howe, K., Hughes, M. and Thomas, G. (2013) *The Social Work Portfolio: A Student's Guide to Evidencing Your Practice*. Maidenhead: Open University Press/ McGraw-Hill.

You will find this book helpful in relation to portfolio construction.

INTERNET RESOURCES

British Association of Social Workers (BASW): www.basw.co.uk

BASW membership provides access to a range of resources. In addition, the BASW website contains many freely available resources and also advertises social work vacancies.

BASW provides some extremely useful advice on looking for employment, including a list of dos and don'ts for interviews and advice on how to best present yourself at interview: www.basw.co.uk/social-work-careers/your-guide-to-finding-a-job/

In recognising that NQSWs are uniquely positioned in relation to employment and that, increasingly, finding a job can be problematic, the BASW website offers advice and guidance specific to NQSWs: http://cdn.basw.co.uk/upload/basw_105901-4.pdf

Skills for Care and Department for Education – ASYE: www.skillsforcare.org.uk/socialwork/ introductionsw.aspx

Skills for Care and the Department for Education have jointly published advice and guidance about the ASYE which can be found on the Skills for Care website page, which in turn provides links to pages about the purpose of ASYE, registration, support available, the process of holistic assessment and decision-making processes.

The College of Social Work: e-portfolio www.collegeofsocialwork.org/

The College of Social Work (TCSW) offers an e-portfolio for all of its members which will be useful once qualified for providing evidence to the HCPC of your continuing professional development. There are various components within the e-portfolio which allow you to document and reflect on your learning, including sections on CVs, a reflective journal and planning future learning needs.

8

KNOWLEDGE, SKILLS AND VALUES

Chapter summary

When you have worked through this chapter, you will be able to:

- Understand the different types of loss experienced by service users;
- Recognise the impact of change and loss;
- Use a range of theories and theoretical concepts to assist your understanding of change;
- Think creatively about theory and how it could be included in your portfolio.

INTRODUCTION

In this final chapter we draw on the practical information contained in Chapter 7 and discuss a number of theoretical models that explore the interlinked concepts of 'loss', 'change' and 'transition'. We also make connections to the core professional values and key skills highlighted in the PCF that you will need to demonstrate as a practitioner. At this concluding point in your placement you will have a range of practical issues to address relating to closure and endings, but it is also important to maintain concentration on your portfolio construction and ensure that your writing fully reflects the work you have undertaken. As our previous chapter emphasises, at this critical time in your professional development you need to take time to reflect on your placement, evidence your portfolio and look forward to an exciting and fulfilling future as a qualified social worker. Consequently, there are a number of transitions, losses and changes that you will be personally experiencing at this time, but we want to shift the emphasis away from you and encourage you to think about these issues from a service user's perspective. In this final chapter, then, we will concentrate on developing a theoretical understanding of loss and change.

CHANGE AND TRANSITION

As you will have discovered from your practice on placement, social work is often concerned with the promotion or management of change and transition in the lives of service users, their families and in the wider community. Many of the legal processes or organisational procedures we use as practitioners force or compel service users to undergo potentially profound changes. For example, the instigation of care proceedings and the consequent removal of a child from its family can lead to a chain reaction of consequences, transitions and changes for a whole range of people. Some of these changes can be predicted and planned for, whilst other changes may be unanticipated and more difficult to manage. As an integral component of your placement experience we expect that you will have been involved in the facilitation and management of change. In order to help us to analyse the dynamics of change and transition we invite you to think back over the course of your placement and reflect on some of the changes you have witnessed.

Activity 8.1

Recognising change and transition

Make a list of the changes and transitions that you have been involved with over the duration of your placement. Consider the service users and situations you have worked with.

- What changes have you facilitated or noticed as a result of your intervention?
- Have all of the changes been beneficial?
- Has change always been well managed and orderly?
- What other changes have you been aware of?

COMMENT

It is likely that you have been able to identify a number of incidents or interventions which have led to direct and significant change. Whether these changes will be viewed as being beneficial or harmful will often depend on perspective and we must be careful to be balanced in our judgements about the outcomes of our work – rarely is change all 'good' or all 'bad'. For example, we may decide for sound organisational and professional reasons that moving a child from one set of foster parents to another is a 'good' decision which will produce positive results. Academic research, however, and more importantly the testimony of children who have experience of the care system, tells us that the repeated moves experienced by many children in care can be profoundly disruptive and unsettling (Barn, 2010; Stein, 2005). Consequently, whether the outcomes of change are seen to be 'good' or 'bad' will depend on a range of factors, not least the perspective of the people involved in the transition. Equally, we need to recognise that often change can be small scale and difficult to see and sometimes the effectiveness of what we do as social workers can be hard to measure.

Whilst this initial exercise guided you towards a consideration of changes you have observed in the lives of service users, some of you may also have been involved in organisational change within your placement. For example, it is not unusual for voluntary agencies to lose contracts on which they are financially reliant and have to reduce or reorganise their activities, sometimes leading to considerable disruption. In recent years many statutory organisations have undergone profound changes including staff redundancies, the amalgamation of teams and the reorganisation of management structures. Change and fluidity is very much part of the landscape of social work and often workers will be expected to respond positively to major organisational and team changes.

We also anticipate that you will have noticed changes in yourself as a result of the experiences you have gained on placement. Coming into direct contact with the demands and realities of professional practice, sometimes for the first time, can be a challenging experience which often generates considerable personal and professional learning and development. Many of you will feel more knowledgeable and more confident as a result of the learning you have gained from placement. Others may have changed their views about key issues in social care or have had a moment of revelation when academic work has come 'alive' during practice. Some of you will also have changed your minds about where or how you want to practise. Such changes or transitions are to be expected as social work continually forces you to examine yourself and therefore we should expect placements to be a catalyst for significant self-discovery. Humphrey (2011) supports this view and suggests that the process of becoming a social worker, undergoing professional training and encountering the challenges and growth of practice, propels students towards maturity and transformation.

DIFFERENT TYPES OF LOSS

Having established that change and transition can be significant factors within professional practice and within your learning, we now want to encourage you to critically consider the concept of loss. This is an important exercise as often we find that students completing their portfolios miss an opportunity to increase their level of analysis by using key words such as loss in an unthinking way which does not fully reflect the many potential nuances contained within the word. We know from our own lives that change and transition is often 'messy' leading to both losses and gains. For example, when you commenced your studies at university it is possible that you experienced a series of significant changes creating both losses and gains within your life. You may have moved geographical area and lost contact with some existing friends whilst making new friendships at university. You may have developed new interests or hobbies which meant that you no longer had time to devote to an existing pastime. Whilst these changes may seem 'natural' and very much part of leaving home and growing up, other changes in life are less routine and potentially less welcome.

Activity 8.2

Identifying loss

Mrs Hardy is an 84-year-old widow who lives alone in an owner-occupied bungalow in a suburb of a small town. The bungalow was bought following the retirement of her husband some 20 years ago. Mrs Hardy has one daughter and three grandchildren who live some distance away and rarely visit. They have very busy lives and, whilst not uncaring towards Mrs Hardy, have little time to give to her. Since Mr Hardy died 12 months ago, the family have only visited on three occasions. Mrs Hardy rarely goes out and seems to have no friends. Since the death of her husband, Mrs Hardy appears to be quite confused. Over the last few months she has burnt out several pans on the cooker, has been found wandering aimlessly in the street by neighbours and has telephoned her daughter in the middle of the night on several occasions saying that her husband is missing. As a student on placement you were asked to undertake an initial assessment following a referral from a neighbour. (Adapted from Mathews, 2009)

Write down the different elements of loss that you can identify within this case scenario.

COMMENT

This is a straightforward exercise and we would hope that you have been able to identify a range of losses. For example, the loss that derives from a major bereavement, the loss of memory and the potential loss of relationships within the extended family. There may well be other changes or transitions that you can identify or even some that you might be able to anticipate occurring in the near future due to the physical and mental frailty of Mrs Hardy. As you can see from this example, life can often be significantly influenced by losses that occurred in the past, losses that are ongoing, and even losses that we anticipate happening in the future can have the power to create fears and anxieties. We will return to the case of Mrs Hardy as a working example on a number of occasions throughout this chapter, but we now turn to a discussion of loss which will allow us to discuss some of these nuances. We start our analysis by suggesting that there are a number of different types of loss, all of which are relevant to professional practice.

UNRESOLVED OR AMBIGUOUS LOSS

Boss (2000) argues that sometimes there is an inherent ambiguity within loss, especially when it is not final or clear-cut and where there is not an opportunity to find 'closure' for those involved. An example that Boss (2000) provides is where a person is physically present but psychologically absent from the lives of those around them. This absence could be caused by a number of issues or illnesses such as dementia or brain injury where the person remains physically present but is unable to sustain connections or relationships due to the extent of their cognitive impairment. To return to Mrs Hardy, it could be that one of the reasons why her family find it difficult to visit her is that they have feelings of loss and sadness about her mental decline which are painfully reinforced when they meet. Families sometimes feel that the losses associated with dementia, such as the loss of personality or the inability to hold a conversation, rob them of the person they once knew and loved (Crawford and Walker, 2008).

Boss (2000) further suggests that there may also be occasions where ambiguity and a lack of resolution is created where a person is psychologically present but is physically absent. In terms of practice, you may be able to see this type of loss in a number of situations. For example, when a parent is absent from a child's life due to the imposition of a prison sentence, parental separation or divorce. The parent is physically absent from the life of the child but even in their absence continues to exercise a considerable psychological and emotional influence over the thoughts and life of the child. In our case study of Mrs Hardy, it may be that part of her confusion or her apparent disconnection from daily life is created because she continues to grieve for her husband and is unable 'to let go' or 'move on'. It may be that her thoughts are preoccupied with her husband, the life they previously shared and what he would have done if he were still present. Such thoughts are not uncommon when a person is grieving for the death of someone close – but as practitioners we need to recognise that such feelings may also occur in other types of loss or separation. For example, research tells us that children whose caregivers are removed from the family home following an assessment under the Mental Health Act experience a range of feelings, including grief and loss, which can negatively impact on their sense of identity and wellbeing (Cooklin and Gorell Barnes, 2004; Evans and Fowler, 2008; Manning and Gregoire, 2009). Even here, however, we need to take care not to be assumptive as factors such as the strength of other relationships and the quality of specialist support available can protect the psychological and emotional wellbeing of the child (Office of the Deputy Prime Minister, 2004; Tew, 2011).

UNACKNOWLEDGED OR DISENFRANCHISED LOSS

The second type of loss we want you to consider occurs when the loss experienced by a person is dismissed or not recognised by other people. This unacknowledged loss is particularly relevant to an older person such as Mrs Hardy as losses experienced in older age are frequently trivialised or diminished (Thompson, S., 2002). There is often an ageist assumption made that older people are somehow used to experiencing loss and are therefore more able to withstand the effects and emotions of loss due to their age (Currer, 2007). There are a range of other examples that we could consider where the loss sustained is disregarded by others and the people affected are not seen as being entitled to grieve. Riggs and Willsmore (2012), for example, have written about foster families where looked after children have been unexpectedly removed from their care. This has caused considerable distress and a real sense of loss to families as they have felt that the attachments and relationships they have developed, sometimes over many years, have been disregarded by professional staff. On the other hand, practitioners and fostering agencies may argue that foster parents are professional carers paid to undertake a specific task which is recognised as being of a temporary nature. Therefore it should not be a cause of distress or disruption if a child is removed from their care. Other examples include groups of people who are seen as somehow being immune to grief. We have already mentioned older people who are often considered within this assumption, but children and people with learning difficulties are also sometimes portrayed as being unable to understand loss or death and are seen as not being affected in the same way as 'normal' people. This is perhaps most noticeable when children or people with learning difficulties are not told of the death of a loved one or are not invited to funerals 'because it might upset them'. As practitioners we need to be aware of these oppressive assumptions and ensure that all people are treated with dignity and respect and allowed to express their emotions in an appropriate and meaningful way.

SELF-INDUCED LOSS

The final type of loss that we would like you to consider is that of self-induced loss. This is where a loss and the feelings associated with it are minimised or disregarded because the person is seen as being undeserving of support and sympathy because of the choices they have made. Often in these situations a person is seen to have either chosen the loss or 'to have brought it on themselves'. For example, where a woman chooses to terminate a pregnancy, when a person becomes ill from a sexually transmitted infection, or when an abusive parent loses a child. These examples go to the heart of one of the great ethical debates within society; namely, who 'deserves' and who does 'not deserve' to receive sympathy, support and understanding. This highly emotive debate reaches back to the Poor Law era where legislation differentiated between people who were seen to have an entitlement to support whilst others, often due to their feckless and irresponsible behaviour, were seen as being undeserving. This categorisation continues to be current as we frequently hear prejudicial comments about 'benefit scroungers', 'asylum seekers' and others who are portrayed in the media as receiving payments or services to which they are not seen to be entitled.

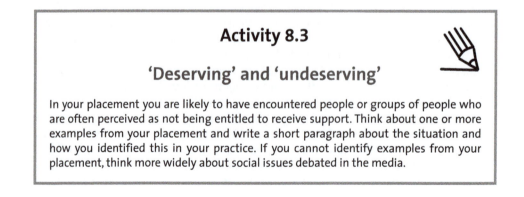

Activity 8.3

'Deserving' and 'undeserving'

In your placement you are likely to have encountered people or groups of people who are often perceived as not being entitled to receive support. Think about one or more examples from your placement and write a short paragraph about the situation and how you identified this in your practice. If you cannot identify examples from your placement, think more widely about social issues debated in the media.

COMMENT

You may have been able to identify some situations from practice or to relate this question to items you have encountered in the news. In a portfolio we recently read, the student described the response she received when she took a service user to the accident and emergency department at the local hospital on a busy Friday evening. The service user had self-harmed and had cut their arms and thighs. The reaction of staff was profoundly unsatisfactory as they voiced their views that the service user was wasting valuable NHS time and resources by their 'attention-seeking behaviour'. According to the staff, the service user did not deserve to receive a service as she had chosen to self-harm and therefore should take responsibility for her own actions. As part of our reflection on this case example, we need to take a balanced view as to how much 'choice' many of our service users have when they make decisions which to other people would seem to be unwise. Often we work with people who have limited personal resources who routinely experience oppression or abuse. For example, many writers, particularly those who come from a service user or social model perspective in mental health, would argue that self-harming behaviour is no more than a logical reaction to the pressures of a mad world and the abuses of psychiatry (Tew, 2002, 2011). To return to one of our previous examples, it could be that a woman's 'choice' to terminate her pregnancy is forced on her by economic, social, cultural, religious or family pressures. Consequently, we need to take care when describing a loss as being 'self-induced' as there may be many contextual factors and issues which contribute to the choice being taken.

Top tips – Thinking about loss

- Develop a critical understanding of the different types of loss that you might encounter in practice

- Critically self-reflect on your value base and your view on who deserves, and who does not deserve, to receive support and empathy

- Recognise that sometimes people who make what could be seen as unwise decisions have few options

- Adopt a balanced view of the losses and gains associated with loss

- Ensure that your understanding of loss and change is fully explored in your portfolio.

We hope that you can see from this analysis that loss is a complex concept which has a number of nuances and meanings that can be usefully explored within your portfolio. In order to help you to develop even greater criticality we now turn to a discussion of theory which helps to explain the processes that occur in loss.

THEORETICAL UNDERSTANDINGS OF LOSS AND TRANSITION

There are a number of theories and theoretical concepts concerning loss and transition which could be used to inform practice and to enhance the level of analysis within your portfolio. One of the most widely used and referenced was devised by Elisabeth Kübler-Ross (1926–2004), a Swiss-American psychiatrist who was influential in the development of the hospice movement in the United States in the 1960s. Kübler-Ross undertook research into the thoughts and feelings of patients resident in hospices who were diagnosed with a terminal illness. The model has subsequently been re-worked on a number of occasions and can be applied to a range of practice issues where major loss is being experienced. Whilst we need to take care not to misuse or overuse a particular theory by attempting to relate it to every casework situation we encounter, it is permissible to think creatively about how theory may be used to explore similar situations. This theory suggests that people move through a number of discrete stages as they psychologically and emotionally work their way through their final illness (see Figure 8.1).

STAGE 1 – DENIAL

According to Kübler-Ross (Kübler-Ross, 1970; Kübler-Ross and Kessler, 2005), in the first stage of the psychological processing of loss a person often denies the reality of the situation they face. Research tells us that denial can either be a conscious or an unconscious defence mechanism which protects people from potentially damaging psychological effects (Currer, 2007; Leander, 2010; Wong and Tomer, 2011). To briefly return to the case example of Mrs Hardy that we used at the beginning of this chapter, it may be that her family is in denial. They do not want to recognise her mental and physical deterioration as this would be extremely painful for them; so they deny to themselves and possibly others that there are any problems. Consequently, they do not to visit Mrs Hardy as seeing her would force them to recognise the difficulties and would contradict their denial. We need to be aware, however, that denial is not always problematical as it can be a psychologically healthy way of avoiding reality. Academic interest in the positive benefits of denial were shaped by the lived experiences of survivors of Nazi concentration camps in the Second World War which demonstrated that a denial of reality could be an important protective factor which enabled some people to survive – often against great odds (Frankl, 1959).

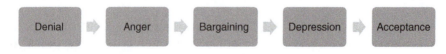

Figure 8.1　The five stages of grief (Kübler-Ross, 1970)

STAGE 2 — ANGER

In this second stage, denying the reality of the situation is no longer an option and there is a tendency for the person to become angry and to express their feelings. This anger can be misplaced and typically be aimed at those who are emotionally and physically closest to the patient. In Kübler-Ross's model this was often people like doctors or nurses who were involved in the day-to-day care of terminally ill patients. Relatives and friends could also be on the receiving end of anger, often in a haphazard or illogical way, as the person tries to understand and manage their limited prognosis. You may also consider that those close to a person who is dying may also be going through the same psychological process as the patient. In other words, it is not uncommon for family members to deny the extent of their loved one's illness or to become angry at medical staff. Again you may reflect that expressing anger is not necessarily a negative response or a 'bad' thing for a person who has experienced, or is in the process of experiencing, significant loss. As Thompson (2012) explains, people who are dying often experience a range of emotions such as resentment, guilt and anger, all of which need to be recognised and valued if a measure of acceptance and emotional calm is to be achieved. To widen our discussion to other practice areas, you may reflect that social workers often face anger and resentment when subjecting service users to interventions which lead to significant loss or change.

STAGE 3 — BARGAINING

The third stage identified by Kübler-Ross sees the person attempting to bargain with those in authority in order to extend their life. Often this will involve trying to strike a bargain with hospital or medical staff who may be asked to provide innovative or expensive treatment in exchange for a donation. Alternatively, the bargaining may be with a religious figure who is seen as having the power to intercede with a higher authority. Typically, the patient may promise a reformed life dedicated to service to a particular religion or faith in exchange for healing.

It is important for you to note that in many other areas of practice, service users attempt to bargain with social workers in an attempt to avert a promised course of action, or to prevent a particular outcome. Reder et al. (1993), in their pivotal book on the failures of the child protection system, use the term 'disguised compliance'. By this they mean where a family appears to comply with the interventions of health and social care agencies which disguises the fact that they are continuing to abuse or neglect children in their care. Reder et al. (1993) quote the example of Kimberley Carlile, a five-year-old child from Greenwich, London, who was murdered by her mother's partner after several years of systematic abuse. When Kimberley's family moved to Greenwich from another part of the country her stepfather aggressively refused an approach from child protection services who had been asked to monitor Kimberley's wellbeing. Her mother, however, spontaneously visited the local health clinic and impressed the health visitor with the level of her openness and cooperation (Reder et al., 1993: 106). In a sense, the family was bargaining with the various agencies by offering limited cooperation with one, knowing that the other would be informed and consequently would be less likely to intervene.

STAGE 4 – DEPRESSION

According to Kübler-Ross the next stage is where the dying person begins to recognise and process the certainty of death. In this phase, the person feels a range of emotions including sadness, regret, fear and uncertainty. There is a sense that the person is now 'coming to terms' with the reality of their situation and is beginning to gain a measure of acceptance. They may be profoundly unhappy with what is happening to them but nonetheless are psychologically able to move forward with their thinking and planning. Schneider (2000, 2006), however, argues that there is a danger that professionals tend to 'medicalise' and pathologise feelings of lowness that may exhibit themselves at times of profound loss and challenge. He argues that grieving for something significant that has been lost, or is being lost, is a natural human process which should not be confused with depression with its medical and clinical overtones. This is an important point as there is a risk that practitioners begin to interpret extreme but common feelings and emotions, such as euphoria or lowness of mood, as being problematical and in need of eradication. Tew (2011) goes further and argues that even what could be considered as unusual mental experiences, such as hearing voices, should not necessarily be seen as being 'bad' or abnormal. This view derives from a perspective which values the interpretations of the individual in distress and sees their view of what is happening to them as being more valid than the classification of symptoms and medical diagnosis.

STAGE 5 – ACCEPTANCE

The final stage in the model depicts the person as accepting the reality of their position and learning to live with it. This may be a time of activity where practical plans are put in place such as making a will or planning the funeral. This stage represents the end point of the process and it is often assumed that acceptance means that psychological resolution or a state of peace has been achieved. This is by no means always the case as we know that people face the consequences of loss and transition in a variety of ways.

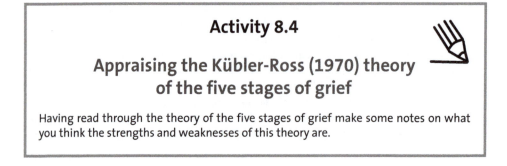

Activity 8.4

Appraising the Kübler-Ross (1970) theory of the five stages of grief

Having read through the theory of the five stages of grief make some notes on what you think the strengths and weaknesses of this theory are.

COMMENT

The main criticism that has been made of Kübler-Ross's theory is that it does not adequately reflect the complexity and ambiguity of grief and loss. Critics such as Neimeyer (2000), Attig (2011) and Thompson (2012) argue that there is no evidence base for suggesting that stages occur in the grieving process, and to talk of prescribed emotions when considering grief is unhelpful. There is also little to suggest that people who undergo transition and loss experience all of the emotions described in the model. It may be more accurate to say that some people experience some, or all, of these feelings whilst others do not. In terms of strengths, however, we need to recognise that this model was amongst the first to try and offer a theoretical understanding of loss and does succeed in describing at least some of the feelings and processes which we can recognise in transition. We have already suggested that another criticism might be that this model is overly optimistic, assuming as it does that there is a final stage of psychological adjustment and acceptance. Whilst this final stage may be contested, we also need to guard against the opposite view that loss, change and transition, even if significant and unwelcome, are necessarily 'bad' and damaging to health and wellbeing. A number of writers, for example Calhoun and Tedeschi (2001), suggest that loss can be transformational. By this they mean that whilst loss can be extremely painful it can also be the catalyst for significant positive changes in a person's life.

Activity 8.5

Identifying positive loss

Reflect on your work with service users or situations that you have experienced on placement where a loss has occurred. Identify and describe losses that may have been positive or even 'transformational'.

COMMENT

This is difficult as you may remember that we started this chapter by suggesting that we need to adopt a balanced view when working with loss and transition and recognise that few losses are all 'bad' or 'good'. Nonetheless, there may be times when a loss can be an opportunity for a person to review their life and to make positive changes that lead to enhanced self-esteem, increased options and a greater sense of wellbeing. For example, if we return to the case study of Mrs Hardy, it could have been that her husband was domineering and perhaps even violent towards her. Consequently, his death, whilst unwanted and a source of unhappiness, could represent a real turning point in her life. For the first time in many years she could go out and make new friendships or take up new hobbies. Perhaps she could make plans to go on holiday with her family or generally experience a level of freedom and opportunity that was simply unattainable whilst her husband was alive. We appreciate that the detail contained in the case study does not especially support this scenario, but there are other losses that you may have encountered in practice where the changes that have occurred as a result of a loss have been beneficial. Here are some examples encountered by students whilst on placement.

Positive loss

- A woman who is misusing substances seeks professional help to manage, reduce and eventually cease her reliance on illegal drugs. As a result she loses her partner and many former friends who were also substance misusers, but is able to renew contact with her children who had been subject to care proceedings due to her history.

- A young child who is subject to emotional abuse and neglect is removed from his parents. This results in him losing contact with his immediate family including his parents, siblings and cousins. Due to the complexity of his needs, he is placed with specialist foster parents in a different geographical location and is forced to move school. Whilst these losses are substantial he gradually begins to rebuild his life. For the first time, he begins to achieve extremely good results at school, develops an interest in sport and joins the Scouts. More obviously, he gains an environment where he is free from harm and can thrive as an individual.

- A service user who is experiencing domestic violence is involved in a road traffic accident in which her abusive partner is killed. As a result of his death, she loses a considerable amount, not least her home which was rented in his name and access to some welfare benefits. She gains the opportunity, however, to re-evaluate her life and comes to some major decisions. She successfully applies to go to university, qualifies as a teacher and gains a job as a primary school teacher. All of these changes would not have been possible if her partner, who controlled all aspects of her life, had still been alive.

To summarise, loss, change and transition are complex terms that merit thoughtful use and exploration within your portfolio. So far, we have concentrated on the feelings and emotions that can occur during a period of profound change or loss, and have briefly looked at some of the potential consequences of change. We now consider another well-known theoretical model which explores further the processes that can occur at times of change and transition.

THE 'WHEEL OF CHANGE'

This model was developed by Prochaska and DiClemente (1994) and is widely used in social work with drug and substance misusers (Goodman, 2009). Like the work

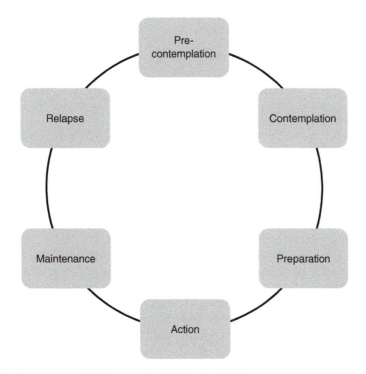

Figure 8.2 Prochaska and DiClemente's (1994) wheel of change

of Kübler-Ross (1970; Kübler-Ross and Kessler, 2005) it describes a number of stages that people encounter whilst undergoing change and sees change as being a process that occurs over a period of time, rather than being a single event. This theory concentrates on the motivational readiness of the person to embrace change and the challenges that change will inevitably bring to their lives.

According to Prochaska and DiClemente (1994), the process of change is characterised by six stages (see Figure 8.2).

The first stage is where the person experiences a period of *pre-contemplation*, in which they do not view their behaviour or their situation as being problematical and do not see any reason to change. Consequently, they have no motivation for engaging with services or for accepting professional intervention. Professionals in health and social care often work with people who are resistant to intervention and it is necessary to acknowledge that there are a range of reasons why this may be the case. Killick (2011: 69–70) suggests the following reasons as being of potential significance;

- Family loyalty;
- A fear of damaging relationships;
- Dependence on family or a carer;

- Distrust of professionals;

- A desire for privacy;

- A desire to retain control;

- Shame;

- Powerlessness;

- A fear of reprisal.

To this list we could add denial and we would encourage you to consider that there are links between this stage of pre-contemplation and the work of Kübler-Ross (1970; Kübler-Ross and Kessler, 2005). If a person denies that there is a problem clearly they will be resistant to intervention and their views will mirror many of the features of pre-contemplation.

There then follows a period of *contemplation*. This is where the person remains ambivalent about change but is at least open to the possibility that changing certain aspects of their life might be worthwhile. No positive action is taken and time is needed to consider the advantages and disadvantages of the proposed changes. This is where social work needs to be undertaken in a skilful and sensitive manner as people need to be encouraged to reflect on their options. You will recall that the PCF domain on 'Intervention skills' highlights a number of key skills that need to be utilised in such casework situations:

> Social workers engage with individuals, families, groups and communities, working alongside people to assess and intervene. They enable effective relationships and are effective communicators, using appropriate skills. Using their professional judgement, they employ a range of interventions: promoting independence, providing support and protection, taking preventative action and ensuring safety whilst balancing rights and risks. They understand and take account of differentials in power, and are able to use authority appropriately. (TCSW, 2012c)

In particular, we would ask you to note that all of these skills directly link to the core values of social work. The reason why social workers seek to 'work alongside people', 'enable effective relationships' and 'promote independence' is because practice is driven by values which emphasise the provision of choice, the need to preserve and enhance human dignity, the right to receive a respectful response and, of course, the empowerment of the powerless.

In the third stage, entitled *preparation*, the person has concluded their period of contemplation and is now preparing to take action to embrace change. Their preparation may involve making practical plans that will facilitate change or they may address emotional and psychological issues that stand in the way of success. As we have previously noted, this model is most often used with people who misuse substances and in public health programmes such as smoking cessation campaigns. Taking this last example, preparation may involve making arrangements to attend smoking cessation classes, telling friends of the plan to stop smoking and setting a date when smoking is to cease.

Goodman suggests that again there is a need for thoughtful social work intervention at this stage as 'change does not occur overnight but has to be planned' (2009: 113). This is perhaps an understatement when we consider that he is referring to service users with significant histories of substance misuse. Nonetheless, he rightly identifies that part of the role of social work is to enable people to set manageable and achievable goals that can lead to real and lasting change. Again there are clear links to Kübler-Ross (1970; Kübler-Ross and Kessler, 2005) here as the final stages of her theory also identify the importance of accepting the reality of the situation and 'moving forward'.

The fourth stage is that of *action*, where a person is sufficiently motivated to make changes and to move forward by incorporating the changes into their daily routine. Again, the difficulties surrounding this move should not be underestimated. Care needs to be taken to provide a supportive context to change and to ensure that the risks and losses associated with change are understood. As we noted at the beginning of this chapter, social workers often force or facilitate people, many of whom have limited personal and emotional resources, to undertake profound changes in their lives. Whilst for a social worker moving a child between foster placements or admitting an older person into nursing home care may just be 'another day at the office', for the service user they can be defining moments in their lives.

Sometimes people have real difficulty deciding to change, as is emphasised by the terminology used in this theoretical model. On the other hand, sometimes there is a crisis or a turning point that increases motivation causing change to rapidly occur. In the following extract from a student's portfolio, the student describes her work with a young girl who we will call Alice. In this case study, Alice has a number of complex needs and does not receive consistent support from her father who lives apart from the family. At the time of writing Alice is continuing to see her father but needs to make some far-reaching decisions about her future.

Alice

CASE STUDY

'During our meeting, Alice shared with me her feelings and wishes around future contact with her father. Alice disclosed that her dad had continually pressurised her into agreeing to go and live with him during their contact time and that he had not stopped until Alice agreed to tell her mum that she wanted to live with her father. Alice described how her dad had become very angry towards her and she thought he would walk off and leave her or that he would hit her. Alice had gone home and become aggressive towards her mum and siblings; then began inflicting self harming injuries to her face.

'We talked through what Alice thought had made her feel so angry towards her mum and what she was feeling before and after she started self harming herself in her bedroom. Alice described wanting a hug from her mum when she returned but instead had started shouting at her. I was able to talk through with Alice where her anger may have come from and ways in which she could express and share her anger in the future. Alice was very clear on what her wishes and feelings were around future contact with her father.'

Whilst this incident could be seen as being a typical example of social work intervention, it was also the turning point that enabled Alice to take action to make significant changes in her life, not least assisting the courts and Children's Services to formalise her living arrangements and her contact with her father. In a sense, this single event, albeit as a component part of a much longer process, encapsulates the preparation and action stages of Prochaska and DiClemente's (1994) model. Alice had previously been thinking about, or contemplating, her options but this event increased her level of motivation and quickened her decision making. A connection you could make here is that this is an example of 'transformational loss' (Calhoun and Tedeschi, 2001) which we discussed earlier. Whilst there are undoubtedly losses and changes that Alice will have to negotiate following her decision, there are also considerable gains that could transform aspects of her life.

As can be seen, the student had some important work to do during the meeting and drew on the skills and values we highlighted earlier from the PCF in order to help Alice make her decisions. The language the student uses to describe her intervention is revealing. For example, she uses the phrase 'I was able to talk through with Alice where her anger may have come from and ways in which she could express and share her anger in the future.' This is an excellent example of a student 'working alongside' and developing an 'effective relationship' with a child to validate and explore their justifiable feelings of anger and distress. Note that the student makes it clear to the reader that they did not merely acknowledge the anger but that they also sought ways in which the anger could be expressed and shared in the future.

The final stage in this theory is that of *maintenance*. This is where the initial enthusiasm for change has diminished and there is recognition that the changes that have been made need to be maintained. To return to our previous example of smoking cessation, the person who has stopped smoking needs to develop and maintain patterns of behaviour that support their decision to quit. For example, not going to the pub with friends who are committed smokers and continuing to attend the smoking cessation support group. This brief example again confirms that we need to be balanced in our thinking when we consider loss and change. The person who has given up smoking could potentially lose friendships and social opportunities due to their decision. Equally, they should make a number of very positive gains, not least an improvement in their general health and financial position.

Finally, this theory is helpful as it recognises that there is the possibility of failure and relapse during times of change. Sometimes, even with the best planning and support people are unable to make changes to their lives. Under those circumstances unless statutory powers suggest otherwise we have to respect people's decisions and learn to live with disappointment.

Top tips – Making the most of theory

- Recognise that some theories have relevancy across a range of different situations

---

- Be creative in how you use and apply theory
- Make links between different theories
- Consider both the strengths and weaknesses of theory
- Do not be afraid of adopting a critical approach to theory
- Reflect on the connections between values and theory
- Recognise the biases and subjectivities that are inherent in theory construction

CONCLUSION

In this chapter we have introduced you to a number of theories and theoretical concepts which help us to analyse loss, change and transition. We have reflected on the commonalities and differences that exist between the different theories and have creatively used their insights to make a range of comments about the key skills and core values that inform and underpin the profession.

FURTHER READING

Adams, J. and Sheard, A. (2013) *Positive Social Work: The Essential Toolkit for NQSWs.* London: Critical Publishing.
This helpful introduction to life as a qualified social worker offers advice on a range of important issues such as emotional intelligence, sources of support and what to expect when you enter practice.

Currer, C. (2007) *Loss and Social Work.* Exeter: Learning Matters.
An excellent introduction to working with grief and loss.

Thompson, N. (2012) *Grief and its Challenges.* Basingstoke: Palgrave Macmillan.
This important book offers a rounded view of grief and the complications that can occur if loss is not effectively managed. It provides a strong theoretical perspective and looks at the issues created by grief to individuals, communities and society.

INTERNET SOURCES

The Elisabeth Kübler-Ross Foundation: www.ekrfoundation.org

This website acts as a tribute to the work of Elisabeth Kübler-Ross and offers advice to professionals about working with people who are terminally ill and their families. The Foundation has also uploaded videos onto YouTube which can be found at: www.youtube.com/user/kenrossaz

The Social Work Podcast and Prochaska and DiClemente's 'Wheel of Change' (Dr Jonathan Singer): http://socialworkpodcast.blogspot.co.uk/2009/10/prochaska-and-diclementes-stages-of.html

Dr Singer provides a podcast on the wheel of change which is accompanied by a written transcript. The podcast discusses each stage of the model.

There are other podcasts by different contributors on various subjects on the main Social Work Podcast site: http://socialworkpodcast.blogspot.co.uk/

CONCLUSION

In reaching the end of this book, it is likely that you have also completed your placement experience and will be either resuming studies or looking for a qualified practitioner post. We hope that your placement(s) went well and that your experiences will provide a solid foundation for your social work career. Not all practice learning experiences run smoothly, but they always offer a valuable source of learning and development.

The chapters of this book were specifically directed to support you in understanding the processes and knowledge you need to engage with at the beginning, middle and end of your placement. You can refer back to these in your next placement or indeed if you find yourself supporting student social workers in the future. The additional reading and sources provide more detailed guidance and knowledge about aspects of social work practice, knowledge or skills and we hope that you will take the time to review some of these.

Practice learning is a complex undertaking and in order to successfully complete placements, you will need to be actively engaged with your learning from 'start to finish' and to embrace the recurring themes within the book, which include:

- The need to understand the context of social work practice learning and assessment, for example the standards set out by the professional regulator, the HCPC, particularly the Standards of Proficiency for Social Work (HCPC, 2012b) and The College of Social Work Professional Capabilities Framework (TCSW, 2012c);

- The importance of preparing for, understanding and engaging with placement processes in order to make the most of practice learning experiences. Completing documents on time and keeping up to date with academic work is particularly important;

- Being assessed as a student social worker is a challenging process and will involve a range of different assessment processes and methods. This can also be an exciting and enjoyable part of your professional training and we advise you to engage with the learning experiences that present themselves;

- The relevance of knowledge, including theory, legislation, service user knowledge, organisational knowledge, your developing practice wisdom in helping you to work effectively with service users and carers;

- The underpinning values of social work that provide a basis for all aspects of social work practice;

- The need to develop skills as a critically reflective practitioner to help you manage the demands and complexities of practice including risk and making defensible decisions, and to help you understand your limits and professional development needs;

- In becoming a reflective practitioner, you also need to be aware of 'self' including the impact of self on working with service users and the importance of developing emotional resilience which will help to protect you from the stresses of working in frontline social work practice;

- Retaining a focus on the best interests of service users should be a guiding principle for practice; importantly service users are also a valuable source of knowledge;

- Social work is not an insular profession and working with other professions and disciplines to obtain better outcomes for service users is central to social work practice;

- Social work practice is characterised by a complex combination of knowledge, values and skills, and social workers need to possess competence in all three areas in order to make assessments, intervene appropriately and manage risk. Skills in communication, building relationships and working in teams and organisations provide the cornerstone for practice.

It is interesting to note that when a group of Directors of Adults and Children's Services were asked what they expect from students on placement and new qualified social workers, they came up with the following list. You may see how the themes in this book reflect many of these points; you may also find it useful to consider how far you meet these expectations as a social work student or newly qualified social worker.

DIRECTORS OF CHILDREN'S AND ADULT SERVICES – EXPECTATIONS OF STUDENTS ON PLACEMENT AND NEWLY QUALIFIED SOCIAL WORKERS

- Do all you can to ensure that you are ready to work in stressful settings and situations;

- You must be able to demonstrate that you can meet deadlines;

- Show that you can engage with families (including those families who are resistant to interventions) and that you can communicate with them effectively;

- You must have the capacity to write well using good structure, correct punctuation and sentence construction;

- You must be able to write coherent and fluent reports;

- You must be able to process and analyse written and verbal information;

- You must present yourself professionally, in appearance and in how you communicate;

- You must be able to evaluate information and to make a decision based on your assessments;

- You need to be able to defend your decisions with clear and accurate evidence;

- You need to understand about the need for cost effectiveness and you need to show that you can analyse costs;

- You need to show imagination in terms of developing services for people so that you do not simply and automatically rely upon existing social work and other services as the only means of support;

- You need to show an awareness of community development approaches so that you can draw on the resources of the community, as well as the local authority and other agencies;

- Show an understanding of the organisational contexts of other disciplines, e.g. Clinical Commissioning Groups;

- You must be prepared to work in the current difficult financial context even when this means there is a conflict between the organisational ethos and the moral purpose of social work.

If you are about to enter qualified practice, the guidance offered in this text about reflection, use of knowledge and how practice is assessed can be transferred to the ASYE. Many of our points about how you might learn, be assessed, apply knowledge to practice and critically reflect will be directly relevant to qualified practice in the immediate and long-term futures. Learning acquired during qualifying training provides you with a toolkit to take with you into employment in order to work effectively with service users, so although your placement has finished, your development is not at an end and you will need to build upon the foundations provided by your placement experiences and academic learning.

Social work is a dynamic, constantly evolving profession and as we conclude this book, the PCF has been introduced for qualifying social work programmes. Even so, the prospect of further change is on the horizon as the government has announced its intention to review social work education (Department of Health, 2013). Change therefore is inevitable. However, whilst some of the frameworks for learning and development may change, the essential skills and knowledge of how to relate to, work with and understand service users remain constant. As practitioners of the future, you will need to constantly review your knowledge and keep up to date with new developments which will be plentiful. Additionally, within the context of continuous change, it is important that social work retains and develops its professional identity; as future social work practitioners, we hope you will be able to embrace this challenge.

GLOSSARY OF TERMS AND ABBREVIATIONS

ASYE – Assessed and Supported Year in Employment: The Assessed and Supported Year in Employment during the first-year post-qualification was one of the recommendations of the Social Work Task Force (2009). The ASYE came into effect in September 2012, replacing previous arrangements under the Newly Qualified Social Workers (NQSW) framework. The AYSE is assessed against the relevant domain levels of the Professional Capabilities Framework and during the first year of employment newly qualified social workers can expect to receive a protected workload, developmental opportunities and a higher level of supervision.

BASW – British Association of Social Workers: The BASW represents social workers across the UK and provides its members with a range of services, including union representation and discounted rates to its peer-reviewed journals. The BASW has produced a code of ethics for social workers.

GSCC – General Social Care Council: Established on 1 October 2001, the GSCC was the regulatory body for social work and was responsible for the registration of social workers and student social workers and for producing a code of conduct for social care staff and employers. The GSCC closed on 31 July 2012, transferring responsibility for the registration of qualified social workers to the HCPC. Some of the guidance documents it developed in relation to practice learning are still relevant and available through The College of Social Work.

HCPC – Health and Care Professions Council: From 1 August 2012, the HCPC became the regulatory body for qualified social workers in England, assuming responsibility from the GSCC. Formerly known as the Health Professions Council (HPC), the organisation was re-named to reflect its regulation of social workers. The title social worker became a protected title in 2005 and only those registered with the HCPC are entitled to refer to themselves as a social worker.

On-site supervisor: Some students will be allocated an on-site supervisor as their practice educator is not directly located in the agency or team in which the placement is based. The on-site supervisor works in the same agency and site and usually the same team as the student and takes day-to-day responsibility for organising and monitoring the placement and the work the student undertakes. The on-site supervisor will allocate work, as well as providing daily guidance and support. They contribute to the student's learning and assessment, writing reports for the portfolio, and whilst they contribute to the final decision about the student's practice, they are not responsible for the final assessment recommendation.

Practice educator: The practice educator is the person who takes overall responsibility for a student's learning and assessment when they are on practice placement. They assess the student against the Professional Capabilities Framework and placement criteria and make a recommendation to the university examination board. Under TCSW's (2012e) standards for practice educators a two-tiered qualification (Stage 1 and Stage 2) for practice educators reflects the experience, knowledge, skills and expertise of individual practice educators and also the differing complexities of placements. Once the changes to practice educator training and standards are fully implemented, only Stage 2 qualified practice educators will be able to assess final placement students and all independent (also known as off-site or long-arm practice educators) will need to be qualified to Stage 2.

PCF – Professional Capabilities Framework: From September 2013, all social work students will be assessed against the nine domains of the Professional Capabilities Framework at the level commensurate with their progress throughout the degree. The PCF will also provide a continuing professional development framework for qualified social work practitioners throughout their careers.

QAPL – Quality Assurance in Practice Learning (TCSW and Skills for Care, 2012): This is the system by which practice learning opportunities, or placements, are monitored, evaluated and quality assured; it includes an evaluation tool used to gather feedback from students and practice educators.

SCIE – Social Care Institute for Excellence: According to its website (www.scie.org. uk), the SCIE sets out to 'improve the lives of people who use care services by sharing knowledge about what works. It is an independent charity working with adults, families and children's social care and social work services across the UK. Working with people who use services and carers, the SCIE gathers and analyses knowledge about what works and translates that knowledge into practical resources, learning materials and services including training and consultancy.'

SWRB – Social Work Reform Board: The SWRB, chaired by Dame Moira Gibb, was established to operationalise the 15 recommendations of the Social Work Task Force. Many of the SWRB publications can be found on TCSW's website.

SWTF – Social Work Task Force: The SWTF was appointed by the Secretaries of State for Health (DOH) also for Children, Schools and Families (DCSF) to provide expert advice and guidance in the light of concerns about social work as a profession. Under the leadership of Dame Moira Gibb, the SWTF made 15 recommendations about the future of the social work profession, leading to wholesale changes and reforms in education, training and continuing professional development for social workers.

Standards of Education and Training: The HCPC's Standards of Education and Training (SETs) set out the standards of education and training that an education programme must meet in order to be approved by the HCPC. These are generic standards for all professional programmes regulated by the HCPC, and they set out to ensure that any person who completes an approved programme meets the standards of proficiency for their profession and is therefore eligible to apply for admission (www.hpc-uk.org/aboutregistration/standards/sets/).

Standards of Proficiency for Social Workers: The HCPC's Standards of Proficiency (SOPs) set out what a social worker in England should know, understand and be able to do when they complete their social work training so that they can register with the HCPC. They set out clear expectations of a social worker's knowledge and abilities when they start practising (www.hpc-uk.org/publications/standards).

TCSW – The College of Social Work: According to their website (www.tcsw.org.uk) the College is 'the centre of excellence for social work, upholding and strengthening standards for the benefit of the public'. TCSW was established following the Social Work Task Force's call for the creation of an independent and strong organisation which would represent and support the social work profession. The College is led by and accountable to its members and exists to uphold the agreed professional standards and promote the profession and the benefits it brings to the general public, the media and policy makers.

REFERENCES

Adams, J. and Sheard, A. (2013) *Positive Social Work. The Essential Toolkit for NQSWs*. London: Critical Publishing.

Advocacy in Action with Charles, M., Clarke, H. and Evans, H. (2006) 'Assessing fitness to practise and managing work-based placement', *Social Work Education,* 25 (4): 373–84.

Alcock, P. and Ferguson, H. (2012) 'Social policy and social work', in Becker, S., Bryman, A. and Ferguson, H. (eds) *Understanding Research for Social Policy and Social Work*, 2nd edn. Bristol: The Policy Press. pp. 1–55.

Arnstein, S.R. (1969) 'A ladder of citizen participation', *Journal of the American Institute of Planners,* 35 (4): 216–24.

Attig, T. (2011) *How We Grieve: Relearning the World*, 2nd edn. Oxford: Oxford University Press.

Barlow, C. and Hall, B.L. (2007) 'What about feelings? A study of emotion and tension in social work field education', *Social Work Education,* 26 (4): 399–413.

Barn, R. (2010) 'Care leavers and social capital: Understanding and negotiating racial and ethnic identity', *Ethnic and Racial Studies,* 33 (5): 832–50.

Barrett, G. and Keeping, C. (2005) 'The processes required for effective interprofessional working', in Barrett, G., Sellman, D. and Thomas, J. (eds) *Interprofessional Working in Health and Social Care*. Basingstoke: Palgrave. pp. 18–31.

Bichard, M. (2004) *The Bichard Inquiry Report*. London: The Stationery Office.

Biestek, F. (1961) *The Casework Relationship*. London: Allen & Allen.

Blackburn, R. (2000) 'Risk assessment and prediction', in McGuire, J., Mason, T. and Okane, A. (eds) *Behaviour, Crime and Legal Processes: A Guide for Forensic Practitioners*. Chichester: John Wiley & Sons. pp. 178–204.

Blewett, J., Lewis, J. and Tunstill, J. (2007) *The Changing Roles and Tasks of Social Work; A literature informed discussion paper*. London: SCIE Available from: www.scie.org.uk/news/files/roles.pdf

Boss, P. (2000) *Ambiguous Loss: Learning to Live with Unresolved Grief*. Cambridge, MA: Harvard University Press.

British Association of Social Workers (2012) *The Code of Ethics for Social Work: Statement of Principles*. Birmingham: BASW.

British Association of Social Workers (2013) *Job Hunting Advice for Social Workers* [Online]. Birmingham: BASW. Available from: www.basw.co.uk/social-work-careers/your-guide-to-finding-a-job/ [accessed 14 April 2013].

British Association of Social Workers (undated) *Advice for Newly Qualified Social Workers: Finding Employment*. Birmingham: BASW.

Broadhurst, K., White, S., Fish, S., Munro, E., Fletcher, K. and Lincoln, H. (2010) *Ten Pitfalls and How to Avoid Them: What Research Tells Us*. London: NSPCC.

Brookfield, S. (2009) 'The concept of critical reflection: Promises and contradictions', *European Journal of Social Work,* 12 (3): 293–304.

Bryman, A. (2008) *Social Research Methods*, 3rd edn. Oxford: Oxford University Press.

Butt, J. (2006) *Race Equality Discussion Paper 03: Are We There Yet? The Characteristics of Organisations that Successfully Promote Diversity*. London: SCIE.

Caldicott Committee (1997) *Report on the Review of Patient-Identifiable Information*. London: Department of Health.

Calhoun, L.G. and Tedeschi, R.G. (2001) 'Posttraumatic growth: The positive lessons of loss', in Neimeyer, R.A. (ed.) *Meaning Reconstruction and the Experience of Loss*. Washington, DC: American Psychological Association. pp. 157–72.

Campbell, D. and Maclean, C. (2002) 'Ethnic identities, social capital and health inequalities: Factors shaping African Caribbean participation in local community networks in the UK', *Social Science and Medicine*, 55 (4): 643–57.

Carson, D. and Bain, A. (2008) *Professional Risk and Working with People: Decision Making in Health, Social Care and Criminal Justice*. London: Jessica Kingsley.

Collins, S. (2007) 'Social workers, resilience, positive emotions and optimism', *Practice: Social Work in Action*, 19 (4): 255–69.

Collins, S. (2008) 'Statutory social workers: Stress, job satisfaction, coping, social support and individual differences', *British Journal of Social Work*, 38 (6): 1173–93.

Consortium for Research on Emotional Intelligence in Organizations (1998) *The Emotional Competence Framework*. The Consortium for Research on Emotional Intelligence in Organizations. Available from: www.eiconsortium.org/reports/emotional_competence_framework.html [accessed on 4 July 2013].

Cooklin, A. and Gorell Barnes, G. (2004) 'Family therapy when a parent suffers from psychiatric disorder', in Seeman, M., Gopfert, M. and Webster, J. (eds) *Parental Psychiatric Disorder*. Cambridge: Cambridge University Press. pp. 306–25.

Cooper, B. and Rai, L. (2011) *Try a Day in the Life of a Social Worker* [Online]. Milton Keynes: Open University. Available from: www.open.edu/openlearn/body-mind/social-care/social-work/day-the-life [accessed 4 February 2013].

Cooper, F. (2012) *Professional Boundaries in Social Work and Social Care*. London: Jessica Kingsley.

Coulshed, V. and Orme, J. (2012) *Social Work Practice*, 5th edn. Basingstoke: Palgrave Macmillan.

Crawford, K. (2012) *Interprofessional Collaboration in Social Work Practice*. London: Sage.

Crawford, K. and Walker, J. (2008) *Social Work with Older People*, 2nd edn. Exeter: Learning Matters.

Currer, C. (2007) *Loss and Social Work*. Exeter: Learning Matters.

D'Cruz, H., Gillingham, P. and Melendez, S. (2007) 'Reflexivity, its meanings and relevance for social work: A critical review of the literature', *British Journal of Social Work*, 37 (1): 73–90.

Department of Health (2013) *Review Announced on Social Work Education*. London: DOH. Available from: www.gov.uk/government/news/review-announced-on-social-work-education [accessed 6 May 2013].

Diggins, M. (2004) *Teaching and Learning Communication Skills in Social Work Education*. London: SCIE.

Dimond, C. and Misch, P. (2002) 'Psychiatric morbidity in children remanded to prison custody: A pilot study', *Journal of Adolescence*, 25 (6): 681–9.

Doel, M. (2010) *Social Work Placements: A Traveller's Guide*. London: Routledge.

Doel, M. and Sawdon, C. (1999) *The Essential Groupworker: Teaching and Learning Creative Groupwork*. London: Jessica Kingsley.

Doel, M., Shardlow, S., Sawdon, C. and Sawdon, D. (1996) *Teaching Social Work Practice: A Programme of Exercises and Activities towards the Practice Teaching Award*. Aldershot: Ashgate.

Doel, M., Deacon, L. and Sawdon, C. (2007) 'Curtain down on act one: Practice learning in the first year of the new social work award', *Social Work Education,* 26 (3): 217–32.

Edwards, C. (1999) 'The public service culture', in Rose, A. and Lawton, A. (eds) *Public Services Management.* Harlow: Pearson Education. pp. 278–94.

Elliott, T., Frazer, T., Garrard, D., Hickinbotham, J., Horton, V., Mann, J., Soper, S., Turner, J., Turner, M. and Whiteford, A. (2005) 'Practice learning and assessment on BSc (Hons) Social Work: "Service user conversations" ', *Social Work Education,* 24 (4): 451–66.

Evans, J. and Fowler, R. (2008) *Family Minded: Supporting Children in Families Affected by Mental Illness.* Ilford: Barnardo's.

Fanthome, C. (2004) *Work Placements: A Survival Guide for Students.* Basingstoke: Palgrave Macmillan.

Fauth, R., Jelicic, H., Hart, D., Burton, S. and Shemmings, D. (2010) *Effective Practice to Protect Children Living in 'Highly Resistant' Families.* London: Centre for Excellence and Outcomes in Children and Young People's Services.

Fenge, L.A., Howe, K., Hughes, M. and Thomas, G. (2013) *The Social Work Portfolio: A Student's Guide to Evidencing Your Practice.* Maidenhead: Open University Press/ McGraw-Hill.

Ferguson, H. (2007) 'Abused and looked after children as "moral dirt": Child abuse and institutional care in historical perspective', *Journal of Social Policy,* 36 (1) :123–39.

Ferguson, I. and Woodward, R. (2009) *Radical Social Work in Practice: Making a Difference.* Bristol: The Policy Press.

Fernando, S. (2010) *Mental Health, Race and Culture,* 3rd edn. Basingstoke: Palgrave Macmillan.

Flynn, M.C. (2007) *The Murder of Steven Hoskin: A Serious Case Review: Executive Summary.* Cornwall: Cornwall Adult Protection Committee.

Ford, K. and Jones, A. (1987) *Student Supervision.* Basingstoke: Macmillan.

Frankl, V.E. (1959) *From Death Camp to Existentialism.* New York: Washington Square Press.

Gelman, C.R. (2004) 'Anxiety experienced by foundation year MSW students entering field placement: Implications for admissions, curriculum, and field education', *Journal of Social Work Education,* 40 (1): 39–54.

Gelman, C.R. and Lloyd, C.M. (2008) 'Pre-placement anxiety among foundation-year MSW students: A follow up study', *Journal of Social Work Education,* 44 (1): 173–83.

General Social Care Council (2010) *Quality Assurance for Practice Learning: Quality Assurance Benchmark Statement and Guidance on the Monitoring of Social Work Practice Learning Opportunities (QAPL)* [Online], 2nd edn. Rugby: GSCC. Available from: www. gscc.org.uk/cmsFiles/Education%20and%20Training/QAPL_benchmark_statement_and_ guidance_2nd_ed.pdf [accessed 13 November 2011].

General Social Care Council (2011) *Professional Boundaries: Guidance for Social Workers.* London: GSCC.

Gibbs, G. (1988) *Learning by Doing: A Guide to Teaching and Learning Methods.* London: Further Education Unit.

Goleman, D. (1998) *Working with Emotional Intelligence.* London: Bloomsbury.

Goodman, A. (2009) *Social Work with Drug and Substance Misusers,* 2nd edn. Exeter: Learning Matters.

Haringey Local Safeguarding Children Board (2009) *Serious Case Review: Baby Peter – Executive Summary.* London: Haringey LSCB.

Health and Care Professions Council (2012a) *Guidance on Conduct and Ethics for Students.* London: HCPC.

Health and Care Professions Council (2012b) *Standards of Proficiency: Social Workers in England.* London: HCPC.

Health and Care Professions Council (2012c) *Standards of Education and Training*. London: HCPC.

Higher Education Funding Council for England (2010) *Circular Letter Number 12/2010: Employability Statements* [Online]. Bristol: HEFCE. Available from: www.hefce.ac.uk/pubs/circlets/2010/cl12_10/

Home Office (1998) *Inquiry into the Matters Arising from the Death of Stephen Lawrence*. London: TSO.

Hothersall, S.J. and Maas-Lowit, M. (eds) (2010) *Need, Risk and Protection in Social Work Practice*. Exeter: Learning Matters.

Humphrey, C. (2011) *Becoming a Social Worker: A Guide for Students*. London: Sage.

Hurley, J. (2012) 'Introducing emotional intelligence', in Hurley, J. and Linsley, P. (eds) *Emotional Intelligence in Health and Social Care: A Guide for Improving Human Relationships*. London: Radcliffe Publishing. pp. 1–16.

Hurley, J., Linsley, P. and Stansfield, C. (2012) 'Self-awareness and empathy: Foundational skills for practitioners', in Hurley, J. and Linsley, P. (eds) *Emotional Intelligence in Health and Social Care: A Guide for Improving Human Relationships*. London: Radcliffe Publishing. pp. 29–44.

Information Commissioner's Office (2012) *Latest News Releases* [Online]. Wilmslow: Information Commissioner's Office. Available from: www.ico.gov.uk/news/latest_news.aspx [accessed 27 May 2012].

Ixer, G. (1999) 'There's no such thing as reflection', *British Journal of Social Work*, 29 (6): 513–27.

Jackson, L. (2012) 'Why CAFCASS is now in good health: Making well-being a priority in the workplace has transformed the children and family court's advisory service's sickness record', *Guardian*, 24 October.

Kanno, H. and Koeske, G.F. (2010) 'MSW students' satisfaction with their field placements: The role of preparedness and supervision quality', *Journal of Social Work Education*, 46 (1): 23–38.

Keady, J. and Thompson, R. (2009) 'The community mental health nurse', in Doel, M. and Shardlow, S. (eds) *Educating Professionals: Practice Learning in Health and Social Care*. Farnham: Ashgate. pp. 31–50.

Kemshall, H. and Wilkinson, B. (eds) (2011) *Good Practice in Assessing Risk: Current Knowledge, Issues and Approaches*. London: Jessica Kingsley.

Killick, C. (2011) 'I don't want your help: Ambivalence and resistance in adult protection', in Taylor, B.J. (ed.) *Working with Aggression and Resistance in Social Work*. Exeter: Learning Matters. pp. 66–79.

Kinman, G. and Grant, L. (2011) 'Exploring stress resilience in trainee social workers: The role of emotional and social competencies', *British Journal of Social Work*, 41 (2): 261–75.

Klohen, E.C. (1996) 'Conceptual analysis and measurement of the construct of ego-resiliency', *Journal of Personality and Social Psychology*, 70 (5): 1067–79.

Koprowska, J. (2005) *Communication and Interpersonal Skills in Social Work*. Exeter: Learning Matters.

Kübler-Ross, E. (1970) *On Death and Dying*. London: Routledge.

Kübler-Ross, E. and Kessler, D. (2005) *On Grief and Grieving*. London: Simon & Schuster.

Laming, Lord (2009) *The Protection of Children in England: A Progress Report*, London: The Stationery Office.

Leander, L. (2010) 'Police interviews with child sexual abuse victims: Patterns of reporting, avoidance and denial', *Child Abuse and Neglect: The International Journal*, 34 (3): 192–205.

Lefevre, M. (2005) 'Facilitating practice learning and assessment: The influence of relationship', *Social Work Education*, 24 (5): 565–83.

Lefevre, M. (2010) *Communicating with Children and Young People: Making a Difference.* Bristol: The Policy Press.

Lishman, J. (2009a) 'The social worker', in Doel, M. and Shardlow, S. (eds) *Educating Professionals: Practice Learning in Health and Social Care.* Farnham: Ashgate. pp. 175–91.

Lishman, J. (2009b) *Communication in Social Work.* Basingstoke: Palgrave Macmillan.

Lomax, R., Jones, K., Leigh, S. and Gay, C. (2010) *Surviving Your Social Work Placement.* Basingstoke: Palgrave Macmillan.

Maclean, S. and Caffrey, B. (2009) *Developing a Practice Learning Curriculum.* Rugeley: Kirwin Maclean Associates.

Maclean, S. and Harrison, R. (2009) *Making the Most of your Practice Learning Opportunities: OR ... Everything You Ever Wanted to Know About Social Work Placements.* Rugeley: Kirwin Maclean Associates.

Maclean, S. and Lloyd, I. (2008) *Developing Quality Practice Learning in Social Work: A Straightforward Guide for Practice Teachers and Supervisors.* Rugeley: Kirwin Maclean Associates.

Manning, C. and Gregoire, A. (2009) 'Effects of parental mental illness on children', *Psychiatry*, 8 (1): 7–9.

Mathews, I. (2009) *Social Work and Spirituality.* Exeter: Learning Matters.

Mathews, I. and Crawford, K. (2011) *Evidence Based Practice in Social Work.* Exeter: Learning Matters.

Mathews, I., Simpson, D., Croft, A., McKinna, G. and Lee, M. (2009) 'Unsung heroes: Who supports social work students on placement?', *Journal of Practice Teaching and Learning*, 9 (2): 57–71.

McLaughlin, H. (2007) *Understanding Social Work Research: Key Issues and Concepts.* London: Sage.

Morrison, T. (1999) *Staff Supervision in Social Care.* Brighton: Pavilion.

Morrison, T. (2007) 'Emotional intelligence, emotion and social work: Context, characteristics, complications and contribution', *British Journal of Social Work*, 37 (2): 245–63.

Mulally, R. (1993) *Structural Social Work: Ideology, Theory and Practice.* Toronto: McClelland & Stewart.

Murdoch-Eaton, D.G. and Roberts, T.E. (2009) 'The doctor', in Doel, M. and Shardlow, S. (eds) *Educating Professionals: Practice Learning in Health and Social Care.* Farnham: Ashgate. pp. 51–71.

Nathan, J. (2002) 'The advanced practitioner: Beyond reflective practice', *Journal of Practice Teaching and Learning*, 4 (2): 59–83.

National Archives (1998) *The Data Protection Act 1998.* Kew.

Neimeyer, R.A. (2000) *Lessons of Loss: A Guide to Coping.* Memphis, TN: Center for the Study of Loss and Transition.

Oelofsen, N. (2012) *Developing Reflective Practice: A Guide for Students and Practitioners of Health and Social Care.* Banbury: Lantern Publishing.

Office of the Deputy Prime Minister (2004) *Mental Health and Social Exclusion.* London: HMSO.

Oko, J. (2011) *Understanding and Using Theory in Social Work*, 2nd edn. Exeter: Learning Matters.

Open University (undated) *Introducing Social Work Practice* [Online]. JORUM. Available from: http://dspace.jorum.ac.uk/xmlui/bitstream/handle/10949/791/Items/K113_1_PracticeCards_p65-78.pdf?sequence=77; [accessed 3 February 2013].

O'Sullivan, T. (2011) *Decision Making in Social Work*, 2nd edn. Basingstoke: Palgrave Macmillan.

Parker, J. (2010a) *Effective Practice Learning in Social Work*, 2nd edn. Exeter: Learning Matters.

Parker, J. (2010b) 'When things go wrong! Placement disruption and termination: Power and student perspectives', *British Journal of Social Work*, 40 (3): 983–99.

Parker, J. and Bradley, G. (2010) *Social Work Practice: Assessment, Planning, Intervention and Review*, 3rd edn. Exeter: Learning Matters.

Parsons, C. (2007) 'The dignity of risk: Challenges in moving on', in Neami (ed.) *17th Annual Conference*, Melbourne, September 2007. Melbourne: Neami.

Pawson, R., Boaz, A., Grayson, L., Long, A. and Barnes, C. (2003) *Types and Quality of Knowledge in Social Care: Knowledge Review 3*. London: SCIE.

Payne, M. (2005) *Modern Social Work Theory*, 3rd edn. Basingstoke: Palgrave Macmillan.

Perske, R. (1972) 'The dignity of risk', in Wolfensberger, W. (ed.) *Normalization: The Principle of Normalization in Human Services*. Toronto: National Institute on Mental Retardation. pp. 194–200.

Prochaska, J. and DiClemente, C. (1994) *The Transtheoretical Approach: Crossing Traditional Boundaries of Therapy*. Malabar, FL: Krieger Publishing Company.

Quality Assurance Agency (QAA) (2008) *Social Work Subject Benchmarks*. Mansfield: Quality Assurance Agency for Higher Education

Reder, P., Duncan, S. and Gray, M. (1993) *Beyond Blame: Child Abuse Tragedies Revisited*. London: Routledge.

Richards, M., Payne, C. and Shepperd, A. (1990) *Staff Supervision in Child Protection Work*. London: National Institute for Social Work.

Riggall, S. (2012) *Using Counselling Skills in Social Work*. London: Sage/Learning Matters.

Riggs, D.W. and Willsmore, S. (2012) 'Experiences of disenfranchised grief arising from the unplanned termination of a foster placement: An exploratory South Australian study', *Adoption and Fostering*, 36 (2): 57–66.

Rogers, C. (1961) *On Becoming Person*. Boston, MA: Houghton Mifflin.

Ross, A. (2002) *Institutional Racism: The Experience of Teachers in Schools*. Presented at BERA conference, Exeter, 11–14 September. Available from: www.teacherworld.org.uk/Articles/racism%20BERA%202002.PDF [accessed on 5 July 2013].

Rowan, S.M. and Alsop, A. (2009) 'The occupational therapist', in Doel, M. and Shardlow, S. (eds) *Educating Professionals: Practice Learning in Health and Social Care*. Farnham: Ashgate. pp. 135–56.

Rutter, L. and Brown, K. (2012) *Critical Thinking and Professional Judgement for Social Work*, 3rd edn. Exeter: Learning Matters.

Schneider, J. (2000) *The Overdiagnosis of Depression: Recognising Grief and its Transformative Potential*. Traverse City, MI: Seasons Press.

Schneider, J. (2006) *Transforming Loss: A Discovery Process*. East Lansing, MI: Integra Press.

Schön, D.A. (1983) *The Reflective Practitioner: How Professionals Think in Action*. New York: Basic Books.

Scott, S. (2004) 'Reviewing the research on the mental health of looked after children: Some issues for the development of more evidence informed practice', *International Journal of Child and Family Welfare*, 7 (2–3): 86–97.

Scottish Executive (2006) *Report of the 21st Century Social Work Review: Changing Lives*. Edinburgh: Scottish Executive. Available from: www.scotland.gov.uk/Resource/Doc/91931/0021949.pdf

Shardlow, S. (1991) 'Inspecting social work values', *Practice: Social Work in Action*, 5 (1): 76–85.

Shardlow, S.M. and Doel, M. (2009) 'Health and social care: A complex context for professional education', in Doel, M. and Shardlow, S.M. (eds) *Educating Professionals: Practice
Learning in Health and Social Care*. Farnham: Ashgate. pp. 3–14.

Sheppard, M. (1998) 'Practice validity, reflexivity and knowledge for social work', *British
Journal of Social Work*, 28 (5): 763–81.

Sheppard, M., Newstead, S., Di Caccavo, A. and Ryan, K. (2000) 'Reflexivity and the development of process knowledge in social work: A classification and empirical study', *British
Journal of Social Work*, 30 (4): 465–88.

Siraj-Blatchford, S. (1991) 'A study of black students' perceptions of racism in initial teacher
education', *British Educational Research Journal*, 17 (1): 35–50.

Skills for Care and Department for Education (undated (a)) *AYSE: Support and Assessment*
[Online]. Leeds: Skills for Care. Available from: www.skillsforcare.org.uk/socialwork/
ASYE3Supportandassessment/supportandassessment.aspx?nostats=t [accessed 2 February
2013].

Skills for Care and Department for Education (undated (b)) *ASYE: Informing Judgements
and Processes* [Online]. Leeds: Skills for Care. Available from: www.skillsforcare.org.uk/
socialwork/ASYE5Informingjudgementsandprocesses/informingjudgementsandprocesses.
aspx [accessed 14 April 2013].

Skills for Care and Department for Education (undated (c)) *What is the Assessed and
Supported Year in Employment (ASYE)?* [Online]. Leeds: Skills for Care. Available from:
www.skillsforcare.org.uk/socialwork/ASYE1WhatistheASYE/WhatisASYE.aspx [accessed
14 April 2013].

Smith, R. (2008) *Social Work and Power*. Basingstoke: Palgrave Macmillan.

Social Work Reform Board (2010a) *Building a Safe and Confident Future: One Year On –
Progress Report of the Social Work Reform Board*, London, Department for Education.
Available from: https://www.gov.uk/government/uploads/system/uploads/attachment_
data/file/180510/DFE-00601-2010-1.pdf [accessed: 5 July 2013].

Social Work Reform Board (2010b) *Building a Safe and Confident Future: One Year on –
Improving the Quality and Consistency of the Initial Qualifying Social Work Education
and Training* [Online]. London: Department for Education. Available from: www.education.
gov.uk/publications/eOrderingDownload/5%20Proposals%20for%20the%20social%20
work%20degree.pdf [accessed 5 July 2013].

Social Work Reform Board (2011) *Implementing SWRB Proposals to Improve the Provision
of Social Work Degree Programmes*. London: SWRB.

Social Work Task Force (2009) *Building a Safe and Confident Future*. London: Department of
Health/Department for Children, Schools and Families.

Stein, M. (2005) *Resilience and Young People Leaving Care: Overcoming the Odds*. York:
Joseph Rowntree Foundation.

Taylor, B.J (2013) *Professional Decision Making and Risk in Social Work*, 2nd edn. Exeter:
Learning Matters.

Taylor, C. and White, S. (2000) *Practising Reflexivity in Health and Welfare: Making
Knowledge*. Buckingham: Open University Press.

Tew, J. (2002) *SPN Paper 3: Start Making Sense – Developing Social Models to Understand
and Work with Mental Distress*. Leeds:TOPSS.

Tew, J. (2011) *Social Approaches to Mental Distress*. Basingstoke: Palgrave Macmillan.

The College of Social Work (2012a) *Practice Learning Guidance: Overview of New
Arrangements for Practice Learning*. London: TCSW.

The College of Social Work (2012b) *An Explanation of the Professional Capabilities
Framework (PCF)* [Online]. London: TCSW. Available from: www.collegeofsocialwork.
org/pcf.aspx [accessed 26 January 2013].

The College of Social Work (2012c) *The Professional Capabilities Framework* [Online]. Wilmslow: TCSW. Available from: www.collegeofsocialwork.org/pcf.aspx [accessed 27 May 2012].

The College of Social Work (2012d) *Professional Capability Framework: Readiness for Practice Capabilities* [Online]. London: TCSW. Available from: www.collegeofsocialwork. org/uploadedFiles/PCFNOVReadiness-for-practiceCapabilities.pdf [accessed 27 May 2012].

The College of Social Work (2012e) *Practice Educator Professional Standards for Social Work*. London: TCSW.

The College of Social Work (2012f) *Professional Capability Framework: Qualifying Social Worker Level Capabilities*. London: TCSW.

The College of Social Work (2012g) *Professional Capability Framework: End of First Placement Level Capabilities* [Online]. London: The College of Social Work. Available from: www. collegeofsocialwork.org/uploadedFiles/PCFNOVEndofFirstPlacementCapabilities.pdf [accessed 27 May 2012].

The College of Social Work (2012h) *Understanding What is Meant by Holistic Assessment*. London: TCSW.

The College of Social Work (undated (a)) *Practice Learning Guidance: Placement Criteria* [Online]. London: TCSW. Available from: www.tcsw.org.uk/uploadedFiles/TheCollege/_ CollegeLibrary/Reform_resources/PlacementCriteria(edref9).pdf

The College of Social Work (undated (b)) *Assessing Social Work Practice Against the PCF: Principles for Gathering and Using Feedback from People Who Use Services and Those That Care for Them*. London: TCSW.

The College of Social Work (undated (c)) *Practice Learning Guidance: 'Developing Skills for Practice' and Assessment of 'Readiness for Direct Practice'*. London: TCSW.

The College of Social Work and Skills for Care (2012) *Quality Assurance in Practice Learning (QAPL): The Social Work Practice Learning Quality Assurance Benchmark Statement, With Supporting Evaluation Tools*, Leeds/London, Skills for Care/The College of Social Work. Available from: www.tcsw.org.uk/uploadedFiles/TheCollege/Resources/QAPLhandbook. pdf [accessed on 28 June 2013].

Thompson, N. (2002) *People Skills*, 2nd edn. Basingstoke: Palgrave Macmillan.

Thompson, S. (2002) 'Older people', in Thompson, N. (ed.) *Loss and Grief*. Basingstoke: Palgrave Macmillan.

Thompson, N. (2006) *Anti-Discriminatory Practice*, 4th edn. Basingstoke: Palgrave Macmillan.

Thompson, N. (2012) *Grief and its Challenges*. Basingstoke: Palgrave Macmillan.

Thompson, S. and Thompson, N. (2008) *The Critically Reflective Practitioner*. Basingstoke: Palgrave Macmillan.

Tickle, L. (2009) 'Placement on the frontline', *Community Care*, 3 September.

Trevithick, P. (2008) 'Revisiting the knowledge base of social work: A framework for practice', *British Journal of Social Work*, 38 (6): 1212–37.

Trevithick, P. (2012) *Social Work Skills and Knowledge: A Practice Handbook*, 3rd edn. Maidenhead: Open University Press/McGraw-Hill.

Tummey, R. and Tummey, F. (2008) 'Iatrogenic abuse', in Tummey, R. and Turner, T. (eds) *Critical Issues in Mental Health*. Basingstoke: Palgrave Macmillan. pp. 126–42.

Urbanowski, M. and Dwyer, W. (1988) *Learning Through Field Instruction: A Guide for Teachers and Students*. New York: Family Service America.

Walker, J. and Crawford, K. (2010) *Social Work and Human Development*, 3rd edn. Exeter: Learning Matters.

Walker, J., Crawford, K. and Parker, J. (2008) *Practice Education in Social Work: A Handbook for Practice Teachers, Assessors and Educators*. Exeter: Learning Matters.

Wenger, E. (1998) *Communities of Practice: Learning, Meaning and Identity*. Cambridge: Cambridge University Press.

Williams, S. and Rutter, L. (2010) *The Practice Educator's Handbook*. Exeter: Learning Matters.

Wilson, K., Ruch, G., Lymbery, M., Cooper, A. with Becker, S., Bell, M., Brammer, A., Clawson, R., Littlechild, B., Paylor, I. and Smith, R. (2011) *Social Work: An Introduction to Contemporary Practice*, 2nd edn. Harlow: Pearson.

Wong, P.T.P. and Tomer, A. (2011) 'Beyond terror and denial: The positive psychology of death acceptance', *Death Studies,* 35 (2): 99–106.

Younghusband, E. (Chair) (1959) *Report of the Working Party on Social Workers in the Local Authority Health and Welfare Services*. London: HMSO.

INDEX

Page numbers in **bold** indicate a glossary entry